Quick In

Disneyland Resort Address

1313 S. Harbor Boulevard
Anaheim, CA 92802

Halloween Information
General Halloween: disneyland.com/halloween
Halloween Facebook Page: facebook.com/DisneylandHalloween
Mickey's Halloween Party: disneyland.disney.go.com/events-tours/mickeys-halloween-party/

Customer Service
Ask Otto (Automated Attraction & Dining Info.): (714) 520-7090

Live & Recorded Customer Service: (714) 781-4565, then press 0

Mobile Website: m.disneyland.com
Events & Hours: disneyland.disney.go.com/calendar/

Twitter
Disneyland Park: twitter.com/DisneylandToday
Disneyland Resort: twitter.com/Disneyland

Grand Californian Hotel (714) 635-2300, then press 5
1600 S. Disneyland Drive, Anaheim, CA 92802

Disneyland Hotel (714) 778-6600, then press 3
1150 Magic Way, Anaheim, CA 92802

Paradise Pier Hotel (714) 999-0990, then press 3
1717 S. Disneyland Drive, Anaheim, CA 92802

Dining Reservations
(714) 781-DINE [3463] then press 4
disneyland.disney.go.com/dining/

Annual Passes
Block Out Dates: disneyland.disney.go.com/passes/blockout-dates/

Annual Pass News: Disneyland.com/AP
facebook.com/DisneylandPassholders • twitter.com/DisneylandAP

Maps

Halloween
at the
Disneyland Resort

September 11 - November 1
2015

The Ultimate Unauthorized Quick Guide to Halloween at
Disneyland • California Adventure • Downtown Disney • Resort Hotels

by

John Glass

100 BOOKS
a division of Alternative Travel Press (USA) Los Angeles

Author: John Glass
Editor: Linda Ray
Cover Design: M. Thomas
Map Illustrations: Ted Freely

Version 1.23 | Updated 10.16.2015

Published by 100 Books, a division of Alternative Travel Press

This Is an Unauthorized Travel Guide
This book is not authorized, endorsed, or in any way associated with the Disney company, any of it's affiliates, or any of the other companies, businesses, or products mentioned inside. All products and services mentioned in this book are trademarks of their respective companies.

Tell Us What You Think
Disneyland is a constantly evolving place. While every effort has been made to make this book as accurate as possible at the date of publication, minor changes to the park may render some information out of date by the time you receive this book. If you think we left something out of this book, please let us know. We may even include your suggestion in future editions. Please eMail the publisher from our website with any comments, corrections, or suggestions. We look forward to hearing from you.

www.alternativetravelpress.com

Table of Contents

Introduction

Halloween is a magical time at the Disneyland Resort, and Disney goes all out with it's decorations, shows, special food, themed merchandise, and most importantly, incredible transformations of a few of the park's most popular attractions. In this quick guide to Halloween at the resort I will take you through all of the magic that transforms your typical Disneyland Resort experience into the spooky frightfest known as *Halloween Time at the Disneyland Resort*.

In the chapters that follow I will explore every attraction, show, restaurant, and shop in the park. The details that add a spooky Halloween flair to the these places have been added to their respective chapters, and a special section in the front of the book gives you quick access to the best Halloween experiences in the Resort. You will find the best Halloween themed attractions, shows, foods, and souvenirs listed there. A complete set of maps in the front of the book will guide you to all Halloween and non-Halloween destinations mentioned throughout the book, and checklists give you a quick way to keep track of your visit to the resort.

Keep in mind that this is a quick guide to Halloween in the Disneyland Resort, and it trades brevity for the lengthy detailed articles found in our more complete travel guides. This is a book for people who don't have the time or inclination to read through a long travel book, and just want quick access to this information. From the well known to the obscure, these are the things you don't want to miss while visiting the Disneyland Resort during the Halloween season. I wrote this book for you, my readers, so that you could get as much fun out of the parks as I do. I hope you enjoy it!

About the Author

John Glass is a travel blogger, founder of the Southern California travel magazine SoCal Secrets, and author of the fan site Disney Parks Club. View more travel information on his websites:

www.socalsecrets.com
www.disneyparksclub.com

About the Publisher

Alternative Travel Press strives to bring a unique perspective to your travel adventures. Look for books on a wide variety of travel topics on the publisher's website:

www.alternativetravelpress.com

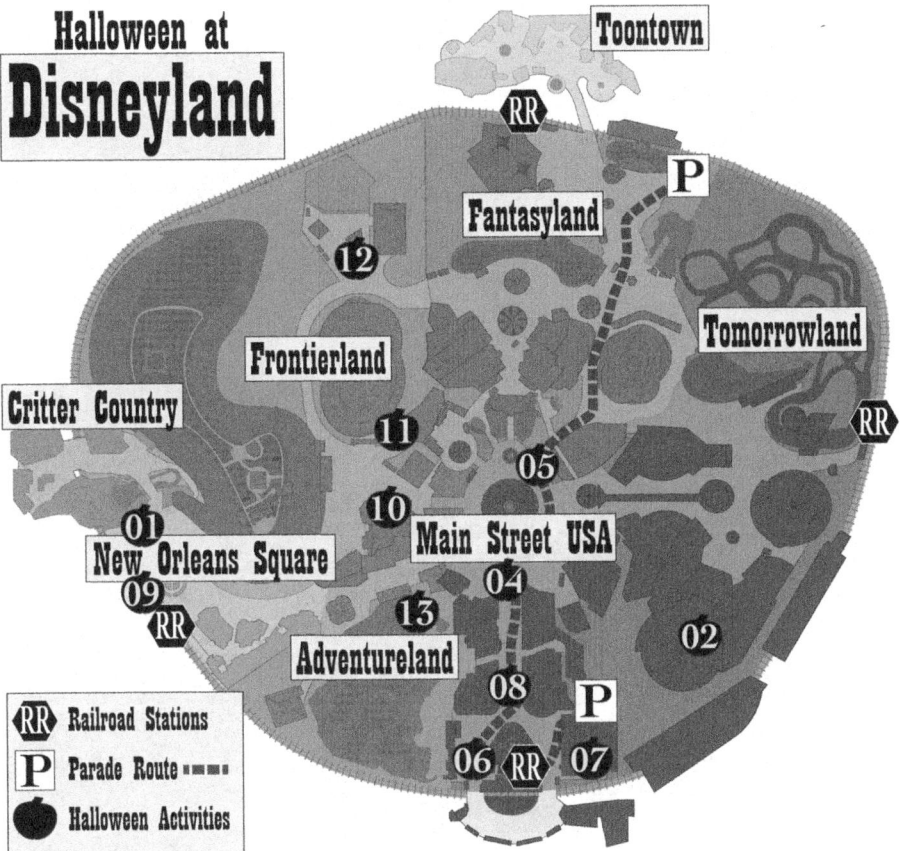

Halloween at Disneyland

Attractions
- ☐ 01 Haunted Mansion Holiday
- ☐ 02 Space Mountain Ghost Galaxy

Events & Activities
- ☐ 04 Mickey's Halloween Party
- ☐ 05 Halloween Magic Shots
- ☐ 06 Disney's Happiest Haunts Tour
- ☐ 07 Spooky Gallery Exhibits
- ☐ 08 Main Street USA Pumpkin Festival
- ☐ 09 Meet Jack Skellington
- ☐ 10 The Halloween Tree
- ☐ 11 Dia de los Muertos
- ☐ 12 Big Thunder Ranch Halloween
- ☐ 13 Sunrise Safari Breakfast
- ☐ 14 Halloween In-Room Celebrations

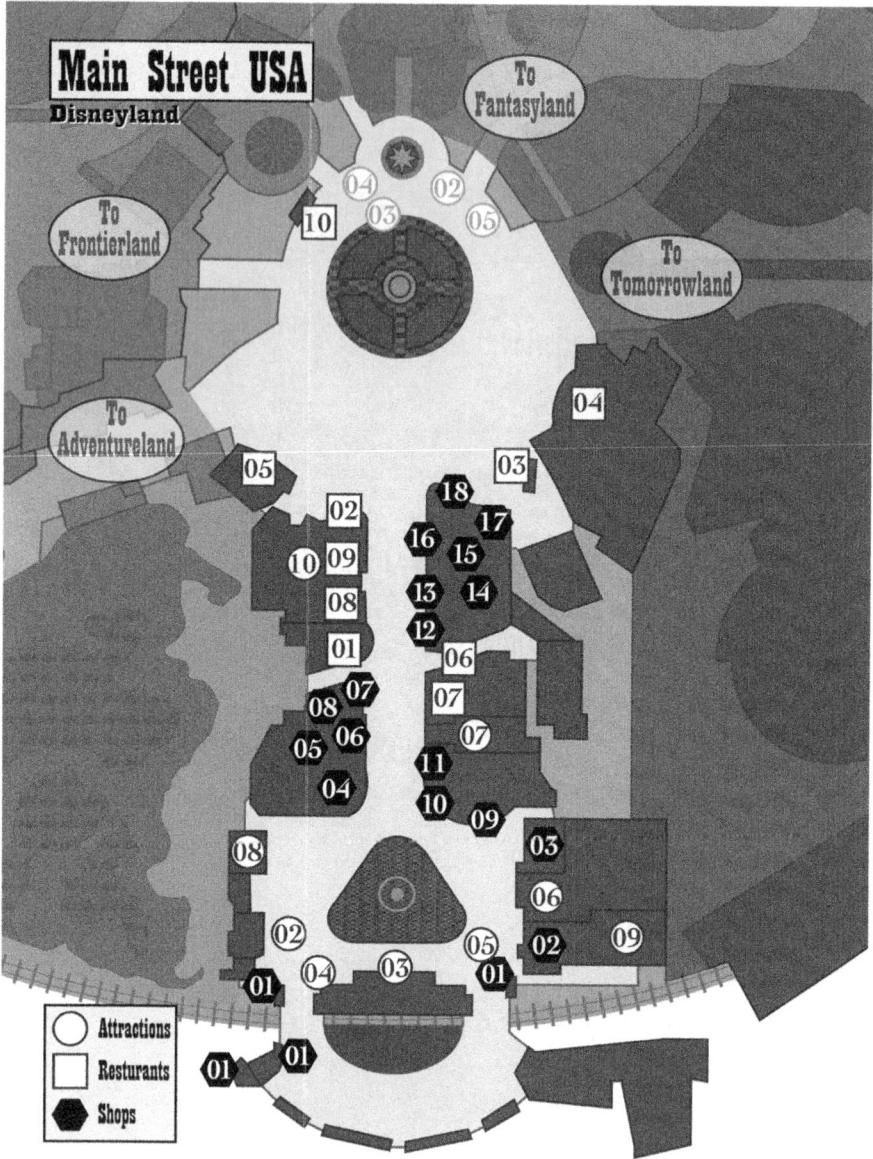

Attractions & Activities

- ☐ 02 Fire Engine
- ☐ 03 Horse-Drawn Streetcar
- ☐ 04 Horseless Carriage
- ☐ 05 Omnibus
- ☐ 06 The Disneyland Story Presenting Great Moments with Mr. Lincoln
- ☐ 07 Main Street Cinema
- ☐ 08 The Fire Station
- ☐ 09 The Disney Gallery
- ☐ 10 The Penny Arcade

Shows

- ☐ 04 The Dapper Dans
- ☐ 05 The Hook and Ladder Co.
- ☐ 06 The Strawhatters
- ☐ 07 Main St Piano Player
- ☐ 08 The Disneyland Band
- ☐ 09 Pearly Band
- ☐ 10 Flag Retreat Ceremony

Restaurants

Full Service

01 Carnation Café

Quick Service

02 Coca-Cola Refreshment Corner

03 Little Red Wagon

04 Plaza Inn

05 Jolly Holiday Bakery Café

Carts

06 Main Street Fruit Cart

Coffee & Dessert

07 Market House

08 Gibson Girl Ice Cream Parlor

09 Candy Palace & Penny Arcade

10 Central Plaza Cappuccino Cart

Shops

01 Newsstands
02 Disneyana & The Disney Gallery
03 The Mad Hatter
04 Disneyland Emporium
05 Crystal Arcade
06 Jewelry Shop
07 Fortuosity Shop
08 The Storybook Store
09 Disney Showcase
10 Main Street Magic Shop
11 20th Century Music Company
12 Disney Clothiers, Ltd
13 Castle Bros.
14 Chester Drawer's
15 Crystal Arts
16 Silhouette Studio
17 China Closet
18 Main Street Photo Supply Co.

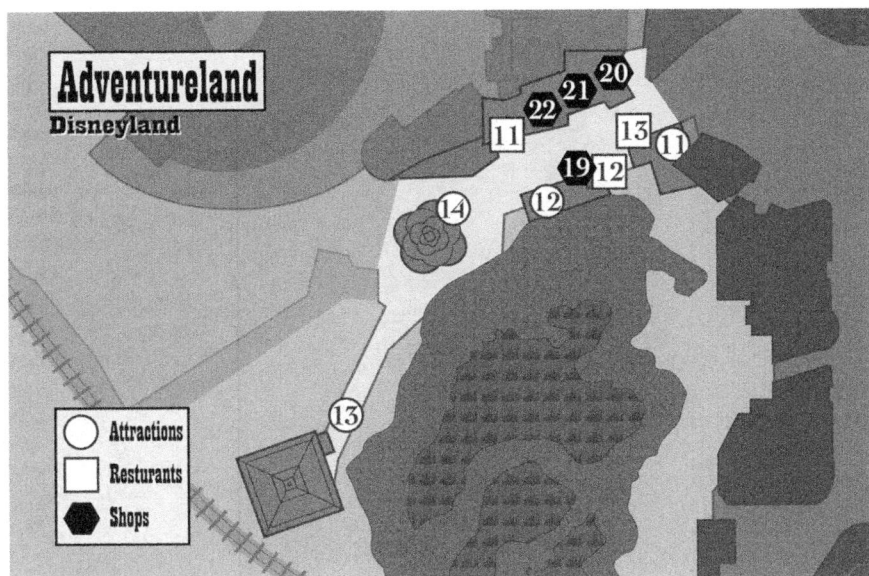

Attractions & Activities

- ☐ 11 Enchanted Tiki Room
- ☐ 12 Jungle Cruise
- ☐ 13 Indiana Jones Adventure
- ☐ 14 Tarzan's Treehouse

Restaurants

Quick Service

11 Bengal Barbecue

Carts

12 Tropical Imports

Coffee & Dessert

13 Tiki Juice Bar

Shops

19 Tropical Imports
20 Adventureland Bazaar
21 South Seas Traders
22 Indiana Jones Adventure Outpost

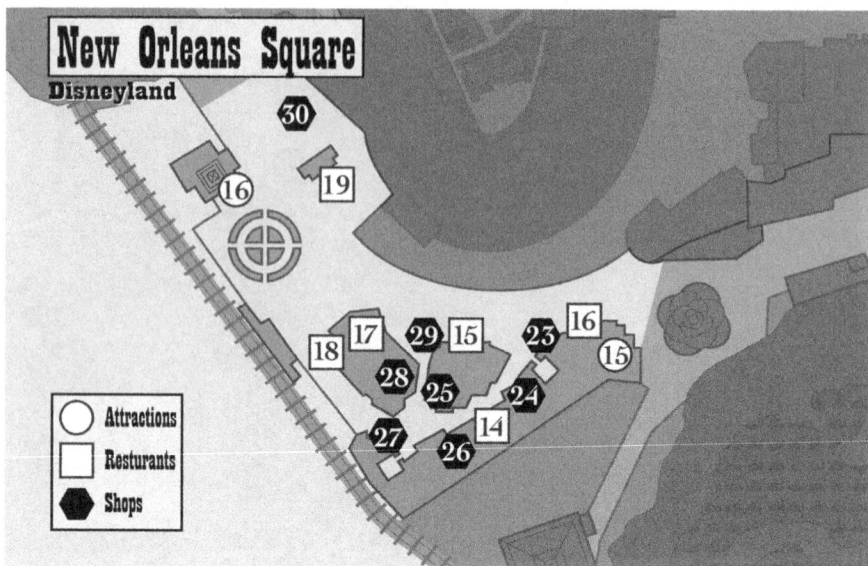

Attractions & Activities
☐ 15 Pirates of the Caribbean
☐ 16 Haunted Mansion

Shows
☐ 11 Royal Street Bachelors
☐ 12 The Bootstrappers
☐ 13 Jambalaya Jazz

Restaurants
Full Service
14 Blue Bayou
15 Café Orléans

Quick Service
16 Royal Street Veranda
17 French Market Restaurant

Coffee & Dessert
18 Mint Julep Bar
19 New Orleans Square Coffee Cart

Shops

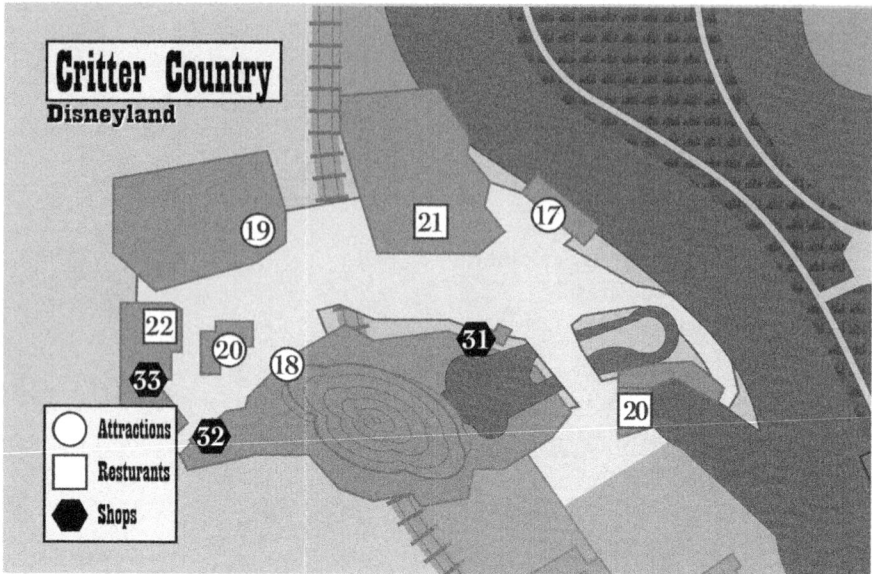

Attractions & Activities
Rides

- ☐ 17 Davy Crockett's Explorer Canoes
- ☐ 18 Splash Mountain
- ☐ 19 The Many Adventures of Winnie the Pooh
- ☐ 20 Winnie the Pooh's Thinking Spot

Restaurants
Quick Service

20 Harbour Galley

21 Hungry Bear Restaurant

Dessert

22 Pooh Corner

Shops

31 Briar Patch

32 Prof. Barnaby Owl's Photographic Art Studio

33 Pooh Corner

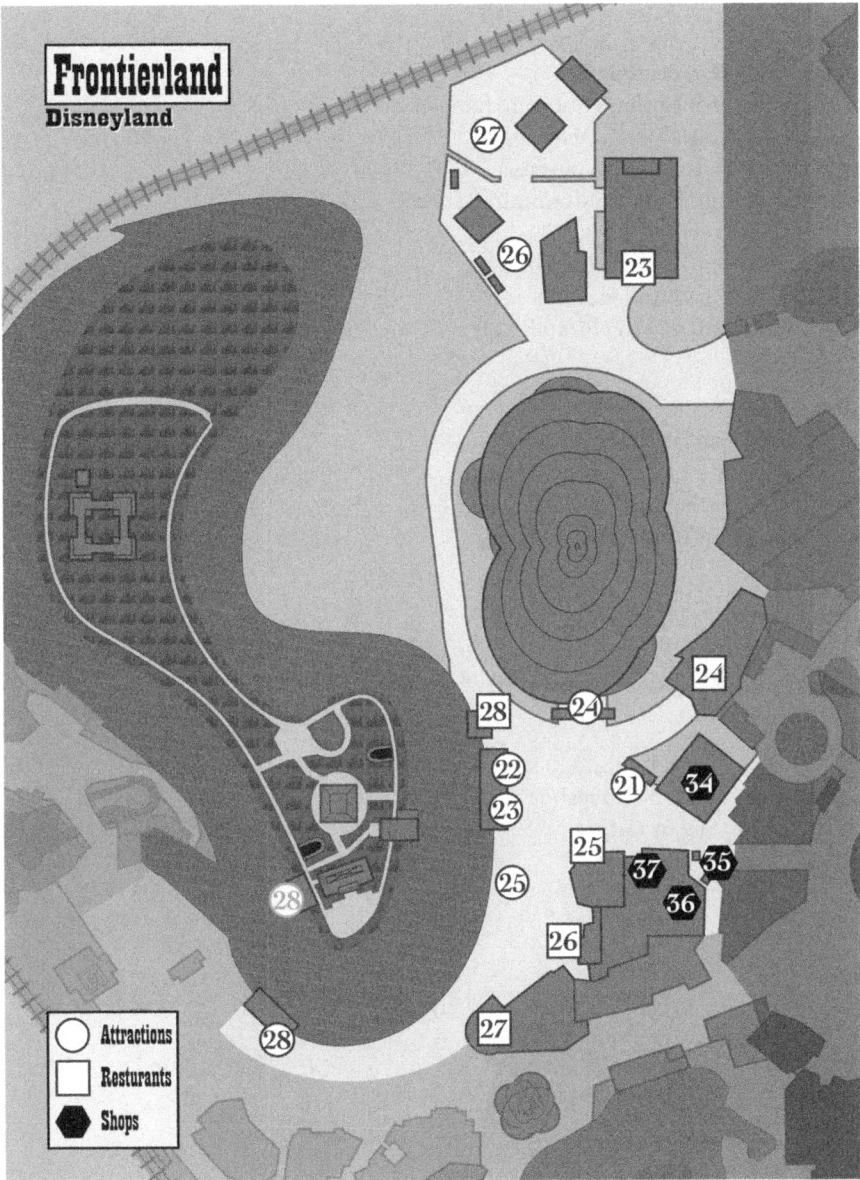

Frontierland
Disneyland

Attractions
Resturants
Shops

Attractions & Activities
- ☐ 21 Frontierland Shootin' Exposition
- ☐ 22 Mark Twain Riverboat
- ☐ 23 Sailing Ship Columbia
- ☐ 24 Big Thunder Mountain Railroad
- ☐ 25 Petrified Tree
- ☐ 26 Big Thunder Ranch
- ☐ 27 Big Thunder Jamboree
- ☐ 28 Rafts to the Pirate's Lair on Tom Sawyer Island

Shows
- ☐ 14 Fantasmic!
- ☐ 15 The Laughing Stock Co.
- ☐ 16 Farley the Fiddler
- ☐ 17 Big Thunder Ranch Stage

Restaurants
Full Service

23 Big Thunder Ranch Barbecue

Quick Service

24 Rancho del Zocalo Restaurante
25 The Golden Horseshoe
26 Stage Door Café
27 River Belle Terrace
28 Shipping Office

Shops
34 Westward Ho Trading Company
35 The Leather Shop
36 Pioneer Mercantile
37 Bonanza Outfitters

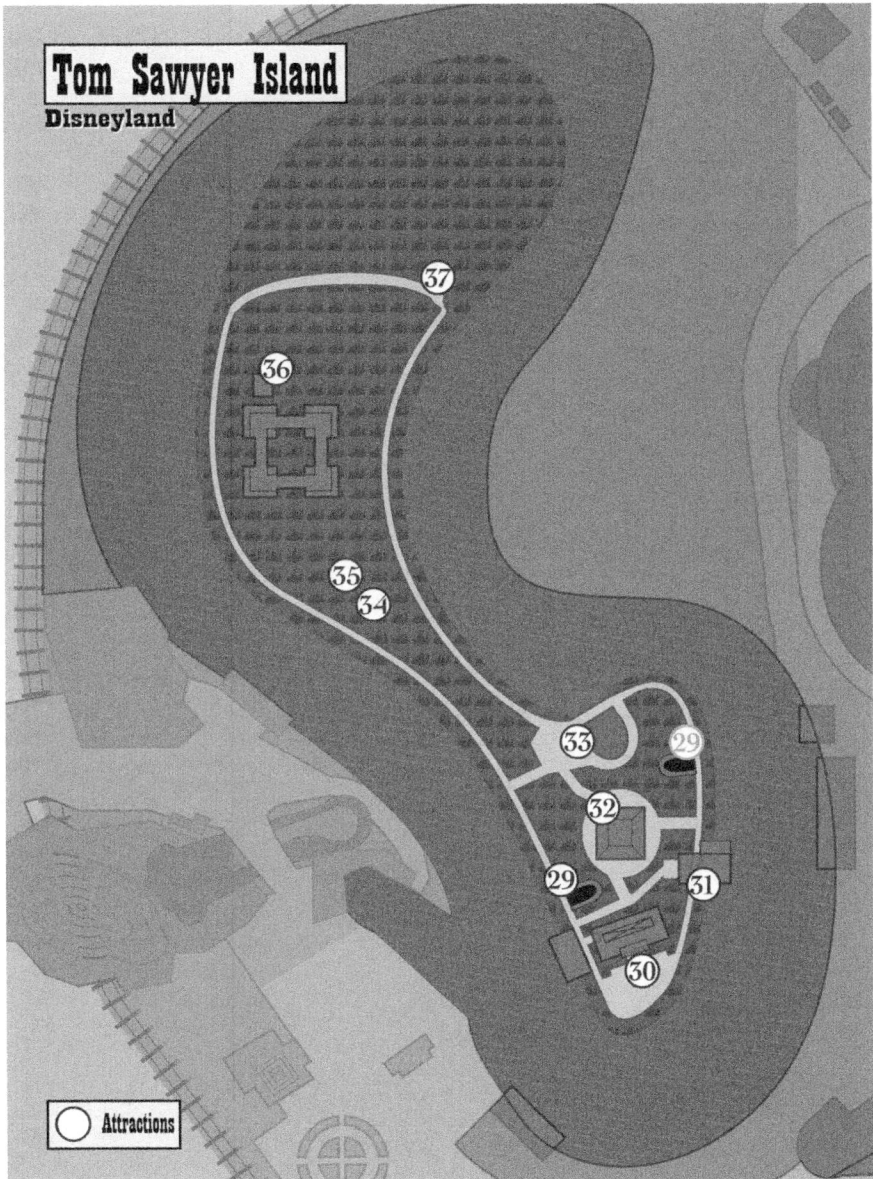

Tom Sawyer Island
Disneyland

37

36

35
34

33   29

32

29   31

30

◯ Attractions

Attractions & Activities

- ☐ 29 Dead Man's Grotto
- ☐ 30 Lafitte's Tavern & Pirate Point
- ☐ 31 Will Turner's Blacksmith Shop
- ☐ 32 Tom & Huck's Tree House
- ☐ 33 Smuggler's Cove
- ☐ 34 Castle Rock
- ☐ 35 Shipwreck & Pirate's Den
- ☐ 36 The Graveyard
- ☐ 37 Captain's Treasure

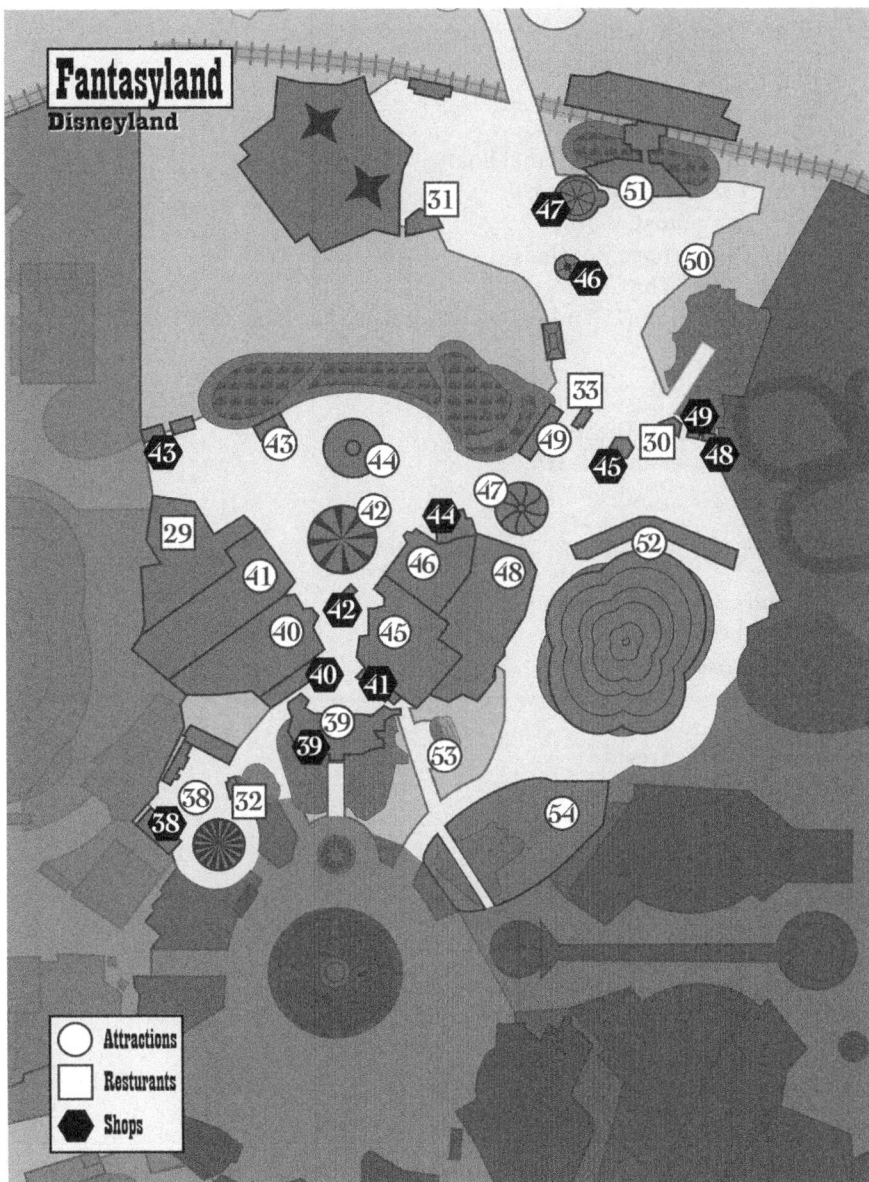

Fantasyland
Disneyland

Legend:
- ○ Attractions
- □ Resturants
- ⬡ Shops

Attractions & Activities

☐ 38 Fantasy Faire
☐ 39 Sleeping Beauty Castle Walkthrough
☐ 40 Snow White's Scary Adventures
☐ 41 Pinocchio's Daring Journey
☐ 42 King Arthur Carrousel
☐ 43 Casey Jr. Circus Train

☐ 44 Dumbo the Flying Elephant
☐ 45 Peter Pan's Flight
☐ 46 Mr. Toad's Wild Ride
☐ 47 Mad Tea Party
☐ 48 Alice in Wonderland
☐ 49 Storybook Land Canal Boats
☐ 50 Brave Meet & Greet
☐ 51 It's a Small World
☐ 52 Matterhorn Bobsleds
☐ 53 Snow White's Grotto
☐ 54 Pixie Hollow: Tinker Bell & Her Fairy Friends

Shows
☐ 18 The Royal Theatre
☐ 19 Fantasyland Theatre

Restaurants
Quick Service
29 Village Haus Restaurant
30 Edelweiss Snacks
31 Troubadour Tavern

Carts
32 Maurice's Treats

Coffee & Dessert
33 Fantasia Freeze

Shops
38 Fairy Tale Treasures
39 Enchanted Chamber
40 Bibbidi Bobbidi Boutique
41 Castle Heraldry Shoppe
42 Carrousel Candies
43 Stromboli's Wagon
44 Mad Hatter
45 Le Petit Chalet
46 Fantasy Faire Gifts
47 "it's a small world" Toy Shop
48 Fairytale Faces
49 Fairytale Scripts

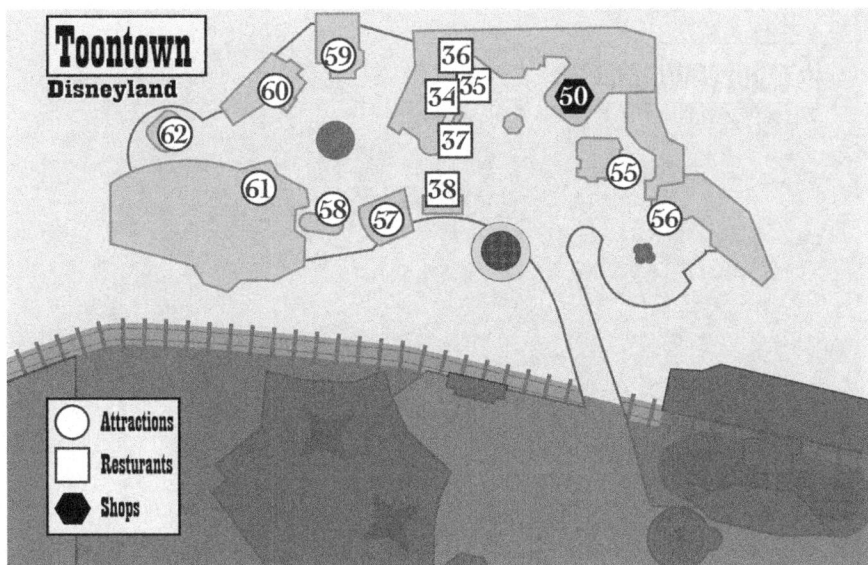

Attractions & Activities

- ☐ 55 Downtown Toontown
- ☐ 56 Roger Rabbit's Cartoon Spin
- ☐ 57 Goofy's Playhouse
- ☐ 58 Donald's Boat
- ☐ 59 Minnie's House
- ☐ 60 Mickey's House
- ☐ 61 Gadget's Go Coaster
- ☐ 62 Chip 'n' Dale Treehouse

Restaurants

Quick Service

34 Daisy's Diner

35 Pluto's Dog House

36 Clarabelle's

Carts

37 Toon Up Treats at Goofy's Gas Station

Coffee & Dessert

38 Goofy's Freez Time

Shops

50 Gag Factory / Toontown Five & Dime

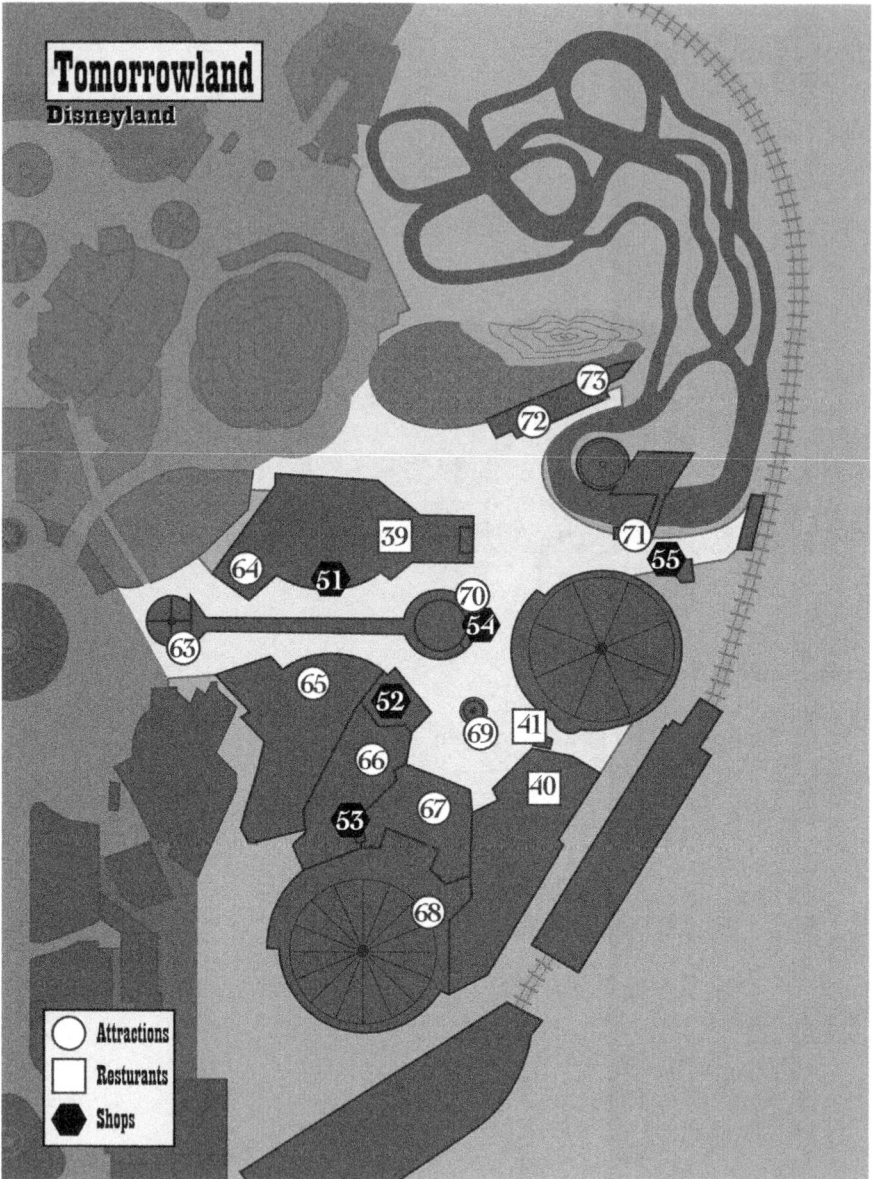

Tomorrowland
Disneyland

Attractions
Resturants
Shops

Attractions & Activities

- ☐ 63 Astro Orbitor
- ☐ 64 Buzz Lightyear Astro Blasters
- ☐ 65 Star Tours – The Adventures Continue
- ☐ 66 Starcade
- ☐ 67 Tomorrowland Theater
- ☐ 68 Space Mountain
- ☐ 69 Cosmic Waves
- ☐ 70 Marvel Action Heros Meet & Greet
- ☐ 71 Autopia
- ☐ 72 Finding Nemo Submarine Voyage
- ☐ 73 Disneyland Monorail

Shows

- ☐ 20 Tomorrowland Terrace Bands
- ☐ 21 Jedi Training Academy At Tomorrowland Terrace

Restaurants

Quick Service

39 Tomorrowland Terrace

40 Redd Rockett's Pizza Port

Carts

41 The Spirit of Refreshment at the Moonliner Rocket

Shops

51 Little Green Men Store Command

52 The Star Trader

53 Spaceport Document Control

54 Tomorrow Landing

55 Autopia Winner's Circle

Halloween at Disney California Adventure

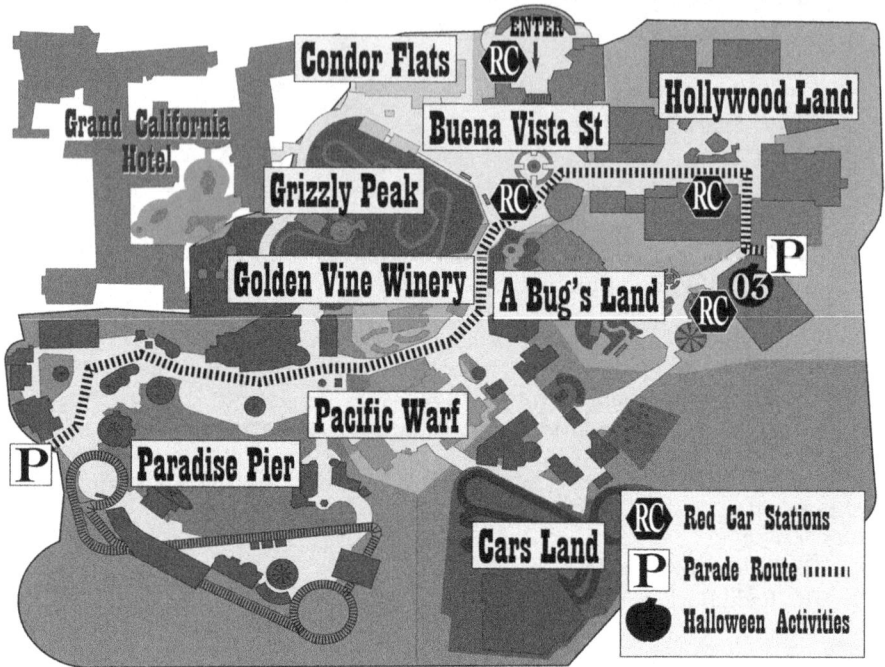

Condor Flats

Grand California Hotel

Buena Vista St

Hollywood Land

Grizzly Peak

Golden Vine Winery

A Bug's Land

03

P

Pacific Warf

Paradise Pier

Cars Land

RC Red Car Stations

P Parade Route ....

Halloween Activities

ENTER

Halloween at Disney California Adventure
Attractions
- ☐ 03 The Twilight Zone Tower of Terror

Park Transportation
- ☐ *RC* Red Car Trolley

Shows
- ☐ *P* Pixar Play Parade

Attractions & Activities
- ☐ 02 Meet Oswald The Lucky Rabbit
- ☐ 03 Buena Vista Bugle
- ☐ 04 The Citizens of Buena Vista Street

Shows
- ☐ 02 Red Car News Boys
- ☐ 03 Five & Dime

Dining
Full Service

01 Carthay Circle Restaurant

02 Carthay Circle Lounge

Quick Service

03 Fiddler, Fifer & Practical Café

04 Mortimer's Market

Dessert

05 Clarabelle's Hand-Scooped Ice Cream

06 Trolley Treats

Shops

    01 Oswald's Tires
    02 Los Feliz Five & Dime
    03 Big Top Toys
    04 Youth Dept. at Elias & Co.
    05 Woman's Dept. at Elias & Co.
    06 Men's Dept. at Elias & Co.
    07 Jewelry Dept. at Elias & Co.
    08 Kingswell Camera Shop
    09 Julius Katz & Sons
    10 Atwater Ink & Paint

Hollywood Land

California Adventure

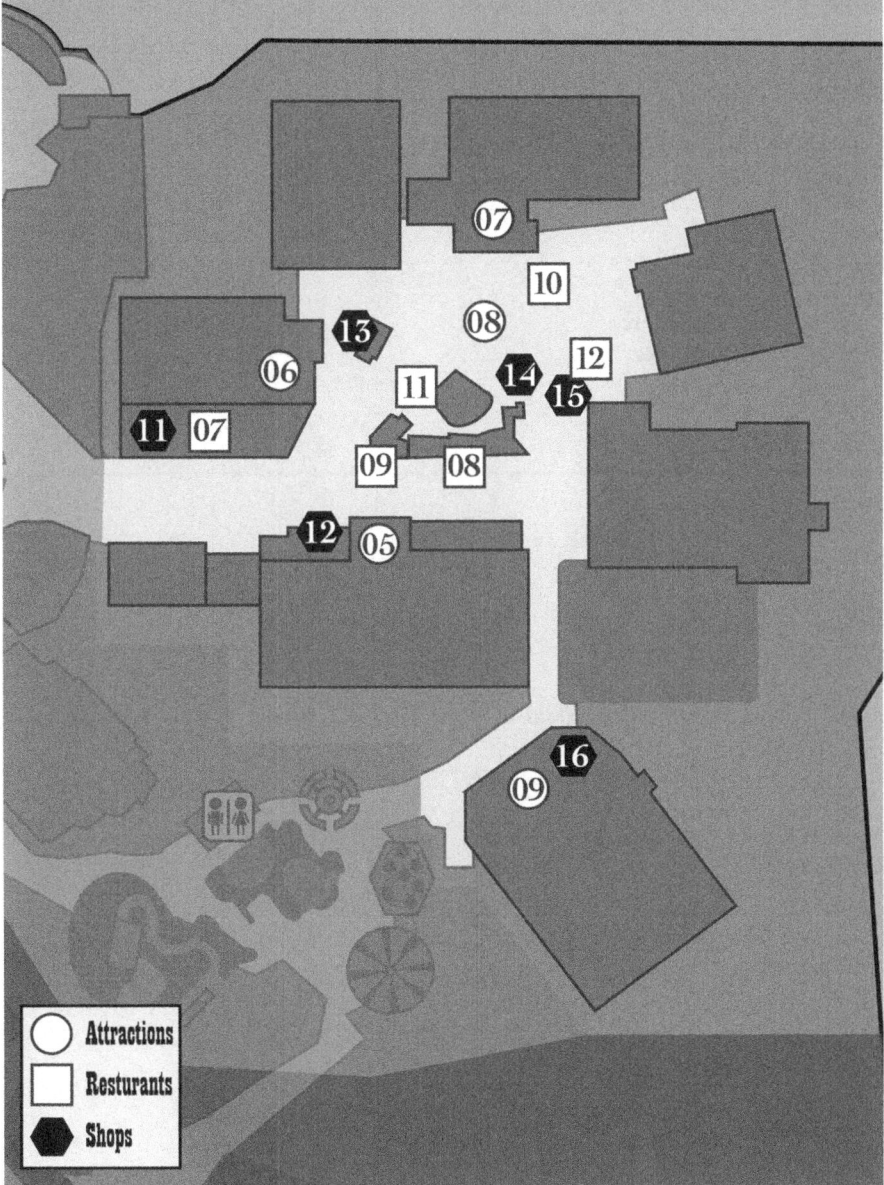

07

10

08

13

06

12

11

15

11 07

09 08

12 05

16

09

Attractions
Resturants
Shops

Attractions & Activities
- ☐ 05 Disney Animation
- ☐ 06 Frozen Fun
- ☐ 07 Monsters, Inc. Mike & Sulley to the Rescue!
- ☐ 08 Diamond Mad T Party
- ☐ 09 The Twilight Zone Tower of Terror

Shows
- ☐ 04 Disney Junior Live on Stage
- ☐ 05 Disney Performing Arts Stage
- ☐ 06 Disney's Aladdin: Musical Spectacular

Dining
Quick Service
- 07 Award Wieners
- 08 Fairfax Market
- 09 Schmoozies

Mad Tea Party Event Stands
- 10 House of Cards
- 11 Drink Me
- 12 Fuze Catering Truck

Shops
- 11 Gone Hollywood
- 12 Off the Page
- 13 Wandering Oaken's Trading Post
- 14 Mad T Party Face Painting
- 15 Disney Diamond Anniversary Gifts
- 16 Tower Hotel Gifts

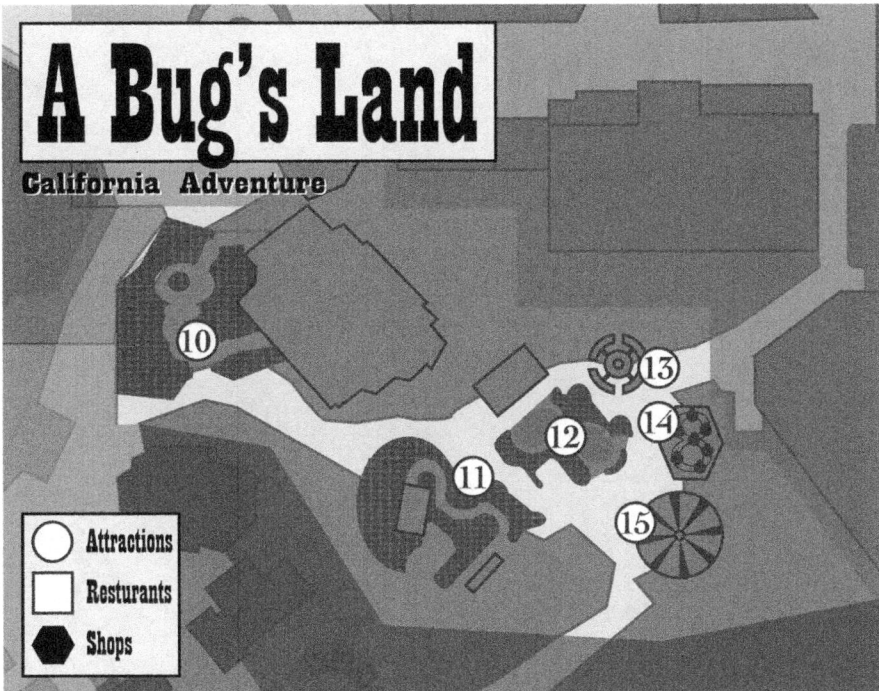

Attractions & Activities

- [ ] 10 It's Tough to Be a Bug!
- [ ] 11 Heimlich's Chew Chew Train
- [ ] 12 Princess Dot Puddle Park
- [ ] 13 Flik's Flyers
- [ ] 14 Francis' Ladybug Boogie
- [ ] 15 Tuck and Roll's Drive 'Em Buggies

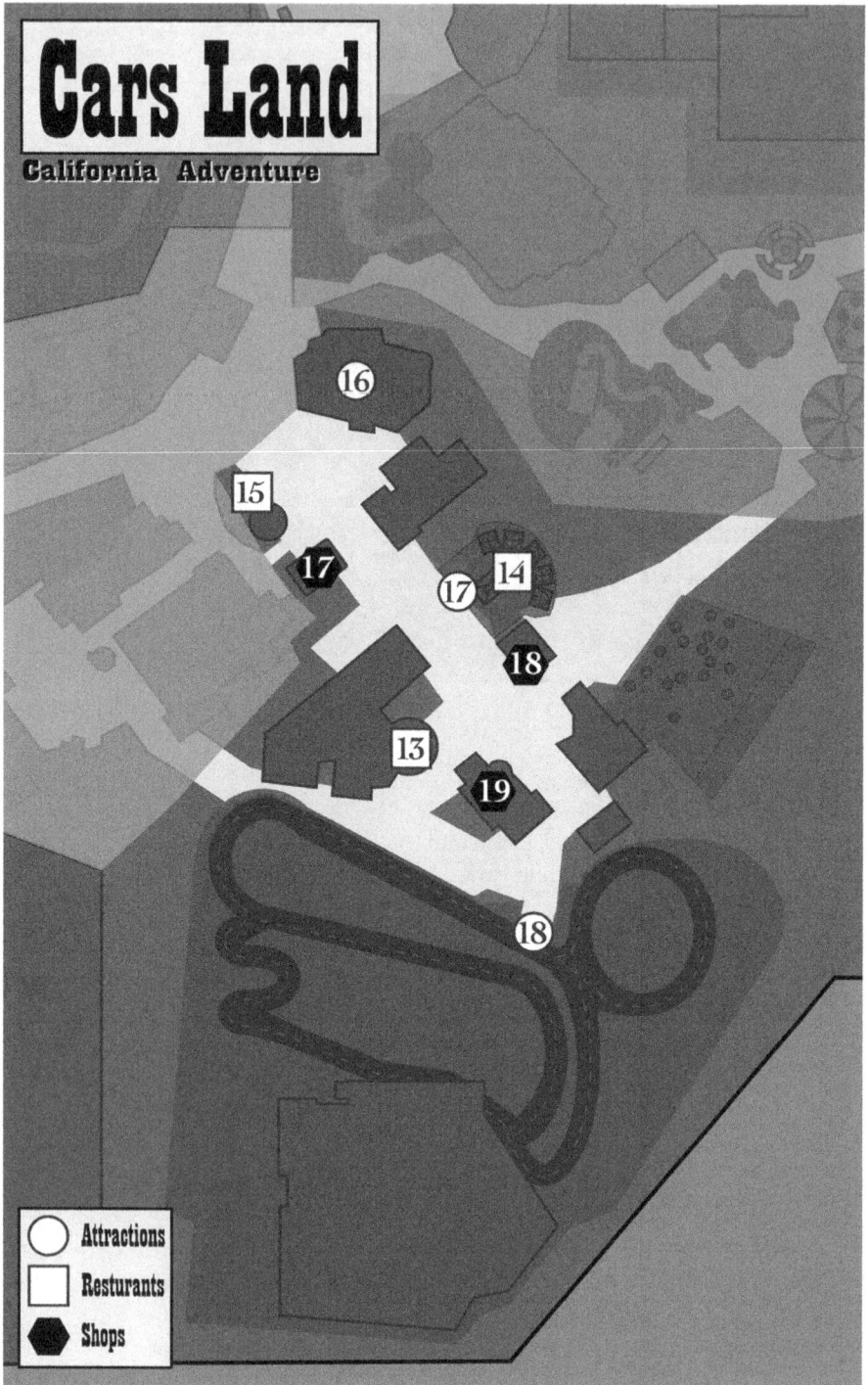

Cars Land
California Adventure

16

15

17

14

17

18

13

19

18

○ Attractions
□ Resturants
⬡ Shops

Attractions & Activities
- ☐ 16 Mater's Junkyard Jamboree
- ☐ 17 Meet Cars Characters
- ☐ 18 Radiator Springs Racers

Shows
- ☐ 07 Red to the Rescue
- ☐ 08 DJ's Dance 'n Drive

Dining
Quick Service

13 Flo's V8 Café

14 Cozy Cone Motel

15 Fillmore's Taste-In

Shops

17 Sarge's Surplus Hut

18 Radiator Springs Curios

19 Ramone's House of Body Art

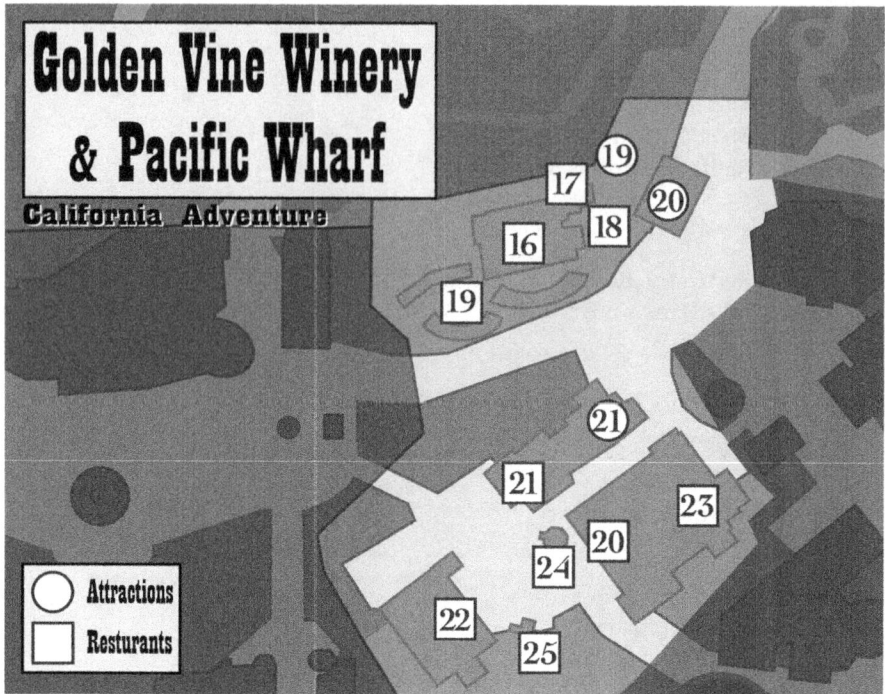

Golden Vine Winery & Pacific Wharf
California Adventure

Attractions & Activities
- ☐ 19 Explore the Vineyards
- ☐ 20 Blue Sky Cellar
- ☐ 21 Boudin Bakery Tour

Shows
- ☐ 09 Mariachi Divas

Dining
Full Service
- 16 Wine Country Trattoria
- 17 Alfresco Tasting Terrace

Quick Service
- 18 Mendocino Terrace
- 19 Sonoma Terrace
- 20 Lucky Fortune Cookery
- 21 Pacific Wharf Café
- 22 Cocina Cucamonga Mexican Grill
- 23 Ghirardelli Soda Fountain
- 24 Rita's Baja Blenders
- 25 Pacific Wharf Distribution Co.

Attractions & Activities

- ☐ 22 Caricature Drawings & Full Color Portraits
- ☐ 23 Meet Donald Duck
- ☐ 24 California Screamin'
- ☐ 25 King Triton's Carousel
- ☐ 26 Toy Story Midway Mania!
- ☐ 27 Meet The Characters From Toy Story
- ☐ 28 Games of the Boardwalk
- ☐ 29 Face Painting & Henna Tattoos
- ☐ 30 Mickey's Fun Wheel
- ☐ 31 Silly Symphony Swings
- ☐ 32 Goofy's Sky School
- ☐ 33 Jumpin' Jellyfish
- ☐ 34 Golden Zephyr
- ☐ 35 The Little Mermaid: Ariel's Undersea Adventure
- ☐ 36 Fun Wheel Challenge

Shows
- ☐ 10 World of Color – Celebrate!
- ☐ 11 Just Add Water: Instant Concert!
- ☐ 12 Operation: Playtime! With The Green Army Men
- ☐ 13 Paradise Gardens Bandstand
- ☐ 14 Phineas & Ferb's Rockin' Rollin' Dance Party

Dining
Full Service
26 Ariel's Grotto

Full Service Dining & Bar
27 Cove Bar

Quick Service
28 Boardwalk Pizza & Pasta
29 Paradise Garden Grill
30 Corn Dog Castle
31 Don Toma's
32 Hot Dog Hut

Coffee & Dessert
33 Paradise Pier Ice Cream Co.
34 Gourmet Coffee

Outdoor Bar
35 Bayside Brews

Shops
21 Laod Bhang's Pin Traders
22 Treasures in Paradise
23 California Scream Cam
24 Midway Mercantile
25 Point Mugu Tattoo
26 Boardwalk Bazaar
27 Sideshow Shirts
28 Embarcadero Gifts
29 Seaside Souvenirs
30 Paradise Pier Sunglass Hut

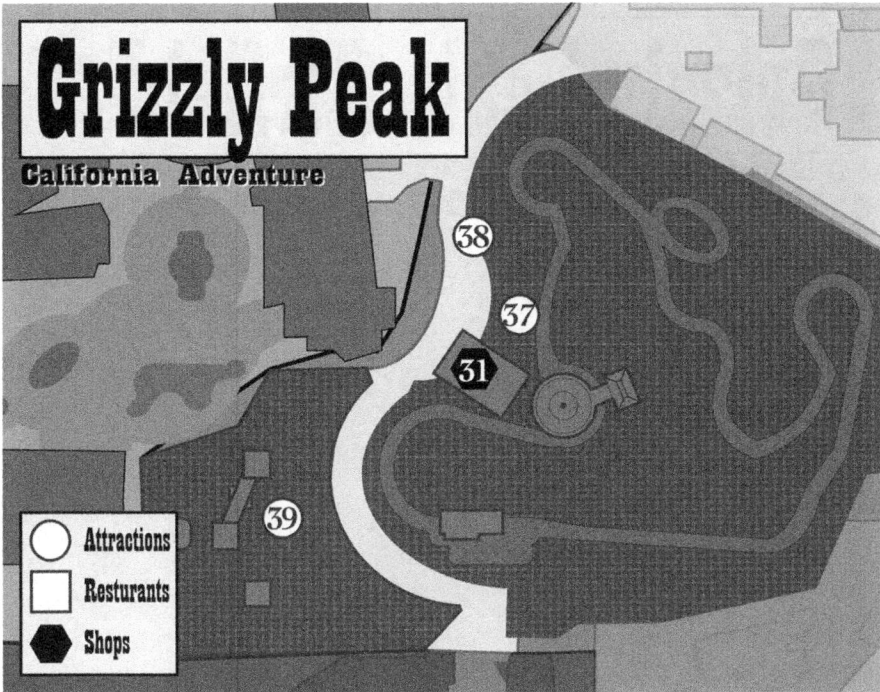

Attractions & Activities
- ☐ 37 Grizzly River Run
- ☐ 38 Route 49 Binoculars
- ☐ 39 Redwood Creek Challenge Trail

Shows
- ☐ 15 The Happy Camper Sing Along

Shops
31 Rushin' River Outfitters

Attractions & Activities
☐ 40 Soarin' Over California

Dining
Quick Service
36 Smokejumpers Grill

Carts
37 Popcorn
38 Refreshment Point

Shops
32 Humphrey's Service & Supplies

Preparation

Purchasing Tickets

Tickets to Disneyland may be purchased at on-site ticket booths, online through the Disneyland website, through discount ticket brokers, through private travel agents, or through the student travel services at many universities.

Ticket Booths

Tickets may be purchased at the Disneyland Resort from the ticket booths located in the plaza between Disneyland and California Adventure. One advantage to buying tickets here are the highly trained cast members manning the booths. They can answer just about any question you have about your Disneyland trip.

Online Ticket Sales

Tickets to Disneyland may also be purchased in advance from the Disneyland Ticket Website. Guests can receive a discount by buying certain multi-day ticket packages online.

disneyland.disney.go.com/tickets/

Ticket Types

Single Park Tickets

Entrance into only one Disneyland Resort Park, either Disneyland or Disney's California Adventure.

Park Hopper Tickets

Admission to both parks, guests may change parks as often as they wish.

Mickey's Halloween Party Tickets

Admission to Mickey's Halloween Party requires a special ticket, even if you have a general admission ticket to the park earlier in the day. See the Mickey's Halloween Party in the Top Halloween Activities section later in this book for event dates and admission prices. You may purchase your tickets in advanced by clicking on the *Special Event Tickets* tab at:

disneyland.com/tickets/events/

Early Admission

Some ticket packages include entry into the theme parks an hour before the general public is allowed in. More information about these programs can be found here:

disneyland.disney.go.com/calendar/early-admission/

Magic Mornings

This promotion provides guests with the ability to enter Disneyland one hour early on one of the days they visit the park. These special tickets are available to Disneyland Resort guests with 3-day or longer theme park tickets, special promotional "bonus" tickets, or a 2015 Southern California CityPASS. See the Disneyland website or on-site ticket booths for details.

http://disneyland.disney.go.com/guest-services/magic-morning-early-admission/

Extra Magic Hour

This promotion gives registered Disneyland Resort hotel guests Early admission to either Disneyland or California Adventure one hour before the park opens to the general public on every day of their hotel stay. Schedules and details for this program are also available at the Disneyland website or on-site ticket booths.

https://disneyland.disney.go.com/guest-services/extra-magic-hour-early-admission/

Halloween Costume Guidelines

Guests may dress up in a Halloween costume only if they have tickets to Mickey's Halloween Party. This includes adults and kids. To handle this policy Disney has come up with a set of guidelines that must be followed by any guest that wears a costume inside Disneyland during the event. Please note that any guest wearing a costume that does not meet these guidelines may be refused entry into the theme parks.

- Costumes must be child-friendly.

- They should not be obstructive, offensive, or violent.

- They cannot drag on the ground.

- They may not contain sharp objects, pointed objects, or materials that may accidentally strike another guest.

- They cannot contain any weapons which resemble or could easily be mistaken for an actual weapon.

- Masks may be worn, but they must not obstruct vision, and eyes must be visible at all times.

- Guests who dress like disney characters may not pose for pictures or sign autographs.

Choosing a Parking Lot

The Disneyland Resort has several different parking lots for guests to choose from, but the Mickey & Friends Parking Structure is the largest and most commonly used. Both the Disneyland park and Disney California Adventure share the same parking lots and parking fees:

$17.00/day: cars & motorcycles

$22.00/day: oversized vehicles including motor homes
$27.00/day: buses

The parking structures and lots for the two Disneyland Resort theme parks usually open one hour before the parks. Trams from the various parking lots to the park's *Entry Plaza* typically begin running when each parking lot opens. For guests who have early admission to the parks with *Magic Mornings* tickets, the Mickey & Friends parking structure typically opens 90 minutes before the Disneyland park officially opens on magic morning days. Parking may be paid for at the various parking lots as guests enter, or in advance on the Disneyland Resort Ticket Website:

disneyland.disney.go.com/tickets

Cash, Credit Cards (Visa, Mastercard, Discover, American Express, JCB, & Diner's Club), Disney Rewards Redemption Cards, Disney Gift Cards, Disney Dollars, and Pre-Paid Parking Vouchers are accepted as payment for parking fees at all Disneyland Resort Parking Lots.

Parking at Disneyland Resort lots other than those used specifically for the theme parks, such as the various hotel parking lots and the lots for Downtown Disney, charge different fees than those listed above. For more information on parking, visit:

disneyland.disney.go.com/guest-services/parking/

Mickey & Friends Parking Structure

As the largest and most popular parking lot for the resorts' two theme parks, guests are most likely to use this gigantic multi-level parking structure. Escalators and stairs take guests to the ground floor where they may take the FREE parking tram to the theme parks' front gates. Fees for parking in this structure follow the standard $17/$22/$27 theme park parking fee schedule listed above.

From inside the parking structure, follow signs to the tram. Trams typically begin running when the parking lot opens, and continue running for about an hour after the park closes. Guests who miss the tram operating hours may walk back to the Mickey & Friends Parking Structure by following the pedestrian sidewalks and walkways back to the lot. Follow the cemented pedestrian path to the left of the tram boarding area alongside the back of the Downtown Disney shops and the Parking Tram route until you reach the path's end at Disneyland Dr, and then turn right onto Disneyland Dr. and proceed until you reach Magic Way. Finally, turn left and cross the street onto Magic Way, and follow it until you reach the pedestrian entrance to the Mickey and Friends parking structure on your right. It's a long walk, so... Don't miss the parking tram.

Pinocchio Parking Lot

Located right next to the Mickey & Friends Parking Structure, this lot shares access to the same FREE parking tram to Disneyland. Often oversized vehicles such as motor homes or trailers are directed into this lot. It follows the same $17/$22/$27 per day parking fee schedule as the Mickey & Friends Parking Structure listed above.

Pumbaa Parking Lot

The Pumbaa parking lot is located to the east of the Disneyland Resort on Disney

Way, across the street from the Anaheim Garden Walk. This lot offers easy access to the Anaheim Garden Walk shopping mall, several local Good Neighbor hotels and is about two blocks away from the Disneyland Entry Plaza. Some guests prefer this lot because of its proximity to Disneyland's entrance and the added bonus of being able to escape parking structure traffic jams at the end of the day. The fees for parking in this lot follow the standard $17/$22/$27 per day theme park parking fee schedule listed above.

Simba Parking Lot

The Simba parking lot is bordered by S. Walnut St. to the west, West Katella Ave to the south and Disneyland Drive (also known as West St) to the east. This large lot is located just to the south-west of the Paradise Pier hotel, and offers access to this hotel as wells as Downtown Disney, but it's fairly far way from the theme parks. The lot is entered on Disneyland Drive (West St), and parking fees follow the standard $17/$22/$27 theme park parking fee schedule listed above.

Toy Story Parking Lot

This lot is located on the west side of S. Harbor Blvd., just below the Katella Cast Member Parking Lot. It is two blocks away from the Anaheim Convention Center and is the farthest parking lot from Disneyland. A free parking shuttle delivers guests to the front of the Disneyland *Entry Plaza*, making this lot a convenient option for many Disneyland insiders. The fees for parking in the Toy Story lot follow the standard $17/$22/$27 theme park parking fee schedule listed above. The FREE shuttle located inside the Toy Story Parking Lot brings guests directly to the Disneyland Resort's East Shuttle Area next to the theme parks' *Entry Plaza*, offering convenient access to ticket booths and entry gates.

Downtown Disney Self Parking

This lot is located next to the Downtown Disney shopping district at the west end of the mall. Follow the signs to Downtown Disney to use these lots. Intended for use by guests of the Downtown Disney shopping district, these lots charge different fees than the Theme Park parking lots: 3 hours FREE parking without validation, 5 hours FREE parking WITH VALIDATION, and $6 each additional Hour ($30 maximum per day).

The Downtown Disney parking lots offer easy access to the Downtown Disney shopping mall, the Disneyland *Monorail* and the Disneyland Hotel. With a validated parking ticket, the lot can offer guests a great FREE alternative to parking fees if they are only visiting the Disneyland Resort for less than 5 hours. Guests with disabilities may park in the 'Disabled' parking spots at the front of the main parking lot. Valet service is typically available from 5pm to 2am and costs $6 in addition to the hourly self parking rates.

Disneyland Hotel Parking

Parking at the Disneyland Hotel parking lot is intended for hotel guests, and in most circumstances is not included in your room fees. However, Anyone can still park in this lot if they choose. The fee for parking at the Disneyland Hotel is $17 per evening for guests with room reservations, and $17 for the first hour plus $9 for each additional hour for guests not staying at the hotel. *Valet Parking is* $25/

evening registered hotel guests, $25 for the first hour plus $9/ additional hour non-registered guests.

Grand California Hotel Parking

Guests staying at the Grand California Hotel pay $17 per evening for self parking. Guests not staying at the hotel pay $17 for the first hour, and $9 each additional hour for self parking. If you do not have a room booked at the hotel these parking rates are very expensive compared to parking at the rest of the park. The Grand California Hotel parking lot offers quick easy access to the hotel, it's restaurants/bars, Downtown Disney, and a special hotel entrance into the California Adventure theme park. *Valet Parking is* $25/evening registered hotel guests, $25 for the first hour plus $9/ additional hour non-registered guests.

Paradise Pier Hotel Parking

This parking lot is also intended for hotel guests, but anyone can park here who is willing to pay the steep parking fees. Guests staying at the hotel pay $17 per evening for self parking, and guests not staying at the hotel pay $17 for the first hour, and $9 each additional hour for self parking. The Paradise Pier Hotel parking lot offers convenient access only to the hotel and the restaurants inside. Unless you specifically want to go to this hotel this parking lot is not really worth the visit. *Valet Parking is* $25/evening registered hotel guests, $25 for the first hour plus $9/ additional hour non-registered guests.

Entering the Parks

The Disneyland Resort offers guests several options for how they get to and enter Disneyland or California Adventure. Sometimes the way you arrive to the park can be just as much fun as what you do inside the park. Start the fun before you even enter the front gates with these arrival options.

Take a FREE Ride on the Monorail

This futuristic single track train system transports guests back and fourth between Downtown Disney (near the Disneyland Hotel) and Tomorrowland (inside the Disneyland Park). The monorail is always free, but you must have a Disneyland Park ticket to ride it. It usually opens at the same time the Disneyland park opens. This futuristic train is not only fun to ride, it's a great time-saving way to enter the park, particularly in the morning when crowds form at the Disneyland entry gates. Find the monorail station near the west end of Downtown Disney. You can also use the monorail to leave the park and return to Downtown Disney for a quick lunch, a stop at your hotel, or to exit the park at the end of the day.

Ride the Mickey & Friends Parking Tram Before the Park Opens

The FREE parking tram picks up guests from the Mickey & Friends Parking Structure and delivers them to the front gates of both Disneyland and Disney California Adventure. This open air tram tour through some of the back areas of the Disneyland property is as much fun to ride on as it is useful. It's like getting a bonus park ride in before the gates even open, and kids love it. But I'll let you in on a little secret; Adults love it too.

If you have a lot of time to kill before the gates open and you truly want to do everything there is to do at Disneyland, you can park in the Mickey & Friends Parking Structure and take the parking tram to Disneyland's front gates. From there you can walk through Downtown Disney to the Monorail station and take the Monorail into the park. If you are staying in one of the Disneyland resort hotels or parked in another lot you can walk to the Mickey & Friends Parking Structure and catch the free parking tram.

Buy Your Tickets Beforehand
The best way to make use of all these fun transportation options (and get into the park quickly in the morning) is to purchase your tickets before you arrive at the park. This can be done online at the Disneyland website or at the park's main ticket booths the night before. The ticket booths are located right outside the entrance to the park and they stay open late, usually an hour after the park closes. This way when you arrive in the morning you can just hop aboard the *Monorail* or jump in line at the entry gates without having to wait in the long ticket purchase lines.

https://disneyland.disney.go.com/tickets/

The Gates Open Early for Everyone
The downside to using the *Monorail* to enter the park is that you arrive inside Disneyland after the gates open. If you enter through the main gates you can be inside Disneyland on Main Street before the park's official opening time, a full half hour before. You only get access to Main Street, but this gives you the chance to get breakfast, do a little morning Shopping, and be in the best location possible when they lower the rope and let guests into the rest of the park. All regular restaurants and shops on Main Street Should be open at this time, but the attractions such as the *Main Street Cinema* will not open until the park's official opening time.

To make use of this extra time, simply line up at the regular entry gates a little more than half an hour before the park's opening time, and at the half hour mark the gates will open and you can enjoy Disneyland's most famous boulevard. Opening times change daily, see the Disneyland website for current opening times:

https://disneyland.disney.go.com/calendars/

Halloween Ambiance & Decorations

Throughout Main Street USA

Disneyland goes all out with it's yearly celebration of Halloween, and the decorations seem to come out earlier and earlier each year. Look for fall themed decorations throughout the Main Street USA area. Below are a few of my favorite Halloween spots on Main Street.

Town Square

Town Square at the south end of Main Street (the area closest to the entry plaza where you entered the park) features the park's traditional giant Mickey jack-o-lantern complete with mouse ears. Be sure to stop by and have your picture taken in front of it, a park photographer will be standing by to take it for you.

Partners Statue

Don't miss the carved pumpkins placed in a circle around the statue of Mickey Mouse and Walt Disney in the center of the Central Hub (at the north end of Main Street.) There is a pumpkin carved to represent each of the lands in Disneyland. Circle the whole display to see them all. Also note the beautiful fall flower arrangements surrounding the pumpkins. Be sure to have your photo taken in front of the statue while you are there.

Frontierland

Frontierland in Disneyland also gets into the Halloween spirit with decorations throughout the land's streets, restaurants, and shops. Look for an extra helping of Halloween decorations in these top locations:

- The Halloween Tree
- Big Thunder Ranch

Assorted Shops & Restaurants

The shops and restaurants up and down main street really get into the Halloween spirit. Take a look at all the fall flowers, ribbons, and Halloween decorations as you travel inside and outside the buildings here. Other restaurants and shops throughout the park get in on the spirit by offering their own brand of decorations and specialty Halloween items.

Disneyana & The Disney Gallery (Main Street USA, DL)

The Ghostly Materials art show in The Disney Gallery features amazing original Haunted Mansion themed art works for sale and viewing. Be sure to stop by and take a look at the ghoulish collection of original paintings, prints, dioramas, and hand crafted figurines found here.

Fortuosity Shop (Main Street USA, DL)

This store goes all out with it's Halloween decorations, and it's famous for its hundreds of black ravens looking down from perches high within the shop.

Port Royal (New Orleans Square, DL)

Look above merchandise shelves and up along the ceiling for a myriad of spooky skulls, jack-o-lanterns, cob webs, and other Halloween decorations.

Le Bat en Rouge (New Orleans Square, DL)

This shop maintains a spooky Halloween feel year round, be sure not to miss it.

French Market Restaurant (New Orleans Square, DL)

Take in *The Nightmare Before Christmas* (1993) and other Halloween themed decorations along the restaurant's outer fence and seating area.

Tower Hotel Gifts (Hollywood Land, DCA)

Be sure to take a look at the display windows full of spooky Halloween artifacts set up in front of the store.

World of Disney (Downtown Disney)

Look for special Halloween decorations and displays throughout the massive store.

Marceline's Confectionery (Downtown Disney)

Look for *The Nightmare Before Christmas* (1993) and other Halloween decorations hanging throughout the shop.

Halloween Attractions

01 • Haunted Mansion Holiday
Haunted Mansion, New Orleans Square, Disneyland
Spooky Mild Ride • FastPass

Towards the back edge of New Orleans Square sits an ominous old mansion, just waiting for it's next group of victims to set foot inside. Although the Haunted Mansion appears frightening, it's family-friendly. Once inside you can try to escape a stretching room with no exit, take a walk down a haunted corridor and ride in a "Doom Buggy" that guides you through the rest of the mansion. But look out, because ghosts can be found lurking around any corner, and if you're not careful some of them may follow you home.

The Nightmare Before Christmas

The largest Halloween transformation in the park takes place at the *Haunted Mansion*, which becomes a 'Nightmare Before Christmas'-themed Haunted Holiday attraction. Nearly every aspect of the mansion is converted into 'Nightmare Before Christmas' decorations, props, and characters. People travel across the globe just to see this yearly transformation. The 'Nightmare Before Christmas' theme at the Haunted Mansion typically opens in early October and lasts until New Years Day.

Don't miss the best aspects of the Haunted Mansion Holiday:

- *Outside the Mansion:* Take a look at all of *The Nightmare Before Christmas* (1993) decorations that have transformed the outside of the mansion, particularly the countdown clock. Have your photo taken in front of the Halloween decorated hearse wagon if you can.

- *The Stretching Room:* The changes in this room get more elaborate every year. Pay close attention to the paintings as they stretch to reveal new designs and watch the center of the ceiling closely, even after you think that part of the show is over. You may see a character familiar to die-hard Haunted Mansion fans appear for a moment after *The Nightmare Before Christmas* (1993) part of the effect is over.

- *Haunted Hallway:* Not only are the paintings in this hallway transforming before your very eyes, but an observant guest will notice that Zero the ghost dog is subtly jumping from one painting to another. Watch these ghoulish works of art carefully as you walk down the hallway towards the ride's loading platform.

- *Boarding Area:* Watch carefully as the displays behind the boarding platform come to life and move periodically. Pay particular attention to the many different moving shadows that appear in the moon from time to time.

- *The Gingerbread House Design:* A new gingerbread house is created with a different theme each year, and the designs get more elaborate with every season. This year's theme is based on a House of Cards game. Look for this amazing yearly creation on the table in the Main Ball Room portion of the ride. Then make sure you sniff the air for the potent smell of gingerbread that fills the room.

- *Gift Labels & List Names:* Guests young and old love to look for their names on gift packages and *Naughty or Nice* lists throughout the *Attic* portion of the ride. See if you can find your name here. I'm able to find my name every year.

- *Return of the Hatbox Ghost*: Look for this menacing creature at the very start of the Graveyard room, just after you exit the Attic. He will perform a special trick for you using his Hatbox, and it is terrifying. This effect has been missing from the Haunted Mansion since it was removed just after the attraction opened in 1969.

02 • Space Mountain Ghost Galaxy

Space Mountain, New Orleans Square, Disneyland
Thrill Ride • FastPass • Rider Swap • Height Requirement 40"

This high-speed roller coaster ride through outer space takes guests on a wild trip through the stars. After walking through a space station guests board a four seat rocket and blast off through a launch tube into outer space. The entire tubular steel track is housed inside a large darkened building allowing you only to see the stars and planets as you wind around curving tracks at high speeds.

Ghost Galaxy

Space Mountain is transformed into *Ghost Mountain* during the Halloween season. There's spooky projections inside and out - and watch out for the space ghost taunting you everywhere you turn. But be careful, the space ghost likes to chase travelers on their voyage through space, and I don't know what happens if he catches you!

In-Ride Photo

An automated camera will snap a photo of you at the end of the ride just as you enter the final lighted tunnel. View your photo on monitors near the exit to the attraction building and purchase prints if you like. Remember that automated attraction cameras are monitored, and anything deemed inappropriate will be erased.

03 • The Twilight Zone Tower of Terror
Hollywood Land, Disney California Adventure
Spooky Thrill Ride • FastPass • Rider Swap • Height Requirement 40"

At the far end of Sunset Blvd you will find what's left of the creepy, abandoned *Hollywood Tower Hotel*, but are you brave enough to enter and discover the secrets it holds inside? This combination walk-through attraction and thrill ride will scare you with its spooky ambience and creepy story before thrusting you up and down in a caged parachute-drop-style ride. Small children and people sensitive to rapid up and down motions may want to sit this one out.

Spooky Ambiance

There is a lot to see while walking through the hotel. Keep your eye out for abandoned luggage and other artifacts of long lost guests in the hotel lobby. The library is full of interesting artifacts to find, but you will have to make multiple trips to see it all. Listen for the motors running and pipes clanging in the boiler room. Even the gift shop is full of references and puns if you look hard enough.

In-Ride Photo

A photo of everyone in the elevator will be taken the first time you reach the top floor of the hotel and the doors open for a moment to the world outside.

In Front of the Hotel

Look for a California Adventure staff photographer on *Sunset Blvd* out in front of the hotel. They can take a wonderful photo of you with the spooky Hollywood Tower Hotel in the background.

Other Spooky Attractions
Throughout Disneyland & Disney California Adventure

These attractions may not be changed specifically for *Halloween Time at Disneyland*, but they are spooky year round and should not be missed when you visit the park this season. Make sure you allow some time to experience these other spooky classics.

- Jungle Cruise (Adventureland, DL)
- Indiana Jones Adventure (Adventureland, DL)
- Pirates of the Caribbean (New Orleans Square, DL)
- Splash Mountain (Critter Country, DL)
- Frontierland Shootin' Exposition (Frontierland, DL)
- Big Thunder Mountain Railroad (Frontierland, DL)
- Dead Man's Grotto (Tom Sawyer Island, DL)
- Smuggler's Cove (Tom Sawyer Island, DL)
- The Graveyard (Tom Sawyer Island, DL)
- Snow White's Scary Adventures (Fantasyland, DL)
- Pinocchio's Daring Journey (Fantasyland, DL)
- Mr Toad's Wild Ride (Fantasyland, DL)
- Alice in Wonderland (Fantasyland, DL)
- Matterhorn Bobsleds (Fantasyland, DL)

- Monsters, Inc Mike & Sulley to the Rescue! (Hollywood Land, DCA)
- It's Tough to Be a Bug! (A Bug's Land, DCA)
- Ariel's Undersea Adventure (Paradise Pier, DCA)

Halloween Events & Activities

04 • Mickey's Halloween Party
Disneyland

This is Disney's take on a time-honored Halloween tradition. Trick-or-Treat stations are set up throughout the park for the kids, and everyone is allowed to wear Halloween costumes. This nighttime event requires a special admission ticket, it's not included in the general admission. It does however offer special activities not found during the park's regular hours. Take a look at my list of favorite Mickey's Halloween Party activities below.

Mickey's Hide-and-Go-Treat Trails

Step up to more than 50 different Trick-or-Treat locations throughout the park and get a sweet surprise. You don't have to be in costume, but it's more fun if you are.

Disney Characters in Halloween Costumes

See your favorite Disney characters dressed up for Halloween throughout the park.

Disney Villains Encounters

A rare opportunity to meet many of Disney's seldom-seen villains roaming the park. Don't forget to get photos and autographs when you meet them.

Creepy Crafts

These Halloween crafts are suitable for the whole family, so keep an eye out for them.

Spooky Foods

Special Halloween themed foods can be found throughout the event.

Mystical Spirits of the Blue Bayou

This special Halloween event combines a three-course New Orleans style dinner with live entertainment. Dr. Facilier himself (The Princess & the Frog, 2009) will even be in attendance. Guests even receive a special parting gift. Tickets to this event must be purchased separately. Reservations are highly recommended.

Paint the Night

This year *Mickey's Costume Party* has been replaced by the spectacular *Paint the Night* parade in honor of Disneyland's 60th Anniversary. See *Paint the Night* in the *Shows & Performances* section of this book for details.

Tomorrowland Terrace Dance Party

Join the fun and dance the night away at *Tomorrowland Terrace* in Tomorrowland. You'll get to see Disney characters compete in a Scare-Off while you are there.

Other Dance Parties

Check the *Disneyland Entertainment Times Guide* as you enter the park for even more dance parties and other fun activities.

The Cadaver Dans

Look for Disneyland's classic *Dapper Dans* in spooky outfits performing Halloween tunes aboard a drifting graveyard raft on the Rivers of America.

Halloween Screams Fireworks Show

Disneyland offers a special fireworks show created just for Mickey's Halloween Party. In past years it has been truly spectacular.

Enter the Park Three Hours Before the Event Starts

Guests with paid tickets to Mickey's Halloween Party can get up to three hours of regular Disneyland park time before the event begins. This would be a good time to enjoy the few rides and restaurants that will be closed during the event.

A Smoking-Free Environment

This is an interesting departure from the park's normal rules, but during Mickey's Halloween Party the usual smoking sections inside the park will we closed. Smoking will not be permitted anywhere in Disneyland during the event, but you may step outside the park into the esplanade between Disneyland and California Adventure to smoke if you need to.

Parking is Included

Normally parking costs an additional $17 at the Disneyland Resort, but for Mickey's Halloween Party it is included in your ticket price.

2015 Admission Dates, Times, & Prices

Admission to Mickey's Halloween Party requires a separate fee, even if you have a valid ticket for admission to Disneyland earlier in that day. The fees change according to the date, and discounts are offered for purchasing the ticket in advance or having an Annual Pass. Below I list all dates and times for the 2015 event, followed by the ticket price for Advance Purchase, Annual Passholder Advance Purchase, and price at the gate (in that order). Note that the closer you get to Halloween, thee higher the ticket prices go. No admission ticket is required for guests 2 and under.

Friday, September 26 • 7:00pm to midnight • $63.00 $56.00 $70.00

Friday, September 25 • 7:00pm to midnight • $69.00 $69.00 $77.00

Monday, September 28 • 6:00pm to 11:00pm • $69.00 $63.00 $77.00

Wednesday, September 30 • 6:00pm to 11:00pm • $69.00 $63.00 $77.00

Friday, October 2 • 7:00pm to midnight • $77.00 $77.00 $77.00

Monday, October 5 • 6:00pm to 11:00pm • $69.00 $63.00 $77.00

Wednesday, October 7 • 6:00pm to 11:00pm • $69.00 $63.00 $77.00

Friday, October 9 • 7:00pm to midnight • $77.00 $77.00 $77.00

Monday, October 12 • 6:00pm to 11:00pm • $69.00 $63.00 $77.00

Wednesday, October 14 • 6:00pm to 11:00pm • $69.00 $63.00 $77.00

Friday, October 16 • 7:00pm to midnight • $77.00 $77.00 $77.00

Monday, October 19 • 6:00pm to 11:00pm • $69.00 $63.00 $77.00

Thursday, October 22 • 6:00pm to 11:00pm • $77.00 $77.00 $77.00

Friday, October 23 • 7:00pm to midnight • $77.00 $77.00 $77.00

Sunday, October 25 • 6:00pm to 11:00pm • $69.00 $63.00 $77.00

Tuesday, October 27 • 6:00pm to 11:00pm • $77.00 $77.00 $77.00

Thursday, October 29 • 6:00pm to 11:00pm • $84.00 $84.00 $84.00

Saturday, October 31 • 7:00pm to midnight • $84.00 $84.00 $84.00

05 • Halloween Magic Shots
Throughout Disneyland and California Adventure

Disneyland photographers can use a special digital technique that places animated characters or objects into photos of you as they take them. This allows the photographers to pose guests in ways that capitalize on the animated images, such as posing you as if you were in a sword fight with an animated villain (which happens to be my favorite Magic Shot photo). During the Halloween season three limited-time spooky Magic Shots are added to the photographer's repertoire. The normal selection of Magic Shot photos are also available at this time. These special photos can make a one of a kind keepsake that can be viewed and printed either at the *Main Street Photo Supply Co.* or later online at the Disney photopass Website.

http://www.disneyphotopass.com

The Magic Shot photos are only available at certain park locations. Ask any Disneyland Resort photographer about taking Magic Shot photos. Below is a list of my favorite Halloween themed Magic Shots available this season inside the Disneyland Resort them parks.

Poison Apple

Have your photo taken as you dangle a poisoned apple over a bubbling cauldron. I found this Magic Shot in front of the giant Mickey Jack-o'-lantern on *Main Street USA*, near the entrance to *Sleeping Beauty Castle*, and in the courtyard just inside the castle. It can also be found at various other locations throughout Disneyland and California Adventure.

Zero the Dog

Have your photo taken as you pet Zero, the ghost dog from *The Nightmare Before Christmas* (1993). I found this Magic Shot in front of the Partners Statue at the north end of Main Street, but it can also be found at various locations throughout Disneyland and California Adventure.

06 • Disney's Happiest Haunts Tour
Disneyland
Available Seasonally Only
Offered nightly September 14 - October 31

During the Halloween season this special tour guides you through the park as you listen to spooky stories, learn new facts about Halloween at Disneyland, and get an inside look at how the Disneyland park is prepared for the holiday. You will also receive a special souvenir tour pin that is redesigned each year. This tour is available only at Halloween time. Join the tour at the *Guided Tour Kiosk* next to *City Hall* on Main Street USA. Tours may be booked up to 30 days in advance. Call (714) 781-TOUR [8687] to make a reservation.

Tour Time: 3 Hours
Cost: $85 per guest 3 years old and older, free for guests 2 and under.
(Annual Passholders receive a 20% discount on this tour.)

VIP Tour Services

VIP tours handle all aspects of a guest's Disneyland experience. They include a private guide throughout the park, assistance with dining reservations, VIP viewing of parades and shows, and ultimate Fastpasses access (instant access to the Fastpass lines of all attractions at any time.)

Guests may call the special VIP Tour Services line at (714) 300-7710 to book a VIP tour up to 90 days in advance. Until recently the park offered two different levels of VIP tours, but they have now been combined into a single tour package. The price of the tour changes seasonally, costing $360 per hour on non-peak days and up to $500 per hour on peak days. This hourly tour price includes up to ten guests. Get more information at the website below.

Cost: $360/$500 PER HOUR, with a 6 HOUR MINIMUM.

disneyland.disney.go.com/events-tours/vip-tour-services/

07 • Spooky Gallery Exhibits
The Disney Gallery, Main Street USA, Disneyland

Disneyland typically allows frightening collections of art take over The *Disney Gallery* at Halloween time. 2014 saw a collection of *Haunted Mansion* themed artwork that featured unique paintings, statues, figurines, and dioramas from accomplished Disney artists. And the art is now only for viewing, it can be purchased at the show as well. Be sure to stop by The Disney Gallery to see what is in store for you this Halloween season.

08 • Main Street USA Pumpkin Festival
Disneyland

Walk down Main Street and take in all the pumpkins lining the street. Each one is hand carved, and no two are alike.

09 • Meet Jack Skellington
New Orleans Square, Disneyland

Look for Jack from the *The Nightmare Before Christmas* (1993) outside the Haunted Mansion. Ask him questions, get an autograph, and have your picture taken. He's quite a playful character, so don't be surprised by his silly antics before he poses for a photo with you.

10 • The Halloween Tree
Frontierland, Disneyland

Be sure to take a look at the famous Halloween Tree located on along the main path through Frontierland. The tree has become a Disneyland tradition with it's branches decorated with lights and pumpkins. The tree was created in 2007 to honor the vision of author Ray Bradbury, and has been prominently displayed in Frontierland every year since. A plaque below the tree explains it's significance. Look for it in front of Frontierland's main row of shops across the walkway from the *Rancho del Zocalo* restaurant.

11 • Dia de los Muertos
Frontierland, Disneyland

Come celebrate the traditional Latin American holiday 'Day of the Dead' in *Zocolo Park* with decorations, historical displays and special face painting. The holiday focuses on family and friends gathering together to remember and pray for lost loved ones. In Mexico Día de los Muertos is celebrated as a national holiday and all banks are closed. The holiday is celebrated at Disneyland throughout the Halloween Holidays, but the Day of the Dead is celebrated throughout the rest of world from about October 31 through November 2.

Learn About the Holiday

Information plaques can be found throughout the area, and the cast members manning the activities here are a wealth of information.

FREE Dia de los Muertos face or body painting
Step of to the face painting booth and get a unique *Day of the Dead* design hand painted on your face. The artwork is smaller that typical face painting designs, and you can choose to have it painted on your arms as well.

Photo Opportunities
Several beautiful large Dia de los Muertos displays make for wonderful photo backdrops, so be sure to have your photo snapped in front of them. Choose between the Dia de los Muertos flower sign above a rock formation or the Day of the Dead skeleton band, or have photos taken at both locations.

12 • Big Thunder Ranch Halloween
Frontierland, Disneyland
The *Big Thunder Ranch* went all out this year with Fall decorations, Outfits for the animals, and plenty of Halloween photo opportunities. Stop by and take a look around. Unfortunately both the *Halloween Carnival* and *The Pirate League* in the *Big Thunder Ranch Jamboree* area have been canceled this year. The entire *Big Thunder Ranch Jamboree* area will no longer be used by Disneyland at all, due to the preparation for the construction of *Star Wars Land* starting in 2016.

Scare-Dy-Crow Shack
Take in the spooky Fall decorations inside this old country farm shack. Then pose for pictures with the Jack-o'-lantern woman next to the old piano, the two Jack-o'-lantern scarecrows playing a game of cards, and the Jack-o'-lantern sheriff and robber siting at a table.

Petting Zoo
Disncyland's goats and other friendly animals are all dressed up to celebrate Fall. Stop by to pet them, and have your photo taken while you are there.

Halloween Diorama
Be sure to have your photo taken in front of the Diorama at the entrance to Big Thunder Ranch. It features a pumpkins, Jack-o'-lantern scarecrows, black cats, fall colored flowers, and other fall themes all in front of a spooky backdrop. It's perfect for a memorable photo.

Halloween Roundup
Take in the Fall themed decorations throughout the area, sit down to some all you can eat BBQ, and take in a live Halloween themed stage show at this unique Frontierland venue. Lunch includes all the BBQ Chicken, Ribs, Cookie's Cole Slaw, Ranch Beans, and Corn Bread you can eat. Dinner includes lunch menu plus Smoked Sausage and Corn Cob Wheels. See the *Restaurant* section of this book for more details on the lunch and dinner served at the Big Thunder Ranch Barbecue.
Live musical acts that get the guests involved in the show start at the venue's Halloween decorated stage and then move outward through the crowd.
Be sure not to miss the antique surrey wagon covered in Fall flowers, leaves, and other Halloween season decorations. Pose in front of this beautiful wagon for a

memorable photo. It's found along the path from the back of the *Big Thunder Ranch Barbecue* that leads to the *Big Thunder Ranch Jamboree* area.

13 • Sunrise Safari Breakfast
Jungle Cruise, Adventureland, Disneyland

Have a wild breakfast experience including pastries, fruit and chia parfaits, eggs, glazed pork belly bacon, pan-seared sausage, roasted gold potato and onion hash, an assortment of juices, freshly brewed coffee, and specialty teas. Then set out on a private Jungle Cruise adventure where YOU will get to act as skipper. At the end you will even receive a special tribal mask keepsake to commemorate your adventure. *Cost:* $300 per person.

14 • Halloween In-Room Celebrations
Disneyland Resort Hotels

The Disneyland Resort's new "A Disney Villainous Halloween" celebration fills your hotel room with Halloween themed items while you are out. A light-up pumpkin door sash, creepy candelabras, a spooky woven blanket, a villainous picture frame, a one-of-a-kind monopoly game, and a large black box full of secret surprises will await you. Reserve it up to 60 days in advance. *Cost:* $399.95

You can also order a Halloween themed *Disney Family Treats Tote* featuring either Mickey or Minnie Mouse ($99.95) filled to the brim with candy and treats, or a Halloween themed Mickey Mouse *My First Disney Visit* kit ($75.95) full of all sorts of surprises. The tote bag can even be personalized with your family's name on it for an additional fee. All delivered to your hotel room for you.

(714) 781-GIFT | disneyland.disneyfloralandgifts.com

Other Events During the Halloween Season

Force Friday - *September 4, 2015* [official Disney event]
Celebrate the opening of *The Force Awakens* (2015) at this ticketed Star Wars merchandise event. Be among the first fans to purchase new Star Wars and Disney themed merchandise. Reservations open August 26, 2015 at the site below.

www.DisneyParksMerchandise.com

Dapper Day - *September 18 - 19, 2015* [Disney-supported event]
At this stylish dress-up event guests are encouraged to wear elegant vintage-inspired or chic-contemporary fashions inside the Disney parks. Dapper Day happens twice a year at three different Disney resorts; the Disneyland Resort in California, The Walt Disney World Resort in Florida, and Disneyland Paris. Usually a spring all-day event and a fall evening affair are held each year. Although no special tickets are required to participate in the event, discounted park tickets can be purchased from the Dapper Day website. Active and retired military are urged to wear their uniforms. This year's fall Dapper Day features a classic car show for the first time ever.

www.dapperday.com

Shiny Day in the Parks - *September 20, 2015* [unofficial fan event]
Browncoats and Alliance folks unite in celebration the cult sci-fi classic Firefly (TV series 2002 – 2003, *"Serenity"* film 2005). Join them for an all-day event this September. Visit's the groups Facebook page for details.

www.facebook.com/ShinyDayinthePark

Tiki Day - *Sunday September 27, 2015* [unofficial fan event]
Meet fellow Tiki fans at Disneyland for the fourth annual Tiki Day celebration. Guests will have two different group photo opportunities in front of Sleeping Beauty Castle, a group ride on the *Mark Twain Riverboat*, and meet-ups at the *Enchanted Tiki Room*, *Jungle Cruise*, and *Trader Sam's Enchanted Tiki Bar*. See the group's Facebook page for more details.

www.facebook.com/TikiDayAtThePark

Gay Days Anaheim - *October 2 – 4* [Disney-supported event]
Put on a red t-shirt and support LGBT pride with activity-filled days in the resort. Discounted park tickets are available for participants.
www.gaydaysanaheim.com | facebook.com/GayDaysAnaheim

CHOC Walk - *October 11, 2015* [official Disney event]
The annual fund raiser for Children's Hospital Orange County takes place as a charity walk both inside and outside the Disneyland park every October. The walk passes through Disneyland and Disney's California Adventure, terminating with festivities in Downtown Disney. Find out more details at:

www.chocwalk.net

Villain's Day - *Sunday October 25, 2015* [unofficial fan event]
Dress up in your best villain attire and join *The Circle of Villains* for an all-day event. (Be sure not to violate the Disneyland dress code when you dress up: disneyland. disney.go.com/faq/parks/dress/.) Stalk the groups Facebook page for details.

www.facebook.com/circleofvillains
www.facebook.com/events/881784468575036/

Epilepsy Awareness Day - *November 4 - 5, 2015* [non-profit event]
Help advance the awareness of epilepsy at the 3nd Annual Epilepsy Awareness Day in Disneyland November 4 - 5, 2015. The event boasts three nonprofit partners: the Division of Pediatric Neurology at Mattel Children's Hospital UCLA, the Chelsea Hutchison Foundation, and the Danny Did Foundation. More than 900 supporters and 30 epilepsy support groups have been in attendance at past events. Find out more details at:

EpilepsyAwarenessDay.org

Galliday - *November 8, 2015* [unofficial fan event]
This unofficial Dr. Who fan day floods the park with some of The Doctor's most ardent fans. Photo Scavenger Hunts, a Tom Sawyer Island romp, the Carousel Takeover, and special photo opportunities fill this day with fun activities. The event's next regeneration occurs November 8, 2015. Visit's galliday.com or the fan groups many other pages for more details.

galliday.tumblr.com | twitter.com/Galliday | facebook.com/Galliday

Avengers Super Heroes Half Marathon - *November 12 - 15, 2015* [official]
Join The Avengers at this 13.1 mile Marathon through the Disneyland resort. Meet The Avengers, enjoy a super hero victory celebration, and bring home an Avengers' "Super Heroes Finisher Medal."

www.rundisney.com/avengers-half-marathon/

Steam Day - *Friday November 13, 2015* [unofficial fan event]
Join fellow Steam Punk fans at Disneyland for this fan-run event. Check the websites below for more details.

www.facebook.com/SteamDay

60th Anniversary
Diamond Celebration

Disneyland first opened it doors on July 17, 1955, which makes 2015 the park's 60th Anniversary. In celebration of this *Diamond Anniversary* you will find a spectacular collection of new events, shows, decorations, and activities throughout the resort, including both Disneyland and Disney California Adventure.

This magical celebration starts *May 22, 2015*, and is expected to last for a long time. Disney has not even announced an end time for the celebration yet. The entire resort will be very crowded during the celebration, and you will want to book your vacation well in advance so you can enjoy the many special activities listed below.

Dazzling Decorations

A major part of the 60th Anniversary Celebration are the glistening new decorations found throughout the park. In *Disneyland* the *Sleeping Beauty Castle* will glisten with special diamond-themed enhancements. The castle will be encrusted with diamonds, bestowed with a giant diamond medallion featuring the Disneyland 'D', and draped in other luxurious decorations. *Main Street USA* will get it's own makeover with festive banners and commemorative décor.

New Entertainment

The most anticipated changes to the parks are the new entertainment opportunities that the celebration brings. Be sure to watch *Paint the Night, Disneyland Forever,* and *World of Color – Celebrate!* while you can. See the *Shows & Performances* section for details.

Special Photo Opportunities

Look for special 60th Anniversary photo opportunities throughout the park. My favorite thus far has been a giant diorama by the *Matterhorn* that lets you look like you're climbing the mountain. Cast members can also be found throughout the park with hand held diamond photo frames ready to help you create a spontaneous photo.

Share Your Personal Photos

The Disneyland Resort has invited guests to post their favorite photos they have taken at the resort. The goal is to share your favorite Disneyland Resort memories with a community of Disney fans and enthusiasts. To participate you simply post your photos to your own Twitter or Instagram account and add the hashtag #Disneyland60Contest when you post them. Disney will keep apprised of the photos being submitted and add their favorite ones to the Disney Parks blog.

disneyparks.disney.go.com/blog/

New Merchandise & Art

The *60th Anniversary Celebration* will introduce Disney fans and collectors to a host of new merchandise opportunities and collectible art. More than 500 new souvenirs, toys, pins, accessories, apparel, headwear, home décor, D-Tech, and collectibles will be hitting Disney stores in May 2015. Expect to see a diamond encrusted toy castle, diamond studded mouse ears, diamond themed jewelry, and much more.

Diamond Celebration Coin Press Machines

Look for these special 60th Anniversary coin presses throughout the park. A detailed guide to the machine's locations can be obtained for FREE at city hall and at information booths throughout the park. New Diamond Celebration coin collection wallets will also be available.

Diamond Pins

A new collection of collectible diamond shaped pins will be released to celebrate the Anniversary. A new pin will be released each month, starting in January 2015. Known as the *DLR - 60th Anniversary Countdown Series*, each of the 6 pins will be a different color and feature a different Walt Disney quote. The pins will also open up to reveal a photo of Walt Disney inside. Release schedules and more information can be found on the Disney Parks Merchandise website.

www.disneyparksmerchandise.com/blog/60th-anniversary-countdown-series-pins/

60th Anniversary Ear Hats

A special 60th Anniversary edition of the wold famous mouse ears will be released during the celebration. The hat is blue with a large number 60 in the front.

Contests

Actual diamonds, private parties, special meals, and coveted nights in the *Disneyland Dream Suite* are being given away on a daily and weekly basis to resort guests. Look for the "Word of the Day" posted in the esplanade between Disneyland and California Adventure, as well as at other resort locations such as the Grand California Hotel entrance into California Adventure. Then text the word to "DISNEY" (347639) to enter the daily contests. Check the website below for updates and details.

disneyland.disney.go.com/events-tours/diamond-days-sweepstakes/

Surprises

The executives and creative teams at Disney promise there will be surprises on top of all of the new activities they have already announced, so keep your eyes out for them. You never know what special experience may show up at the Disneyland Resort's *60th Anniversary Diamond Celebration*. Follow the Disney Parks Blog and check the Disneyland Resort website often for new announcements.

disneyparks.disney.go.com/blog/ | disneyland.com

Top Halloween Dining

Special Halloween menu items are released at different times throughout the Halloween season, so the following items may or may not be available yet when you visit the park. Typically all items are available by October. So be sure to take a break from your screaming long enough to temp your taste buds with the wickedly delicious treats listed below. These special items are only available during the Halloween season, so get them while you can.

Entrees
Sit-Down Meals
Mystical Spirits of the Blue Bayou - Premium Halloween Dining Experience
   A three-course New Orleans style dinner with live entertainment, featuring: a beguiling bayou crab cake with crisp creole slaw and tart remoulade sauce or warm melted goat cheese bon coeur tart; braised bayou short ribs with danish blue-cheese whipped potatoes and baby carrots, bourbon-glazed chicken breast over a bed of smoked-white cheddar polenta, or red fish with crispy rock shrimp; and either a dark chocolate crème brûlée with salted caramel macaroon or an almond praline cheesecake with petit honey beignets.
Blue Bayou (New Orleans Square, DL)

Cajun-Rubbed Pork Chop
   Bone-in pork chop with sautéed spinach, goat cheese mashed potatoes, and a smoked pepper tomato jus.
Blue Bayou (New Orleans Square, DL)

Flat Iron Steak
   Served with peppercorn and cognac sauce, garlic mashed potatoes, butternut squash, and green beans.
Café Orleans (New Orleans Square, DL)

Traditional Shrimp Po' Boy
   Deep-fried popcorn shrimp, lettuce, tomato, vinegar dressing, and cajun remoulade sauce on a toasted potato roll.
French Market Restaurant (New Orleans Square, DL

Seasonal Pork Tamale and Cheese Enchilada Plate
   A pork tamale with rice, refried beans, sour cream, guacamole, and pico de gallo sauce. The Carne Asada option adds sliced carne asada steak and two flour tortilla.
Rancho del Zocalo Restaurante (Frontierland, DL)

Pleasure Island Fiery Chicken Flatbread
Glazed buffalo chicken with Serrano chilies, diced red peppers, tomato sauce, Mozzarella cheese and chipotle sauce.
Village Haus Restaurant (Fantasyland, DL)

Burgers & Sandwiches

Cheeseburger Combo
Cheeseburger with sauce, lettuce, tomato, pickles and grilled onions served with French fries covered in a ghostly Parmesan-ranch "ooze."
Tomorrowland Terrace (Tomorrowland, DL)

Cobweb Style Burgers -or- Chicken Sandwiches
Burgers or chicken sandwiches served "cobweb style" (toped with Swiss cheese, grilled onions, and mushrooms).
Smokejumpers Grill (Grizzly Peak Airfield, DCA)

Pulled Pork Hot Dog
Hot dog topped with pulled pork, citrus coleslaw, fried jalapenos, and fresh cilantro.
Hungry Bear Restaurant (Critter Country, DL)

Mickey's Frightfully Spicy Chicken Sandwich
Fried chicken served with pepper jack cheese, spicy Sriracha sauce, coleslaw, and breaded and fried jalapenos on a brioche bun with a side of French fries.
Carnation Café (Main Street USA, DL)

Pizza

Supernova Pizza Special
Pastrami with mustard oil, Mozzarella cheese, battered pickle chips topped with Horseradish mustard sauce.
Redd Rockett's Pizza Port (Tomorrowland, DL)

Anti-Vampire Chicken Pizza
Roasted garlic sauce, chicken, smoked Gouda, Mozzarella, roasted red peppers, and a tomato Harissa sauce drizzle.
Boardwalk Pizza & Pasta (Paradise Pier, DCA)

Snacks

Caramel Apple Smoothie
Schmoozies (Hollywood Land, DCA)

Jack-o'-Lantern shaped Sourdough Bread Loaf
Mortimer's Market (Buena Vista Street, DCA)
Pacific Wharf Café (Pacific Wharf, DCA)
Boudin Bakery Cart (Pacific Wharf, DCA).

Specialty Drinks

Coffee
Pumpkin Spice Latte
Jolly Holiday Bakery Café (Main Street USA, DL)
The Coffee House (Disneyland Hotel)

Pumpkin Specialty Coffee Drinks
Market House (Main Street USA, DL)
Fiddler, Fifer & Practical Café (Buena Vista Street, DCA)
Downtown Disney Starbucks (Downtown Disney)

Juices & Other Drinks
Caramel Apple Cider
The Coffee House (Disneyland Hotel)

Cocktails
Poison Apple-Tini
    Crown Royal Apple, Dekuyper Pucker Sour Apple Schnapps, and cranberry juice; with an evil-looking poison apple float.
Carthay Circle Restaurant / Lounge (Buena Vista Street, DCA)
Cove Bar (Paradise Pier, DCA)
Steak House 55 (Disneyland Hotel)

Karl Strauss Oktoberfest Beer
Pacific Wharf Distribution Co. (Pacific Wharf, DCA)

Dessert
Pumpkin Beignets Served with Vanilla Crème Anglaise
Café Orléans (New Orleans Square, DL)

Pumpkin Beignets (plain)
Mint Julep Bar (New Orleans Square, DL)

Pumpkin Spice Bread Pudding
Pacific Wharf Café (Pacific Wharf, DCA)

Pumpkin Twist
Maurice's Treats (Fantasy Fair, Fantasyland, DL)
Cozy Cone Motel (Cars Land, DCA)

Pumpkin Cheesecake
Jolly Holiday Bakery Café (Main Street USA, DL)
French Market Restaurant (New Orleans Square, DL)
Boardwalk Pizza & Pasta (Paradise Pier, DCA)

Orange Pumpkin Flan
Rancho del Zocalo Restaurante (Frontierland, DL)

Pumpkin Pie
Plaza Inn (Main Street USA, DL)
Flo's V8 Café (Cars Land, DCA)

Pumpkin Muffin with Streusel Topping
Pacific Wharf Café (Pacific Wharf, DCA)
Whitewater Snacks (Grand California Hotel)
Surfside Lounge (Paradise Pier Hotel)

Pumpkin Muffin (plain)
Central Plaza Cappuccino Cart (New Orleans Square, DL)
The Coffee House (Disneyland Hotel)

Ice Cream Nachos
  "Chips"(waffle cone pieces), choice of ice cream, hot fudge, whipped cream, and a cherry.
The Golden Horseshoe (Frontierland, DL)

Premium Halloween Ice Cream Cone
Gibson Girl Ice Cream Parlor (Main Street USA, DL)

Banana Fritters with crème Anglaise
Royal Street Veranda (New Orleans Square, DL)

Apple Pie Funnel Cake
Hungry Bear Restaurant (Critter Country, DL)

Haunted Mansion Cake
French Market Restaurant (New Orleans Square, DL)

Sugar Cookie Bake
Big Thunder Ranch Barbecue (Frontierland, DL)

Chocolate-Peanut Butter Whoopie Pie
Whitewater Snacks (Grand California Hotel)
The Coffee House (Disneyland Hotel)
Surfside Lounge (Paradise Pier Hotel)

Spiced Bundt Cake
Whitewater Snacks (Grand California Hotel)
The Coffee House (Disneyland Hotel)
Surfside Lounge (Paradise Pier Hotel)

Halloween Themed Gourmet Candy Apples
Candy Palace (Main Street USA, DL)
Pooh Corner (Critter Country, DL)
Trolley Treats (Buena Vista Street, DCA)
Marceline's Confectionery (Downtown Disney)

Ghirardelli Seasonal Chocolates
Seasonal Pumpkin Spice Caramel Chocolate Squares, Halloween themed Premium Chocolate Assortment Tin, and other assorted Halloween themed chocolate collections.
Ghirardelli Soda Fountain & Chocolate Shop (Pacific Wharf, DCA)

Top Halloween Shopping

Every year Disney adds to their special Halloween product line. The enormous amount of products Disney offers makes it impractical to describe them all, but take a look at my list of favorite Halloween items below. Use it to help you find that special Halloween gift or souvenir.

Souvenirs & Collectibles
Haunted Mansion Collectibles
One of the hottest lines of Halloween products for the last few years has been this collection of Haunted Mansion themed collectibles. They are high quality, life-sized reproductions of some of the mansion's most iconic relics. Bulk deals are often available for buying more that one of these collectibles at he same time.

Some of my favorite places to get these collectibles are *China Closet* (Main Street USA, DL), *Disneyland Emporium* (Main Street USA, DL), *Port Royal* (New Orleans Square, DL), *Star Trader* (Tomorrowland, DL), *Julius Katz & Sons* (Buena Vista Street, DCA), *Disney Vault 28* (Downtown Disney), *World of Disney* (Downtown Disney), *Acorns Gifts & Goods* (Grand California Hotel), and *Fantasia Shop* (Disneyland Hotel).

Disneyland Secret - The 1313 Reference: When you go to purchase these items, take a look at their tags. Hidden among the items' descriptions and "Not a toy!" warnings are mysterious references to the number 1313. It's on the tag for every one of these items, but what does it mean? Well, if you have ever had to use Disneyland's official address you know it's 1313 Harbor Blvd., and the number is a reference to that historic address. But the mystery goes deeper.

Walt himself requested that address when he built his theme park among sprawling orange groves in 1955, and ever since then rumors about the meaning behind the numbers have ranged from paranoid ideas about the Masons to obscure numerology references. But the real reason he picked that address has to do with Walt's favorite business partner, Mickey Mouse. What is the 13th letter of the alphabet? There are two 13's in the address, so put those two letters together and who's' initials do you get? Examine the tags on your favorite Halloween souvenir this season and see if you can find the hidden 1313 reference.

Hour Glass
This large decorative hour glass uses purple sand to count down your remaining time in this earthly realm.

Madame Leota Decorative Chest
Keep your jewelry, pins, or other collectibles in this highly decorative chest.

Candle Holder
Let this gargoyle from the Haunted Mansion hold on to two of your candles for you.

Bottle Stopper
This famous Haunted Mansion bat can be used to keep your wine bottles fresh.

Coaster Set
Inside a coffin shaped box sits these stone drink coasters with Haunted Mansion sayings on them.

Haunted Mansion Playing Cards
They have spooky designs on the back, favorite Haunted Mansion characters on the front, and... they glow in the dark. The packaging is a mush fun as the cards - they come in a purple silk lined coffin.

Mugs
Two amazing designs - a sculpted Haunted Mansion cauldron and wall sconce design, and the Haunted Mansion wall paper design - await you here in the earthy realm.

Nightmare Before Christmas Gear

A huge selection of *The Nightmare Before Christmas* (1993) clothing, toys, and collectibles are unleashed on many resort stores during the Halloween season. Find them at *Disney Clothiers Ltd* (Main Street USA, DL), *Port Royal* (New Orleans Square, DL), *Jack Skeleton Carriage Cart* (New Orleans Square, DL), *Tower Hotel Gifts* (Hollywood Land, DCA), *Sideshow Shirts* (Paradise Pier, DCA), and *World of Disney* (Downtown Disney).

Halloween Themed Pokit Pals

These small collectible resin boxes are cast into the shapes of famous Disneyland landmarks or characters such as the emblem from the *Pirates of the Caribbean* attraction or the four stretching paintings from the *Haunted Mansion's* Stretching Room. Each PokitPal costs about $20 - $22. Find out more about the unique Olszewski Studios Pokitpals at the designer's website: www.olszewskistudios.com. Look for them at *Disneyana* (Main Street USA, DL), *Off the Page* (Hollywood Land, DCA), and *World of Disney* (Downtown Disney).

Halloween Plush Animals

Figaro the cat (Pinocchio, 1940) *in a Mickey Mouse Jack-O-Lantern* is the most popular plush this year. But be warned, it's adorably cute, so once you spot it you may have a tough time leaving without buying it. *Mickey and Minnie as Haunted Mansion ghosts* come in as a close second (Pieces of Eight, New Orleans Square, Disneyland). A number of other characters in Halloween garb can also be found throughout the resort.

Collectible Halloween Figurines

Limited edition collectible Halloween figurines are a favorite among Hallowen fans. Look for them at *China Closet* (Main Street USA, DL), *Pioneer Mercantile* (Frontierland, DL), *Off the Page* (Hollywood Land, DCA), and *World of Disney (DTD)*.

Halloween Caricature Drawings

These booths offer hand-painted artwork created while you wait. Choose from Hand-Painted Scenic Art ($32), Hand-Painted Caricatures with a profile view ($17.95 per person), or Hand-Painted Caricatures with a front view ($32 per person). Request a Halloween theme added to your Caricature Drawing, such as your head on a spooky character or inside a Halloween costume. Available at the *Caricature Drawings & Full Color Portraits* stand in New Orleans Square.

Fall Themed Name Art

Name art that uses Fall themed colors and Halloween elements are now available. Have your name spelled out with unique illustrations representing each letter at this small set of specialty stands in Fantasyland. The artwork generally costs from $18 to $40 depending on the number of letters and styles used. Available at the *Fairytale Arts* stand in Fantasyland.

Halloween Build a Bears

Design your own teddy bear from the paw up at this unique specialty shop. Choose from a variety off animal types, sizes, and outfits. Special Halloween themed bears and bear costumes are released throughout the Halloween season, with the first batch arriving in late September. Look for a werewolf in a skeleton suit, a cat in a witch outfit, and many more special Halloween designs. Get them at the *Build a Bear Workshop* in Downtown Disney.

Halloween Pins

A large variety of seasonal Halloween pins and pin sets are available at shops throughout the resort. Collectors may be particularly interested in the *Haunted Mansion* pin set or this year's *Disney Parks* collection of Halloween pins. Look for them where ever Disney pins are sold. Check DisneyPins.com for updates on new pins.

Halloween Vinylmation

Spooky themed Vinylmation figures show up every year. Look for them at *Star Trader* (Tomorrowland, DL) *Off the Page* (Hollywood Land, DCA), *Tower Hotel Gifts* (Hollywood Land, DCA), *Point Mugu Tattoo* (Hollywood Land, DCA), *D Street* (Downtown Disney), and *World of Disney* (Downtown Disney).

Costuming
Princess & Knight Makeovers
Get a Disney dream makeover complete with costumes and makeup at *Bibbidi Bobbidi Boutique* (Fantasyland, DL).

Halloween Themed Henna Tattoos
Henna Tattoos Stand, Paradise Pier, DCA
Celebrate Halloween with a temporary Henna tattoo of a spooky creature or saying. Look for this activity in the same booth as *Face Painting of the Boardwalk*, in front of Point Mugu Tattoo along the boardwalk at Paradise Pier. Henna Tattoos use natural dyes that fade over time, usual lasting for several weeks. The Tattoos cost from $7 - $30 depending on the design, with a rather large selection available from the stand's catalog.

Halloween Themed Face Painting Designs
Children can have their faces painted in a variety of colors, designs and styles at the resort's face-painting booths. Choose your favorite style from the sample photos provided on the booth, and then sit down to have your face turned into a walking work of art. Ask about spooky creatures and Halloween or Fall themed designs before making your selection. Available at *Fairytale Faces* (Fantasyland, DL), a booth at the exit to *Pixie Hollow* (Fantasyland, DL), a stand on the boardwalk at *Paradise Pier* (DCA), and at a booth at the *Mad T Party* (Hollywoodland, DCA) while it is happening.

Costume Weapons
Look for Toy Swords, Guns, and Bows to complement your Halloween costumes at *The Storybook Store* (Main Street USA, DL), *Adventureland Bazaar* (Adventureland, DL), *Indiana Jones Adventure Outpost* (Adventureland, DL), and *Pieces of Eight* (New Orleans Square, DL).

Scary Rubber Creatures
Look for spiders, snakes, and other creepy-crawlies at *Tropical Imports* (Adventureland, DL) and the *Indiana Jones Adventure Outpost* (Adventureland, DL).

Clothing & Apparel
Halloween Ears Hats, Ear Headbands, Disney Themed Hats
Wearing mouse ears with your name embroidered on them is a long-standing Disney Parks tradition going back decades. The hats are available in a variety of styles from the classic black and red design to themes including princesses, wizards, and Star Wars characters. Custom embroidery of your name onto the hat takes just a few minutes to complete and it's done while you wait. Hat prices start at about $14, plus $3 to $7 for embroidery of your name. Stylish mouse ear headbands have also gained in popularity, and a variety of other hats sporting Disney themes have become available as well. Look for special Halloween designs and spooky character themes wherever these hats and headbands are sold. Look for them at the following locations:

The Mad Hatter (Main Street USA, DL)
Disneyland Emporium (Main Street USA, DL)
Mad Hatter, Fantasyland (DL)
Le Petit Chalet Gifts (Fantasyland, DL)
Briar Patch (Critter Country, DL)
Gag Factory, (Toontown, DL)
Tomorrow Landing (Tomorrowland, DL)
The Star Trader (Tomorrowland, DL)
Los Feliz Five & Dime (Buena Vista Street, DCA)
Gone Hollywood (Hollywood Land, DCA)
Off the Page (Hollywood Land, DCA)
Treasures in Paradise (Paradise Pier, DCA)
Seaside Souvenirs (Paradise Pier, DCA)
Boardwalk Bazaar (Paradise Pier, DCA)

Ear Headbands can also be found at: *Bibbidi Bobbidi Boutique* (Fantasyland, DL), *Stromboli's Wagon* (Fantasyland, DL), *Gone Hollywood* (Hollywood Land, DCA), and *Boardwalk Bazaar* (Paradise Pier, DCA).

Spooky Personalized Parasols

Get a personalized, embroidered parasol at the stand towards the end of Orleans St near the French Market Restaurant. Look for hand drawn Halloween designs on display at the parasol cart throughout the season. A large selection is available to choose from including: bats, cobwebs, spiders, grave stones, vampires, werewolves, and more, with many more designs becoming available as it gets closer to Halloween. Ask an artist at the cart about what is currently available. Some artists will also even draw unique costume art on the spot for you. Look for them at the *Parasol Stand* in New Orleans Square.

Día de los Muertos Apparel

Look for tops, tee shirts, and bags that celebrate the Day of the Dead at these resort locations: *Adventureland Bazaar* (Adventureland, DL), *Pieces of Eight* (New Orleans Square, DL), and *Disney Vault 28* (Downtown Disney).

Shows & Performances

The live entertainment at the Disneyland Resort is amazing, and it's been part of the magic since Disney opened it's first theme park in 1955. Look for these shows throughout the resort.

Disneyland

Throughout the Park

#01 Paint the Night

Disneyland's newest parade provides a massive modern update to an old park favorite. *Paint the Night* is like a modernized version of the beloved *Main Street Electrical Parade* that graced the streets of Disneyland from 1972 - 1996. The parade features new LED technology that lights up the night sky with floats that change color, interact with their environment, and even interact with the guests around them. This is the first all-LED parade in Disneyland history, containing more than 1.5 million individually controlled lights. The costumes featured in the parade will also light up in a similar manner, giving guests an amazing new parade experience that conjures up memories of their favorite park tradition.

In the parade you get to see novice artist Mickey Mouse mix the power of his imagination with Tinker Bell's magical pixie dust. The mixture creates a special paint that allows the Mickey to conjure up classic Disney characters and animations before your eyes. Favorite characters such as Anna and Elsa (*Frozen*, 2013,), Ariel (*The Little Mermaid*, 1989), Lightning McQueen (*Cars*, 2006), Mike and Sulley (*Monsters Inc.*, 2001), Peter Pan (*Peter Pan*, 1953) and others will join Mickey in the parade on lavish floats. Listen as Disney music will fill the park as you watch the amazing floats and characters pass by.

#02 Mickey's Soundsational Parade

Earlier in the day guest can still watch *Mickey's Soundsational Parade*, featuring melodies from classic Disney films, Disney characters, dancers, and lavish floats marching down *Main Street* daily. You're sure to spot your favorite character: Mickey, Minnie, Goofy, Pluto, Chip 'n' Dale; characters from The Little Mermaid, The Three Caballeros, The Lion King, The Princess and the Frog, Aladdin, Peter Pan, Mary Poppins, and more. Towards the end of the parade there's a procession of princesses with Snow White, Cinderella, Aurora, Belle and Rapunzel. Parades are changed and updated often, so returning guests can get a completely different parade experience each time they visit the park. The entire parade runs about 40 minutes long.

Frozen Fantasy Pre-Parade
Currently Mickey's Soundsational Parade also features a special Frozen Fantasy Pre-Parade that travels down the parade route before the first parade of the day. This event based on the Disney animated film *Frozen* (2013) features the characters Olaf, Princess Anna, and Queen Elsa on a frozen float of ice and snow.

#03 Disneyland Forever

As the latest installment of Disneyland's famous fireworks show, *Disneyland Forever* does much more than just light up the sky, it plays out through the entire Disneyland park itself. Projections are added to *Sleeping Beauty Castle, Main Street USA* buildings, *Matterhorn Mountain*, the *It's a Small World* building, and other park locations. On *Main Street USA* a new projection mapping technology will project scenes from Disney movies on storefronts and restaurants throughout the area. You will be able to see sparkling pyrotechnics fill the sky and immersive special effects invade the lands below from locations throughout the park.

During the show you will be transported into the many worlds created by Disney, from flying above *Peter Pan's* (1953) London skyline to dancing with The *Jungle Book's* (1967) King Louie. The show features two new songs, "Live the Magic" and "Kiss Goodnight", both of which were written by Disney Legend Richard Sherman.

Glow with the Show Ears
The fireworks show allows you to use your *Glow with the Show* ear hats to become part of the show. Read more about these special ear hats in the *Glow with the Show* section of this book.

The Best Fireworks Viewing Locations

- Along the street and sidewalks of *Main Street USA*. You will want to be on *Main Street* to get the best view of the show's spectacular digital overlay effects. They race across the front of the buildings up and down Main Street.

- *Central Hub* in *Main Street USA*, in front of *Sleeping Beauty Castle* and around the core of the *Hub* by the *Partners Statue*. This gives you the best view of the digital effects projected onto Sleeping Beauty Castle, but it's harder to see the projections moving down Main Street.
- *Town Square* in *Main Street USA*, between the *Main Street Train Station* and the *Fire Station*, or up in the benches on the raised platform in front of the *Main Street Train Station*.
- Towards the rear of *Fantasyland* in front of *It's a Small World*.
- From the banks of the *Rivers of America* in *Frontierland*.

Tips

- Line up early to get the best fireworks viewing spot long before the show starts.
- The areas of *Fantasyland* located behind *Sleeping Beauty Castle* are closed during the fireworks show, so it's best not to try to view the show from inside this part of *Fantasyland*. *Toontown* is also often closed

during the show.

- The *Disneyland Railroad* and *Monorail* are often temporarily shut down while the fireworks go off, so generally it's not a good idea to try to view them from aboard these vehicles.
- Although the view isn't as good, guests can also see the fireworks from inside *Disney's California Adventure* park. One of the most magical moments found at the Disneyland Resort is when fireworks are bursting through the air as you reach the top open level of the *Tower of Terror*, when your gondola reaches the highest point of *Mickey's Fun Wheel*, or in the open air race sequence high atop the mountains of *Radiator Springs Racers*.

Main Street USA
#4 The Dapper Dans
Listen to Disneyland's famous barbershop quartet as they sing in perfect harmony. The Dapper Dans have been providing their unique nostalgic music at Disneyland since 1959. Although this a cappella ensemble is made up of many members, they usually perform as a quartet. These are serious artists devoted to their music, and several group members belong to the Barbershop Harmony Society (www.barbershop.org). Find them in traditional striped outfits at various locations along Main Street. Occasionally they can also be seen harmonizing aboard Main Street vehicles such as the *Horse-Drawn Streetcar*. And if the crowds are low enough, sometimes the Dapper Dans can be seen riding around Main Street on their four-seater bicycle. Ask a cast member or consult your *Disneyland Entertainment Times Guide* for the Dapper Dans performance times.

The Dapper Dans Get Spooky
Halloween music fills the air as *Main Street USA's Dapper Dans* go spooky for the Halloween season. Check the *Disneyland Entertainment Times Guide* for show times and locations.

#5 The Hook and Ladder Co.
This group of fire fighters entertain guests by standing in front of the Disneyland Fire Station and singing classic 1890's songs. Look for "The Hook and Ladder Co." in their traditional fire fighters uniforms singing in front of the *Fire Station* and other locations in Main Street USA's *Town Square*.

Occasionally the Hook and Ladder Co. will be joined by costume characters such as Cruella de Vil, the villain from Disney's *One Hundred and One Dalmatians* (1961) famous for trying to kidnap the Dalmatian puppies for their fur.

#6 The Strawhatters
This five person subgroup of *Disneyland Band* members performs turn-of-the-century Dixieland-style music while wearing traditional straw hats. Find them at various locations along Main Street. Dating all the way back to their first performances in 1956, this musical group has been a big part of Disneyland's history. Walt realized the appeal and importance of music in his theme park from the beginning. Dixieland

musicians like The Strawhatters helped establish Disneyland's nostalgic charm. Although the Strawhatters performance times are often not listed in your *Disneyland Entertainment Times Guide*, ask a cast member about the group's performances.

#7 Main St Piano Player

These piano players can be heard playing classic ragtime tunes in the seating area outside *Coke Corner*. You can enjoy a hot dog and a glass of coke as you listen to classic Disney songs played in a ragtime style. The pianist's name and daily performance schedule can be found on a sign hanging on the side of the piano, or consult your *Disneyland Entertainment Times Guide* for daily performance times.

#8 The Disneyland Band

This long-time Disneyland tradition can be spotted in their classic band uniforms playing joyful music while they march down Main Street. They typically perform about four times a day in various locations throughout Main Street USA. Look for them at the Disneyland *Entry Plaza*, in *Town Square*, in front of *Sleeping Beauty Castle*, or at the *Flag Retreat Ceremony*. Consult your *Disneyland Entertainment Times Guide* for current performance times.

The Band at Halloween

Catch the classic Disneyland Band playing Halloween tunes as they march throughout the park. Check the *Disneyland Entertainment Times Guide* for show times.

#9 Pearly Band

This British-themed band is named after the Mother of Pearl buttons sewn into their uniform. They perform traditional London street music reminiscent of the *London pearly kings and queens* they emulate. They were also featured in the animated sequences of Disney's *Mary Poppins* (1964), and Mary Poppins and Bert can be found joining the band in singing popular tunes from the film. Look for the Pearly Band in front of *Sleeping Beauty Castle* or marching through other Fantasyland locations several times a day.

#10 Flag Retreat Ceremony

Each evening inside the Disneyland Park a ceremony is held to lower and remove the United States flag before sunset. During the ceremony musicians such as the *Dapper Dans* and the *Disneyland Band* play music up and down main street. Usually the Star Spangled Banner can be heard when the flag is lowered. Current and veteran members of the armed forces are also honored during the ceremony. They are called up to the flag by military branch. The whole event usually lasts about 20 minutes depending on the musical acts that are available. The Flag Retreat Ceremony can be found at the flagpole in the center of *Town Square* every evening just before dusk.

New Orleans Square
#11 Royal Street Bachelors
If you're in the mood for jazz, head on over to the stage at the *French Market Restaurant* to hear the Royal Street Bachelors. They can also be found strolling around the streets of New Orleans Square playing the same traditional jazz music the original Bachelors played when the land opened in 1966.

#12 The Bootstrappers
The Bootstrappers are a roving band of singing pirates typically found wandering the streets and corridors of New Orleans Square. These performers like to sing classic sea shanties and pirate songs such as "Yo Ho, Yo Ho, a Pirates Life for Me". Just after *Tom Sawyer Island* was redesigned to incorporate the "Pirate's Lair" concept, guests could find The Bootstrappers singing their favorite shanties in front of *Lafitte's Tavern*. It's rare to find them on the island these days - they're more often found engaging guests with their humorous songs near the *Café Orleans*. This group can be hard to track down, so ask a cast member about daily performance times.

#13 Jambalaya Jazz
This jazz band can be found playing their upbeat music throughout the streets of New Orleans Square in their brightly colored pastel uniforms. Considered one of the most lively performances at Disneyland, the band members like to throw out Mardi Gras beads to their audience on occasion. During Disneyland's *Mardi Gras Celebration* the Jambalaya Jazz can also be seen performing with Queenie near the *French Market* restaurant.

Frontierland
#14 Fantasmic!
This magnificent nighttime spectacular should not be missed. Performed on the southern tip of *Tom Sawyer Island* and in the mighty waters of the *Rivers of America*, this show features singing, dancing, Disney characters, fireworks, projections and amazing special effects. Find a spot along the edge of the Rivers of America to view the show.

New Fastpass Reservation System
This show now features a new Fastpass reservation system, so be sure to stop by the Fastpass distribution center early in the morning if you plan on seeing the show. Viewing the show from the standby viewing areas is a very time-consuming and crowded experience, so a Fastpass is highly recommended.

Look for the Fastpass Distribution center along *Big Thunder Trail*, a path that connects Frontierland to Fantasyland (between *Big Thunder Ranch* and the *Village Haus* restaurant.) Passes are distributed on a first come first served bases, and they do run out quickly. You must have the Disneyland Entry Ticket or Annual Pass from each member in your party with you to reserve spots for them, but the guests themselves need not be with you to make the reservation.

Get VIP Treatment with a Fantasmic Dinner Package

Several fine Dining restaurants inside Disneyland now offer a dinner package that includes VIP-style preferred seating tickets for Fantasmic. At some locations (such as *Aladdin's Oasis*) you may even choose between eating your meal there or takeing it with you to the show. The following locations will offer Fantasmic Dinner Packages:

- *Aladdin's Oasis* - Dine-in or boxed dinner to go.
- *Blue Bayou* - Fine Dining served in the restaurant.
- *River Belle Terrace* - Full service dining.

Reservations may be made up to 60 days in advance and are highly recommended. Call the Disney Dine Line at (714) 781-DINE or visit the Disneyland Dining Website to make a reservation.

disneyland.disney.go.com/dining/disneyland/fantasmic-dinner-packages/

#15 The Laughing Stock Co.

Often found in front of the *Golden Horseshoe Stage* on weekends and inside the *Golden Horseshoe Stage* on select weekdays, this vaudeville style variety show features comedy, singing and music. A variety of different versions of the show exist, so it's possible to see entirely different shows at different performances. Consult your *Disneyland Entertainment Times Guide* for daily performance times.

#16 Farley the Fiddler

You can usually find this fiddle master playing toe-tapping music near the porch of the *Pioneer Mercantile*. He may call out for a square dance, so join in on the fun if you get the chance. Farley will even teach you the moves. Lately he's also been spotted joining the festivities at the *Big Thunder Ranch Jamboree*.

#17 Big Thunder Ranch Stage

The stage inside the *Big Thunder Ranch BBQ* gives guests the chance to view live entertainment while dining at the all-you-can-eat restaurant. Daily musical guests sing and dance around the stage area, and special holiday shows are provided around *Halloween* and *Christmas*.

Fantasyland

#18 The Royal Theatre

A new interactive performance area called the *Royal Theatre* brings to life the stories of Disney's fairy tale heroes and heroines by allowing guests to become part of the story. Nighttime music and dancing at the theatre promises to keep the area alive long after the sun goes down. Look for this theatrical experience under the large circular tent inside the new *Fantasy Faire* area.

Frozen

Join Mr. Smythe and Mr. Jones as they retell the story of Frozen with their own

74

unique spin on the tale. You will also get to see Elsa, Anna, and the Faire Maidens get in on the act.

Jump, Jive, Boogie Swing Party
Sometimes now referred to as *The Royal Swing Big Band Ball*, look for this seasonally occurring swing dance party on warm evenings under the wide circular awning of the Royal Theatre. This swing dance event is aimed more towards adults, but just like everything at Disneyland - kids of all ages are always welcome to dance the night away. Consult your *Disneyland Entertainment Times Guide* to see if this swing party is happening during your visit.

#19 Fantasyland Theatre
This theatre area formerly housed the *Princess Fantasy Fair* until it closed in August 2012. With the *Fantasy Faire* relocated to the former *Carnation Gardens* area on the other side of Fantasyland, the historic Fantasyland Theatre is now free to host another live Disneyland stage show. This large outdoor theater area has been renovated to present an all-new stage show starring Mickey Mouse, utilizing the latest in theatre technology.

Mickey and the Magical Map
This brand new live stage show premiered at the newly refurbished Fantasyland Theatre in the summer of 2013. Titled "Mickey and the Magical Map," the show features Mickey Mouse reprising his role as the Sorcerer's Apprentice from Disney's *Fantasia* (1940) and *Fantasia 2000* (1999) films. In this new story, the wise sorcerer Yen Sid tells Mickey about a magical map with the power to take dreamers to any place imaginable. But when the young apprentice attempts to paint the map's single unfinished spot, he stumbles into a fantastic adventure through worlds of music, color and popular Disney characters.

The show also features appearances by some Disney favorites including King Louie (*The Jungle Book*), Mulan (*Mulan*), Pocahontas (*Pocahontas*), Rapunzel & Flynn Rider (*Tangled*) and Tiana (*The Princess and the Frog*). Consult the *Disneyland Entertainment Times Guide* or the online *Entertainment Schedule* for show details and performance times:

disneyland.disney.go.com/calendar/daily/

Tomorrowland
#20 Tomorrowland Terrace Bands
The Tomorrowland Terrace Stage is located in front of the *Tomorrowland Terrace* restaurant and has been a popular spot to view contemporary musical performances since the late 1960's. The venue is known for it's unique two level concert stage in which the lower level hydraulically lifts out of the ground when performances begin. You can watch contemporary bands playing original modern music or popular cover tunes as you dine on food from the *Tomorrowland Terrace* restaurant. Check your *Disneyland Entertainment Times Guide* for a list of current performers and concert times.

The Rising Stage
Arrive early before the show starts and then watch as the featured band rises up out of the ground on the hydraulically lifted stage.

#21 Jedi Training Academy at Tomorrowland Terrace

Children between the ages of 4 and 12 get the chance to become Padawan Jedi Knights in this interactive stage show at *Tomorrowland Terrace*. Kids are randomly chosen out of the audience to participate in the show and train with Jedi Masters before entering into light saber duels with some of the *Star Wars* franchise's most infamous villains. Check your *Disneyland Entertainment Times Guide* for daily performance times.

How to Get Picked for Training
Arrive early and have your little ones sit in the front row for the best chance at getting picked by the Jedi Masters for Padawan training.

California Adventure

Throughout the Park

#01 Pixar Play Parade

Enjoy watching your favorite characters from memorable Disney/Pixar films such as *A Bug's Life* (1998), *Finding Nemo* (2003), *The Incredibles* (2004), *Monsters, Inc.* (2001) and *Toy Story* (1995) march past you among incredible floats and talented dancers. The parade typically lasts about 40 minutes and runs from the *Twilight Zone Tower of Terror* in Hollywood Land to the *Silly Symphony Swings* in Paradise Pier. Cast members refer to this route as the Performance Corridor, and you can watch the parade from designated viewing stations located along the route.

Inside Out Pre-Parade
The new pre-parade show at California Adventure features the characters from the film *Inside Out* (2015). Experience Joy, Fear, Sadness, Anger, and Disgust as they dance across the parade route for you.

Buena Vista Street

#2 Red Car News Boys

This live musical show erupts spontaneously on Buena Vista Street as newsboys start to sing and dance on the *Red Car Trolley*. The show continues to Carthey Circle as the newsboys get out and perform their rendition of the song "A Suitcase and a Dream" about the arrival of Walt Disney to California in 1923. They then continue performing on the Red Car Trolley as it travels down *Hollywood Blvd* and eventually ends up in front of the *Hollywood Tower Hotel* on *Sunset Blvd*. One of the most interesting aspects of this show is that you can catch different parts of it from different locations throughout *Buena Vista Street* and *Hollywood Land*. See the

California Adventure *Times Guide* for performance times or ask a cast member in Buena Vista Street about the show.

#3 Five & Dime

Find this six-member band performing hep tunes from their makeshift jalopy as they drive down Buena Vista Street. They like to stop in Carthay Circle for a while and perform for the guests there, so stop by and listen to their unique brand of music.

According to the group's backstory a five-member band traveled to Buena Vista Street in a makeshift jalopy to try to make it big with their music. When they arrived there they met Dime working at the *Five & Dime* shop and convinced her to join the band. Now the six of them drive down Buena Vista Street displaying their musical talents while trying to get gigs.

Hollywood Land

#4 Disney Junior Live on Stage

This interactive show was designed for preschoolers. It features singing, dancing, and many of your favorite characters from Disney Junior shows like *Sofia the First*, *Doc MCStuffins*, *Jake and the Never Land Pirates*, and the *Mickey Mouse Clubhouse*. Kids will get the chance to stand up, clap their hands, sing and dance along with the performers. The show is also full of puppets and catchy songs that will keep them entertained. The entire show tends to last about 25 minutes.

#5 Disney Performing Arts Stage

Occasionally special performances are held at the Disney Performing Arts Stage (formerly known as the Hollywood Backlot Stage.) School award shows, school and local bands, church choirs, and a wide variety of other performances have been held here. Find the Disney Performing Arts Stage in the vast space between *Muppet Vision 3D* and *Disney's Aladdin: Musical Spectacular*. Check the California Adventure *Times Guide* to see if any special shows will be performed on the stage during your visit.

#6 Disney's Aladdin: Musical Spectacular

Enjoy this lavish floorshow in the tradition of big Broadway musicals inside the enormous Hyperion Theater. The show is full of music, dancing, and many of your favorite characters from *Aladdin*. And the effects in the show are amazing. You will leave the theater with wonder in your head and the Aladdin theme in your heart.

Three Different Seating Levels

The theater offers three different seating levels, the *Orchestra*, *Mezzanine* and *Balcony*. Where you wait in line determines which seating area you will be in, so make sure you choose the right area to wait in. Each seating area has its own advantages; the *Orchestra* puts you right down in front of the stage in the area where performers interact with the audience, the *Mezzanine* gives you an amazing straight-on view of the stage, and the *Balcony* allows you to see the performance from high above the crowds below.

Behind the Glass Doors & Windows

Have your photo taken while you pose behind the glass double doors of the *Ten Wilshire Drive* building façade built into the front of the Hyperion Theater. Then stand in the window of the *Fontaine Salon* or *Pere Et Fils* and do the same.

Cars Land
#7 Red to the Rescue

Watch as Red the lovable fire engine sounds his sirens, rings his bell, toots his horn, and moves his ladder up and down in this fun character-driven show in Cars Land. You may even be enlisted to help Red in his fire fighting duties. But watch out, Red isn't afraid to use his fire hose and the guests around him often end up getting a little wet. Look for this spontaneous show in front of the Radiator Springs courthouse at the east end of the land. See the California Adventure *Times Guide* or ask a cast member for show times.

Meet Red the Fire Truck

Stop by and visit with Red the friendly fire truck. Red doesn't speak, but he likes to say hi by turning his mirrors in and out. Look for him in front of a large gate along the path between the *Cozy Cone Motel* and the rear entrance to *A Bug's Land*. He only appears there once in a while, so ask a *cast member* when he will be appearing next.

#8 DJ's Dance 'n Drive

Get in on the dancing fun as DJ the troublemaking car supplies the beats in this spontaneous interactive show. DJ lights up in multiple neon colors as he spins music for the crowd around him and pumps it out of his built in tweeters, woofers and subwoofers. During the show kids get dance instruction from cast members dressed as 50's carhop waitresses and get to dance to the beat in the center of a crowd of spectators. Check the California Adventure *Times Guide* for daily show times.

Meet DJ

Sometimes DJ becomes available after the show for some photo ops with his fans. Ask a near by cast member at the end of the show when and where you can get a few photos with the troublemaking car.

Pacific Wharf
#9 Mariachi Divas

Listen to classic Mexican Mariachi music performed live at Pacific Wharf. This is a great source of entertainment while you dine on food from any of the nearby restaurants. Check the California Adventure *Times Guide* to see if the Mariachi Divas will be performing on the day you visit.

Paradise Pier
#10 World of Color – Celebrate!

Enjoy a spectacular water show filled with colorful lights, high-reaching fountains, projections, billowing fire and other magnificent special effects. Watch as many of your favorite Disney characters and movie scenes are projected onto plumes of water that launch more than 200 feet into the air. This show is a favorite attraction of many resort guests, and the characters and animation clips featured in the show are updated often. The amazing music for this show was performed by the London Symphony Orchestra. The show runs for about 30 minutes.

A 2015 reboot of the show features new special effects and narration by Neil Patrick Harris (Doogie Howser MD, 1989–1993; How I Met Your Mother, 2005–2014).

Fastpass Reserved Seating

If you arrive early enough you can get a *Fastpass* to see the World of Color, entitling you a spot in the show's reserved seating section. These Fastpasses run out quickly, so *be sure to get one first thing in the morning* after entering the park. The Fastpasses are distributed in *Grizzly Peak* at the *Grizzly River Run* next to the attraction's own Fastpass machines, rather than at *Paradise Bay* where the show is held. The World of Color *Fastpass* is on a separate network. You can grab a Fastpass to the show first thing in the morning and then still get a Fastpass for any other attraction in the park.

Dinner Packages

Diner packages are available at some of the park's finer restaurants which combine a gourmet meal with a guaranteed seat for the show later in a special premiere viewing area. This is a simple way make sure your family gets to see the show and will save you a lot of wait time. Look for special Dining Packages at the *Carthay Circle Restaurant*, *Wine Country Trattoria*, and *Ariel's Grotto*. These gourmet meals replace the former World of Color Picnic service that used to be available to guests.

Carthay Circle Restaurant Fast Passes

Rather than having to purchase a formal prix fixe dinner, the *Carthay Circle Restaurant* also occasionally offers a special deal where everyone in your party who orders an entrée and either an appetizer or dessert receives a special Fastpass for the show from the restaurant. Ask your restaurant hostess or server if this special deal is available.

Non-ticketed Seating

If you don't have a Fastpass or Dinner Package you can still watch the show, but it will be more difficult. Non-ticked seating areas are available throughout the Paradise Bay area on a first come first serve bases. Guests tend to arrive very early to stake out their seats in these areas, and I highly recommend you do the same.

#11 Just Add Water: Instant Concert!

Watch and listen as Maestro Goofy conducts a spontaneous concert in front of the waters of Paradise Bay. His orchestra may be invisible, but fountains out in the bay respond to the music and Goofy's direction in beautiful ways. The shows only last a few minutes, but they are great to catch if you happen to be in the area. The style of the show was inspired by Goofy's series of "How To" cartoon shorts.

Catch this show from Paradise Park located on the north edge of paradise bay. Check the California Adventure *Times Guide* for daily show times.

Three Different Performances Per Day
Three different music pieces are used, with a different one for each show. So if you like the show, you can return two more times on the same day and see different performances.

#12 Operation: Playtime! With the Green Army Men

Watch the Green Army Men drive around Paradise Pier in their army Jeep, beating their drums and looking for other toys to join their cause. Eventually the jeep stops, the soldiers unpack the rest of their drums and start playing in unison. Sarge picks a few "new recruits" (kids) from the crowd and lets them get in on the act. As Sarge barks out orders, the kids and soldiers respond. Check the California Adventure *Times Guide* for show times for this popular performance.

#13 Paradise Gardens Bandstand

Take in a musical performance while you dine at the nearby restaurants in paradise gardens. Located in the center of the Paradise Gardens outdoor dining tables, this gazebo stage offers a variety of different musical talents year round. A number of different historic and international music styles are represented in the shows. See the *California Adventure Times Guide* for daily performance times.

#14 Phineas & Ferb's Rockin' Rollin' Dance Party

Watch as the *A-Little-Too-Young-To-Drive-O-Matic* truck pulls up and the dance party erupts around it in this interactive performance for kids. Cast members dressed as *Fireside Girls* will lead kids in the dance moves as characters Phineas & Ferb dance along. At one point in the show even adults get to join in the fun and try to hula-hoop to the music.

Find this dance party out in front of *The Little Mermaid: Ariel's Undersea Adventure* attraction several times daily. The show runs about fifteen minutes. Check the California Adventure *Times Guide* for show times.

Grizzly Peak

#15 The Happy Camper Sing Along

Sit back and listen as soothing live music fills the air around the Grizzly Peak area. The Happy Camper plays popular campfire songs on the dulcimer (a string instrument similar to a xylophone), a harmonica and guitar combination, or other musical instruments as guests sit or stand around him listening to his melodic creations along the walking paths of Grizzly Peak.

The Happy Camper usually sets up shop along Route 49 near the entrance to the Redwood Creek Challenge Trail. Check the California Adventure Times Guide for performance dates and times.

Attractions & Activities

You came to the Disneyland Resort for the attractions, right? I mean, the food is delicious, the activities are fun, and the shows can be amazing, but you want to go on the rides! Well don't worry, I dedicate plenty of space in this book to talking about ALL of the attractions in BOTH resort theme parks. But before I get into the descriptions of each individual attraction, I thought I better introduce you to the many special programs that exist to enhance your experience with them. Read through the information below to be sure you understand how each program works, and then look for these special programs listed under the names of the attractions that utilize them. Some of these programs can save you from hours of waiting in line, while others warn you about the requirements necessary to ride the attraction. Then read about each attraction in the resort, organized by theme park, land within the theme park, and then finally by the order in which you are likely to encounter them. I also list the type of attraction under it's name, and the number next to each attraction corresponds to the same number on the maps in the front of the book. Enjoy!

Fastpasses

Getting a Fastpasses is like getting a reservation to a popular attraction. The Fastpass system at the Disneyland Resort can save you from a long wait time but it's important to understand how it works. Fastpasses are always free and available to all guests. To obtain a Fastpass, go to the Fastpass distribution machines for the attraction you wish to ride and insert your Disneyland Ticket or Annual Pass. The machine will print out a Fastpass for you with the time to return in order to use the pass. For example, if your pass is marked 2:00pm to 3:00pm, you must return to the attraction's entrance sometime between 2:00pm and 3:00pm in order to use your Fastpass. Present the pass to the cast member at the entrance to the attraction and they will direct you to a special shorter Fastpass line, often saving you hours off of your wait time. Each person in your party needs their own Fastpass.

Single Rider Lines

This program is one of the greatest secrets at the resort. Guests who are willing to ride alone or split up their party may use this fantastic time saver. By entering the Single Rider Line rather than the Stand-By Line for an attraction, guests are able to fill in empty seats left by odd-numbered groups on the attractions. The Single Rider Line is almost always much shorter that the stand-by line. Ask the cast member at the start of each attraction's queue for details on how to use the Single Rider Line program for that particular attraction. They will usually give you some sort of pass showing that you are a single rider and then tell you where to go from there. Only the following attractions allow you to use the single rider feature:

Rider Swap

If you brought young children with you on your Disneyland adventure you may run into attractions your little ones cannot ride due to height requirements. If you are traveling with at least one other adult, you can take advantage of Disneyland's Rider Swap program. The procedure is simple: one adult waits with the children while the rest go on the ride. When the ride is over, the adults swap. This family friendly program means you don't have to wait in line twice to care for your child. Ask a cast member at each of the attractions listed below for details on the rider swap program:

Height Requirements

For safety reasons several Disneyland attractions have strict height requirements. Children who do not meet these minimum height requirements can't board the attraction, in most cases even if accompanied by an adult. All attractions that have a height requirement will have a cast member standing by to assist in determining if your child reaches the required height or not.

Disneyland

Disneyland Railroad
#01 Ride the Railroad Throughout the Park
Mild Ride

Hop aboard the famous Disneyland Railroad to get around the park, or opt for a round-trip *Grand Circle Tour* of Disneyland. From aboard the train you can catch scenic vistas, wildlife, flowing rivers, native peoples and dinosaurs in their natural habitat.

Four Railroad Destinations

Guests may board and exit the train at any of the four stations: *Main Street Station, New Orleans Square Station, Mickey's Toontown Station,* and *Tomorrowland Station*

The Grand Circle Tour

This is the name given to a full-circle round-trip ride on the railroad; you can start at any of the four Disneyland railroad stations and ride the train throughout the park until it returns back to the same station. The Grand Circle Tour gives guests the chance to see all of the sights along the railroad tracks. There is no need to make any special arrangements to take the tour. Just board and exit the train at the station of your choice.

The Grand Canyon

View the animals and scenic vistas of the Grand Canyon as you pass by this 300 foot wide, 34 foot tall diorama on the route between *Tomorrowland Station* and *Main Street Station*. The Grand Canyon diorama opened in 1958 with a hand-painted scenic backdrop, rock formations, plant life and real taxidermy animals. It's remained pretty much the same since that time.

Primeval World Diorama

Following the tour of the Grand Canyon you're magically transported back in time to the primeval world of dinosaurs in their natural habitat. This magnificent life-sized diorama is one of the last things you see before *Main Street Station*.

Main Street USA

#02 Fire Engine
Mild Ride

This open-air Main Street Vehicle is a re-creation of an early model fire truck. It transports guests between *Town Square* and the *Central Hub* with a motor tour down Main Street. The charming turn of the century fire engine uses a horn and bell instead of a siren, and seats about 8-10 guests in the benches toward the rear of the vehicle. The Fire Engine's drivers are very knowledgeable about the history of the vehicle as well as the park in general, so they're always happy to answer any questions you have when it is safe for them to do so.

#03 Horse-Drawn Streetcar
Mild Ride

As one of Disneyland's original 17 attractions when the park opened in 1955, the Horse-Drawn Streetcar can accommodate about 30 guests at a time on a tour down Main Street. The turn-of-the-century trolleys are each pulled by a single horse.

#04 Horseless Carriage
Mild Ride

This vintage open-air automobile takes guests on a puttering motor-tour down Main Street USA. The red or yellow cars are meticulously modeled after authentic 1903 automobiles.

#05 Omnibus
Mild Ride

This double-decker bus transports guests down Main Street in style. The views from the bus are magnificent, particularly from the second level. Disney Imagineers modeled the vehicle after a 1920 New York City double-decker bus and it holds about 45 guests at a time.

#06 The Disneyland Story Presenting Great Moments with Mr. Lincoln
Theater Attraction

At this historic attraction inside Main Street's Opera House you can learn about the creation of Disneyland, get a history lesson from an *audio-animatronic* Lincoln, and view the biographies of American heroes. The attraction is comprised of four different parts:

The Lobby

As you enter the Opera House building you're greeted by historic Disney artifacts such as the bench Walt Disney sat on in Griffith Park while coming up with the idea of Disneyland. Continuing on into a large room inside the building you can view artifacts and articles about the construction of Disneyland and the park's history up until present day. In late 2013 the lobby was renovated to incorporate part of The *Disney Gallery's* rotating art exhibitions.

The Story of Disneyland

This video hosted by comedian Steve Martin plays on a loop in the lobby to the 'Great Moments with Mr. Lincoln' show. It contains a lot of Disneyland history with a few laughs mixed in -so take a seat and enjoy a few minutes with Steve while waiting for the next 'Great Moments' show to begin.

Great Moments with Mr. Lincoln

This live show takes place inside a grand old theater and features an animatronic version of President Abraham Lincoln. During the show Lincoln gives you a history lesson as he recounts some of the important moments of American history and delivers a portion of his famous Gettysburg Address. The show gives guests a unique opportunity to experience what it may have been like to watch Lincoln deliver his famous address back in 1863.

The Hall of Heroes

After exiting the 'Great Moments with Mr. Lincoln' show guests walk through an exit hallway featuring photographs of many of America's greatest heroes.

#07 Main Street Cinema
Theater Attraction

This reproduction of an old-time movie house features six screens in a single room, with a different early Disney cartoon shown on a loop on each screen simultaneously. By standing inside the theater guests can view any one of the screens they wish.

The cartoons are played on a loop all day long on the cinema's 6 screens. View all six animations if you have the time: *Steamboat Willie* (1928), *Plane Crazy* (1928), *Traffic Troubles* (1931), *The Moose Hunt* (1931), *The Dognapper* (1934), *Mickey's Polo Team* (1936).

#08 The Fire Station
Walk-Through Attraction

Located next to *City Hall*, the Disneyland Fire Station is often overlooked as guests rush toward the park's more glittery attractions, but it's worth a closer look. Here you can explore the fire fighting artifacts on display in the museum, get an up-close look at the old fire wagon and fire equipment, and view historic photos of past fire fighters. You can also climb aboard the old fire wagon on display here and have your photo taken.

#09 The Disney Gallery
Walk-Through Attraction

Guests have the chance to view & purchase original Disney artwork at The Disney Gallery on Main Street. Located inside the former Bank of Main Street building, remnants of Disneyland's long gone financial institution can still be seen in the teller windows and antique full-sized bank vault that now displays rare Disney artwork.

Stop by the gallery and see art on display in one of the building's seasonally changing shows. Art shows are typically held in the room towards the rear of the building. The gallery will often feature a particular theme or artist, which changes several times a year. It's often difficult to get information on future shows, but you can always inquire about the gallery's current theme by calling Disneyland guest services at (714) 781-4565, option 0.

#10 The Penny Arcade
Walk-Through Attraction

The Penny Arcade on Main Street offers a variety of old-time coin operated arcade machines. The majority of the machines still cost only a penny to operate, but a few of them cost a dime or a quarter. You can get change from the change machines located in the arcade. Don't forget to have your fortune read by Esmeralda the coin operated fortune teller before you leave - a time-honored Disneyland tradition.

The location of the machines are moved periodically, and the Penny Arcade itself went through a major renovation in 2012, so if you can't find the arcade machines you are looking for, ask a cast member where they have been relocated to.

Adventureland
#11 Enchanted Tiki Room
Theater Attraction

Sit back and enjoy the show as a cast of more than 150 *audio-animatronic* birds, flowers, masks, totems and other characters sing and dance inside a large Polynesian-themed Tiki Room. The humorous songs and fancifully-choreographed movements of these characters amazed and entranced guests when the attraction first opened in 1963, and for the most part the attraction has remained unchanged since that date. The show runs about 15 mins, but you should also plan to spend up to 15 mins in the waiting area watching the pre-show entertainment.

Pineapple Documentary

While waiting for the show to start, be sure to catch the documentary created by Dole on the history of the pineapple. It can be seen on the back of the *Tiki Juice Bar's* roof from inside the waiting area.

Hawaiian Gods Pre-show

Show up to the Tiki Room waiting area early to catch this special entertainment. Each of the Hawaiian God totems found throughout the courtyard come to life and tell their stories through movement and sound.

Hidden Restroom

Because the Enchanted Tiki Room was originally intended to be a restaurant it happens to be the only attraction at Disneyland that was designed with a restroom inside. Although this restroom does not appear on the *Disneyland Park Guide*, it's still in operation and available for guests to use. It's accessed through the waiting area, after passing though the attraction's front entrance look for it along the east wall of the attraction building.

#12 Jungle Cruise
Mild Ride

Take a tour down a remote jungle river with a wisecracking guide, armed only with dry wit and the occasional shots fired from an antique sidearm. Keep your eyes peeled for exotic animals, dangerous tribesmen and lush jungle fauna as your guide jokes his way down the river. The Jungle Cruise was the first attraction to be built for Adventureland, and it's as fun today as it was on Disneyland's opening day.

Different Jokes with Every Ride

After hearing guests say that they didn't need to ride the Jungle Cruise again because they had already seen everything it had to offer, Walt Disney added comedy to the attraction in the form of quips and puns. Now every trip down the river is a unique guest experience. The river guides' pun-filled speeches continues to add a bit of humor to the adventure that has become the Jungle Cruise's defining element.

Artifacts in the Queue

As you walk through the attraction *queue* be sure look at the artifacts on display. There is a lot to see here.

#13 Indiana Jones Adventure
Thrill Ride • FastPass • Single Rider Line • Rider Swap • Height Requirement 46"

Walk with caution through a newly uncovered archeological dig site, 'The Temple of the Forbidden Eye', as you follow the trail of Indiana Jones. Then board a troupe transport for a wild fast-paced ride through the rough terrain of the temple. While on your adventure you will encounter Mara, a powerful ancient deity who promised great treasures to the pure of heart and death to those foolish enough to gaze into its all-seeing eyes. Discover which of three treasures Mara has decided to grant you: "earthly riches", "eternal youth" or "knowledge of the future". Your fate is different each time you ride. Drive through rat-infested rooms, avoid giant snakes, dodge speeding darts - and if you make it that far try to escape the biggest booby trap of them all. The Indiana Jones Adventure was created as a collaboration between George Lucas and Disney, opening in 1995 with AT&T as the attraction's sponsor for the first 7 years.

A Different Adventure Every Time

Every ride on this attraction is a unique adventure, with three different experiences when you encounter the Mara statue in the beginning of the ride leading to three different possible paths to take into the temple, culminating in many different interactions with Indiana Jones at the ride's conclusion.

Mysteries in the Queue

Explore the areas you pass through while waiting in line to board the attraction. These rooms are full of secrets for you to discover.

#14 Tarzan's Treehouse
Walk-Through Attraction

When touring Tarzan's home you'll find yourself climbing upward inside a gigantic tree before crossing a perilous rope bridge to find spectacular views. Explore the many interactive features, discover hidden surprises and follow along with the story of Tarzan as you eventually make your way back down to the earth below. At first glance Tarzan's Treehouse appears to be an attraction intended for children, but with it's magnificent views and attention to detail, this treehouse can be enjoyed by adults and children alike.

Jane's Journal

Follow the story of Tarzan in Jane's Journal. Look for the journal opened to relevant pages throughout the attraction.

Closes Early

Tarzan's Tree House tends to close early, usually before dusk, so be sure to explore the attraction early in the day.

Rarely a Wait

Although Tarzan's Tree House is rarely empty, it does tend to have fairly short lines throughout the day. This is a good place to visit when other attractions become overcrowded, particularly if you already happen to be in Adventureland.

New Orleans Square
#15 Pirates of the Caribbean
Spooky Mild Ride

Sail through the pirate-infested waters of the Caribbean in a small 24 seat boat through this iconic Disneyland attraction that spawned four major motion pictures. After you board your floating bateau you are guided through several different areas where you experience a fierce naval battle, the pillaging of a seaside village, and the ghostly remnants of a sunken ship littered with the skeletons and treasures of pirates past. Although the ride features a few short waterfall drops, you won't typically get wet on this attraction. This was the last attraction Walt Disney participated in creating, opening just after his death in the spring of 1967.

Blue Bayou Dining Room

The dining room of the *Blue Bayou Restaurant* can be viewed from your boat as you sail past it in the beginning of your voyage. Diners can be seen enjoying their lunch or dinner as they take in the simulated outdoor evening ambiance created inside the attraction.

Bayou Gators

Look to the port (left) side of your bateau for alligators as you travel through the bayou portion of the attraction. They can be hard to spot, but look for their eyes sticking up out of the murky water.

Nighttime Sky

No matter what time you enter the attraction, a nighttime sky is always found over the Pirates of the Caribbean bayou area. Look for stars, moving clouds and other elements of the open nighttime sky above you as you travel down the bayou in your bateau.

#16 Haunted Mansion
Spooky Mild Ride • FastPass

(See <u>Haunted Mansion Holiday</u> in <u>Top Halloween Attractions</u> at the front of this book.)

Critter Country

#17 Davy Crockett's Explorer Canoes
Guest Propelled Mild Ride

These 20 person canoes rely solely on the rowing power of the guests inside to drive them down the *Rivers of America*. Two cast member guides operate each canoe, one in the bow and one in the stern. They make sure the vessel stays on course and avoids any hazardous traffic on the river. As the only free-floating trackless attraction on the *Rivers of America*, the canoes often have to slow down or give right of way to other river ferrying vessels that operate on submerged tracks, such as the *Sailing Ship Columbia*, *Mark Twain Riverboat* and *The Rafts to Tom Sawyer Island*. The canoes serve as an excellent way to get up-close views of the many wonders of the *Rivers of America*, including the variety of animals, foliage, boats, buildings and people found along it's banks.

Limited Hours

The Explorer Canoes close early, usually before sundown, and only operate seasonally. They are usually open on warm days when the Park has high attendance. Call Disneyland Guest Services (714-781-4565, option 0) to find out if the canoes will be operating when you visit.

You Could Get a Little Wet

Riders can get a little wet, so wrap up and put away anything you don't want to have splashed with water. If you are really worried, you can always *rent a locker* to store your valuables.

You Do Actually Have to Row

Be prepared to do your fair share of rowing. The canoes really are entirely people powered. If you don't row, your canoe doesn't go!

#18 Splash Mountain
Thrill Ride • FastPass • Single Rider Line • Rider Swap • Height Requirement 40"

Board a log-shaped boat and glide past woodland creatures singing and dancing along the banks of an unforgiving river in the deep South. If you're looking to cool off, this is the place. Start with some refreshing spray while riding down a few small waterfalls, then get ready for the grand finale - a large 52 foot 40mph soaking plunge towards the base of the mountain. During the ride's finale look for a large ensemble of animatronic woodland creatures singing Disney's famous "Zip-A-Dee-Doo-Dah" song.

You May Get Wet

Guests do tend to get wet on this ride. The amount of water that splashes each rider varies from one trip to the next, and depends on several factors including the total weight occupying the log and your seating location.If you're not in the mood to get wet, ponchos are available for sale at the nearby *Pooh Corner* gift shop for $8.50 (adult size) or $7.50 (child size).

Drop in Again Sometime

Look for the hilarious "Drop in Again Sometime" sign at the base of the hill after the final plunge. Silly woodland creatures!

The Disneyland Railroad

Disneyland's famous railroad can be seen passing through the attraction towards the end of your trip down the waterways. Look for it up and to the left of your boat in the finale room where a large number of animatronic creatures join together in song on an old paddle-driven riverboat.

Automated Attraction Photo

Just as your log begins to fall from the largest drop an automated camera snaps a photo of you. This happens at the top of the fall just after your log begins to free-fall down the waterfall, and typically captures a look of terror on your face as you start down the plunge. The photos may be purchased after exiting the attraction at *Prof. Barnaby Owl's Photographic Art Studio* ranging in price from $14.95 - $24.95.

#19 The Many Adventures of Winnie the Pooh
Mild Ride

In *The Many Adventures of Winnie the Pooh* you can board three row beehive-inspired vehicles called "Beehicles" and glide through the Hundred-Acre Woods where you join Pooh, Tigger, Piglet, Eeyore, Heffalumps, Woozles and others at Pooh's birthday party. This is followed by a colorful yet bizarre dream sequence featuring nightmares about Huffalumps and Woozles stealing Pooh's honey. The attraction replaced the iconic Country Bear Jamboree in 2003, and despite it's somewhat out of the way location and low attendance numbers, it remains a favorite attraction among young children and adults who grew up with the *Winnie the Pooh* book series. Be sure to watch out for all of the little details that went into creating this ride, including the flowing brooks and streams that showcase small models of the character's houses in the Hundred-Acre Wood along the outside of the attraction.

Miniature Houses

Find miniature versions of Pooh's friend's houses along the banks of the stream that runs outside the attraction.

#20 Winnie the Pooh's Thinking Spot
Walk-Through Attraction

Meet Winnie the Pooh and his friends daily at this regular costume character meeting spot. Though not featured on the official map provided by Disneyland, this is a favorite stop for any Winnie the Pooh fans and should not be missed. Take photos, get autographs and ask for a hug if needed. This area is based on the location in the Winnie the Pooh book series where Pooh goes to ponder things, often by lowering his head and saying to himself "Think, think, think." To find out when your favorite characters will be at *Pooh's Thinking Spot* see the *Disneyland Entertainment Times Guide* or ask a cast member for help.

Look for the Single Line Entrance

When multiple characters show up, a single line is usually established to meet all of them. If you see a costume character heading towards Pooh's Thinking Spot, try to get in line as soon as possible, as the line tends to get long quickly. Though the exit to the line is clearly marked with an exit sign, there is often not a sign to mark the start of the line, so look carefully for the line entrance and then quickly head there.

Explore the Dioramas

While you are there, take a look at the artfully designed areas around Pooh's Thinking Spot, including "The Gathering Spot" and "Rabbit's Garden".

Frontierland
#21 Frontierland Shootin' Exposition
Arcade Attraction

This is one of most overlooked and enjoyable attractions in the park. You'll pay 50¢ for the opportunity to unload an old frontier rifle on a variety of targets in a diorama-style display of the old 1850's Western town of Boot Hill. In the early days this attraction featured rifles that shot actual lead pellets, but modernization of the Frontierland Shootin' Exposition led to the installation of electronic rifles emitting infrared light, replacing the pellet-shooting guns of the past. Guests have 18 rifles to choose from. Picking your position on the firing line does matter, as some locations give you easier access to some of the targets than others. So decide what you want to shoot at and pick your spot.

Moving Targets

All of the range's targets cause something to happen when successfully shot with the rifle. For example, if you hit the target on the moving shovel, it causes a skeleton to pop up out of it's grave. Try hitting the various targets and see what happens.

#22 Mark Twain Riverboat
Mild Ride

This steam powered paddle boat takes you on a round trip tour of the *Rivers of America*. While on the river keep your eyes out for Native American villages, evidence of famous American pioneers and a large variety of wildlife.

Operating Hours

The last departure of the Mark Twain Riverboat is listed above the entrance to the dock daily. Stop by anytime to see when the boat's last trip is and make sure you don't miss out on this historic attraction.

Multiple Decks

While on board take a walk through all the decks of the Mark Twain, they are fascinating to see. A poster at the boat dock explains the name and function of each deck.

A History in Flags

A collection of historical flags can be found flying on polls above the Mark Twain's dock. The history of each flag can be found posted below it. Look for famous flags such as the The John Cabbot Flag and The Kings Color Flag, there are 8 flags in all to discover.

#23 Sailing Ship Columbia
Mild Ride

Board the Sailing Ship Columbia for a round trip adventure on the *Rivers of America*. This boat views the same sights as the *Mark Twain Riverboat*, and is used as an alternative way to tour the river. Disneyland's reproduction of the boat contains cannons that fire, authentic looking crew uniforms and even crew's quarters down below deck.

Maritime Museum

There is a Maritime Museum below deck that features weapons, a maritime knots guide, galley, crew quarters and more. Try to take a look at it early in the voyage, as it can get crowded towards the end of the trip. The museum's close quarters make for an uncomfortable tour if too many guests try to go below deck at one time.

Firing of the Cannon

This ship contains reproductions of the cannons used in the late 1700's, and one of these cannons still fires. Make sure you are up on deck for the firing of the cannon, you don't want to miss this incredible reenactment. The cannon that fires is located near the bow (front) of the ship. This cannon is quite loud, however, and guests sensitive to noise may wish to keep their distance.

#24 Big Thunder Mountain Railroad
Thrill Ride • FastPass • Rider Swap • Height Requirement 40"

In this roller coaster ride guests board a rickety old mine train and barrel through rocky caverns and around steep mountains at high speed. There are plenty of sights to see along the way, that is if you're brave enough to have your eyes open.

Population sign

A sign with different population numbers crossed out can be found at a viewing spot to the right of the attraction's entrance, just to the left of the *Rancho del Zocalo Restaurante*. It appears the population of Big Thunder Mountain has been going down steadily, starting at 2,015, and then going down to 247, 89 and finally 38. Note also that they eventually started writing the population number in chalk, presumably to make it easier to change frequently. The sign also mentions that the Big Thunder Mountain's elevation is 135 ft.

Horseshoes

Look for horseshoes above the entrances to two different tunnels as your train speeds through Big Thunder Mountain. Over the first tunnel the horseshoe sits in it's traditional lucky position with the legs of the shoe pointing upward, to keep all the good luck from spilling out. Above the second tunnel the legs of the horseshoe point down, symbolizing that your luck is about to run out. This is the tunnel where you are a subjected to an earthquake, an bit of bad luck indeed.

Critters

Spinning opossums, the dynamite-chewing goat, howling coyotes, snakes, skunks, buzzards, bats and wildlife galore lurk around every corner of your train ride. Keep your eyes out for them as you whip around corners and speed down hills throughout the ride.

Dinosaur Bones

Look for these large rib bones as you pass through them towards the end of the ride.

#25 Petrified Tree
Walk-Through Attraction

Did you know that Disneyland has a tree that is at least 55 million years old? Taken from the Pike Petrified Forest in Colorado, this large petrified tree trunk can be found on Display along the edge of the *Rivers of America* just west of the *Mark Twain* and *Columbia* dock. The Redwood of Sequoia tree trunk is believed to be from 55 to 70 million years old, and was presented to Disneyland by Mrs. Disney in 1957. It's a remarkable artifact of prehistoric nature and should become a quick stop on your adventure through Disneyland when you visit.

#26 Big Thunder Ranch
Walk-Through Attraction

Take a break from thrill-ride attractions, parades and performances by spending some time in this Western ranch just north of *Big Thunder Mountain*. Here guests can find goats inside the petting zoo, a reproduction of a western cabin and other ranch items to explore.

Petting Zoo

Pet a collection of friendly goats inside Big Thunder Ranch's petting zoo area. The small goats here are very used to people and are happy to take a picture with you. A hand washing station is available at the entry to the ranch so that guests may wash their hands after petting the goats.

Other Animals

In addition to the goats in the petting zoo, other animals can be found in pens along the west wall of the ranch. Take a look in the pens and see what other animals are available to meet on the day you visit the ranch. The ranch hands will even bring out some birds for you to visit with when the weather is warm enough.

Miss Chris' Cabin

Inside Big Thunder Ranch is a reproduction of a western rancher's cabin known as Miss Chris' Cabin. In this walk-through cabin exhibit, you'll get the chance to see what life was like a hundred years ago on a western ranch. The cabin is full of artifacts, photos and artwork. Coloring books and baskets of crayons can be found on the tables in the center of the cabin for kids to color with, and comfortable furniture provide adults with a nice place to rest.

#27 Big Thunder Jamboree
Walk-Through Attraction

The *Big Thunder Jamboree* area is slated to be torn down just before Halloween this year, in anticipation of the construction of Star Wars land in 2016. Be sure to enjoy this area while you still can if you get the chance to visit it before then. It offers a variety of county-style entertainments including Disney characters in western wear, pin trading, games, and live stage shows.

Live Entertainment

Several western-themed shows and performances have found a new home inside the Big Thunder Ranch Jamboree. Consult the *Disneyland Entertainment Times Guide* for daily performance times.

Pin Trading

The new hotspot for *pin trading* with cast members is on top of barrels near the Big Thunder Ranch Jamboree's pin wagon. Here guests can find a large pin trading wagon wheel, large books of pins for trading and quite a few cast members wearing pin trading lanyards throughout the area. Pins can also be purchased here at the wagon.

Pin Games

Look for special games involving Disney pins near the pin trading area inside the *jamboree area*. These fun little games are a great distraction from the crowds in other areas of the park.

#28 Rafts to The Pirate's Lair on Tom Sawyer Island
Mild Ride

Take a ride on a wooden raft across the Rivers of America just like the one that carried Tom Sawyer and Huck Finn down the Mississippi River in Mark Twain's famous novels. These cast member-piloted rafts are the only way to reach the sights and activities found on *Tom Sawyer Island*, and provide frequent trips back and fourth across the river while the island is open.

Weapons & Supplies

Each island raft is equipped with weapons such as guns and swords attached to it's hull, as well as barrels and chests of supplies. Look around for these weapons and supplies while on board. Some of these barrels even make a convenient place to sit.

Raft Hours

While the rafts operate consistently whenever the island is open, they do close when the island closes, which is usually just before dusk. The last raft to the island tends to leave Frontierland about 10 minutes before the island closes - the time of the final departure is posted at the raft dock on the Frontierland side of the river. You don't have to worry about missing the last raft from the island back to the mainland, they continue to run until all guests are escorted off the island.

Tom Sawyer Island

#29 Dead Man's Grotto
Walk-Through Attraction

As the largest cave on the island, this is one attraction you won't want to miss. Guests young and old can enjoy walking through this expansive cave and explore the wonders it holds inside. Bottomless pits, pirate ghosts and piles of bountiful treasure are awaiting anyone brave enough to enter. The entrance to the Dead Man's Grotto cave is located just a few steps north of *The Landing* and exits on the other side of the island near *Will Turner's Blacksmith Shop*.

Secret Paths

Many alternate paths can be found inside the cave, some only large enough for children to fit through. Feel free to explore all of the secret routes you find as you make your way through the cave, all paths eventually lead to the same exit on the other side of the island.

Bottomless Pit

It's marked with a warning sign, so keep your eye out for this marvel of nature inside the cave.

#30 Lafitte's Tavern & Pirate Point
Walk-Through Attraction

Lafitte's Tavern sits along the southernmost edge of the island and recreates the feel of a swashbuckling pirate's tavern from long ago. Although you can't actually enter the tavern building, you can enjoy the porch and open deck area that sits along the edge of the busy *Rivers of America*.

Pirate Point is the name given to the area in front of and around Lafitte's Tavern, extending all the way to the edge of the *Rivers of America*. Here you can watch as mighty sailing ships and tiny canoes glide past, take in the scenic river banks, and view the bustling New Orleans Square across the river. From high vantage points located behind the tavern you can get an excellent bird's-eye view of the river and many of the island's features.

Stow Yer Weapons

A collection of old guns, axes, swords and other weapons can be found attached to the wall in front of Lafitte's Tavern.

View from Above Pirate Point

Climb the stairs and trails running around the east side of Lafitte's Tavern until you find a suitable viewpoint from above the building. From here you can look out over Pirate Point and the river surrounding the island.

#31 Will Turner's Blacksmith Shop
Walk-Through Attraction

This blacksmith shop is named after the character William "Will" Turner Jr. who appeared in the first three of the *Pirates of the Caribbean* (2003, 2006, 2007) films as the blacksmith's apprentice working in Port Royal who becomes entangled with the infamous Captain Jack Sparrow. Outside the Blacksmith Shop you'll be treated to a working waterwheel using the force of the flowing river to power the tools inside the building. Inside there's a reproduction of an 18th century working blacksmith shop, with all of the tools and other shop items left out on display. The coals in the kiln even appear to be red hot.

#32 Tom & Huck's Tree House
Climb Through Attraction

Named after young adventurers Tom Sawyer and Huckleberry Finn from the classic novels of Mark Twain, this tree house soars high above the island. Climb a ladder inside a large hollowed-out tree trunk to reach Tom & Huck's Tree House at the top of the tree. From there magnificent views of the *Rivers of America, New Orleans Square* and *Critter Country's Splash Mountain* can be seen through the leaves and branches of this mighty tree. Inside the tree house you'll find the remnants of Tom Sawyer and Huck Finn's adventures in treasure maps, wooden swords and pirate gear.

Tom Sawyer Artifacts

Look around the inside of the tree house for evidence of Tom Sawyer and Huck Finn. You can find a pirate treasure map, wooden swords, pirate masks, and more. An old ships wheel has been mounted by Tom and Huck to add to the tree house's décor. Look for it on the wall inside the tree house, an homage to the items Tom and Huck were always looking to collect in Mark Twain's novels.

"Huck Finn the Red Handed"

Look for these words scrawled across the treasure map that Tom and Huck left hanging in their tree house. It refers to the names Tom Sawyer gave to his friends Huck Finn and Joe Harper when they met up for adventures along the Mississippi River in *The Adventures of Tom Sawyer* (1876). Huck was known as "Huck Finn the Red Handed," Joe as "Joe Harper the Terror of the Seas" and Tom as "Tom Sawyer the Black Avenger of the Spanish Main."

#33 Smuggler's Cove
Walk-Through Attraction

This pirate-themed cove on the east side of the island features sunken treasures, rope bridges, cages made of bone, and other features to explore. Walk across the rope bridge suspended high above the cove if you dare, or attempt to cross the water on a bridge supported by floating barrels. Be sure to explore the area thoroughly, many secrets await those brave enough to seek them out.

Suspension Bridge

Cross the high flying suspension bridge looming over Smuggler's Cove. This bridge has a lot of sway and movement to it, so hold on tight. The Suspension Bridge does have established entry and exit sides, so start out by entering on the West end of the bridge.

Pontoon Bridge
Wooden barrels keep this bridge afloat over the rushing waters below. Hold on tight because crossing this bridge can be a bumpy ride. The Pontoon Bridge leads guests out of Smuggler's Cove and into the central part of the island where you can find more *island caves* to explore, *Castle Rock* and the *Shipwreck*.

Capstan Wheel
Step up to this mighty wheel and give it a turn. Then watch what happens as you continue to turn it, the results may surprise you.

Bilge Pumps & Ships Hold
Work the pumps to push water out of the sunken ships hold. Two people can work each pump at the same time.

Bone Cage
Climb inside a reproduction of the round cage made of bone seen in the feature film *Pirates of the Caribbean: Dead Man's Chest* (2006). Have your picture taken inside the cage, or just explore the cage see what it's like to be inside a prison made of bone.

#34 Castle Rock
Walk-Through Attraction
Found towards the center of the island, this large rock structure stretches up into the sky. Guests can explore the caves down below or climb up a narrow staircase and take in the views from above the rocks. There are several hidden activities to find in Castle Rock as well, so explore the area thoroughly and see what you else you can find there.

Lookout Point
Climb the staircase up into lookout point and gaze upon the sights of Tom Sawyer Island from above.

Spyglasses
Look through the many spyglasses set up at the top of Castle Rock and try to figure out their targets. Find moose on the river, abandoned mine cars and a number of other fascinating sights through these lens-less spyglasses. Through the years weathering and use has knocked some of these spyglasses slightly out of alignment with their targets, but if you really move your eye around inside the spyglasses you can usually figure out what they are supposed to be pointing at.

#35 Shipwreck & Pirate's Den
Walk-Through Attraction
Toward the north end of the *Castle Rock* area the subterranean caves lead to a pirate's shipwreck. This "Pirate's Den" is made up of what's left of an old ship that

has run aground on the island. According to legend the ship crashed here due to an encounter with the Kraken creature featured in the *Pirates of the Caribbean* films. Inside the hull of the ship guests will find weaponry, skeletons, tools and other pirate items littered with barnacles. If you listen carefully you can even hear the ghostly voice of pirate Davy Jones as he whispers warnings to anyone who would dare inspect the wreckage.

Ship's Equipment
Stay on the lookout for various tools, weapons and ancient skeletons inside the shipwreck, particularly in the net-covered ship's hold area.

#36 The Graveyard
Walk-Through Attraction
The old graveyard at Tom Sawyer's island adds to the area's authenticity. Found behind *Fort Wilderness* on the hill overlooking the *Captain's Treasure*, this site contains about 11 gravestones for real and fictitious historical characters. Benches up on the east side of the hill also provides guests with a peaceful, quiet place to rest. This site is an homage to the graveyard that plays a pivotal roll in *The Adventures of Tom Sawyer* (1876).

Fort Wilderness
Although Fort Wilderness has been closed to guests since 2003, the mighty fortress can still be viewed from the outside at the north end of Tom Sawyer Island. You can walk up a path all the way to the fort's main gates, which remain closed at all times, and then around the fort to the structure's rear where you can find the Graveyard and Captain's Treasure areas. The fort's public restrooms are still accessible from the outer wall of the log-built structure.

#37 Captain's Treasure
Walk-Through Attraction
Piles of gold, treasure chests, and Jolly Roger flags await you at the northernmost end of Tom Sawyer Island. Here you can examine Captain Jack Sparrow's pirate bounty and snap a few photos while you are there. Nearby benches also make this location a great resting spot. Adventure seekers can then enter the nearby caves and continue their exploration of the island.

Meet Captain Jack Sparrow
Occasionally the infamous Captain Jack Sparrow will even show up at the Captain's Treasure, ready for photos and autographs. Ask a cast member if the Captain is expected on the day you visit.

Treasure Pile
Have your photo taken among the piles of gold and treasure chests found at the sight of the Captain's Treasure.

Fantasyland

#38 Fantasy Faire
Walk-Through Attraction

Formerly located at the rear of *Fantasyland*, the *NEW Fantasy Faire* opened in Spring 2013 at a new location next to *Sleeping Beauty Castle*, with several new activities to experience and places to explore.

Village Square

The NEW Princess Fantasy Faire features an enchanting village square surrounded by fairytale cottages and pavilions. At the center of the square is Tangled Tower, a tall structure based on the popular Disney animated film *Tangled* (2010). Inside the Village Square guests can participate in a variety of princess-themed activities and enjoy new entertainment such as the Royal Ribbon Parade, a performance in which guests can dance and interact with Belle from *Beauty and the Beast* (1991) or Rapunzel from *Tangled* (2010).

The Royal Hall

You also get the chance to have a character meet and greet with many of your favorite Disney princesses inside the Royal Hall. Get autographs and have you picture taken with each of the princesses. Typically three princesses are available to meet at any one time. Below is a list of the princesses you might meet and the films they stared in:

> Cinderella (*Cinderella*, 1950)
> Princess Aurora (*Sleeping Beauty*,1959)
> Ariel (*The Little Mermaid*, 1989)
> Belle (*Beauty and the Beast*, 1991)
> Princess Jasmine (*Aladdin*, 1992)
> Pocahontas (*Pocahontas*, 1995)
> Mulan (*Mulan* , 1998)
> Tiana (*The Princess and the Frog*, 2009)
> Rapunzel (*Tangled*, 2010)

#39 Sleeping Beauty Castle Walkthrough
Walk-Through Attraction

Take a walking tour through the enchanted castle from the classic Disney film *Sleeping Beauty* (1959). You travel up a winding stone staircase inside Disneyland's iconic castle and enter several small stone rooms and passageways. While inside the castle you can relive the story of Sleeping Beauty through artfully created dioramas. The digitally generated animation inside some of the dioramas are breathtaking and add a modern twist to this classic attraction. The castle also has a few surprises for the inquisitive guest, so be on the lookout for secrets as well.

The Accessible Experience

Guests with mobility impairments or who otherwise do not wish to climb the stone staircase can enjoy a video tour of the attraction in the *Accessible Experience* room located on the ground floor of the castle to the east of the drawbridge. A video screen shows a walkthrough of the entire Sleeping Beauty Castle exhibit without having to climb the attraction's difficult winding staircases.

The Castle Draw Bridge
Guests line up on the castle's drawbridge to have their photos taken by both fellow guests and Disneyland photographers.

#40 Snow White's Scary Adventures
A Little Spooky Mild Ride
Board a wooden vehicle resembling the beds of the seven dwarfs and drive through the world of Snow White in this indoor attraction based on Disney's first feature length animated film. You'll encounter the evil queen, meet the seven dwarfs, view the poison apple and get rescued by Prince Charming in this adventure through the story of Snow White. Like many early Disneyland attractions, this ride was intended to place guests in the role of the story's hero, in this case Snow White, and let you experience the adventure as she would experience it as the ride vehicles propel you through the attraction.

Woodland Creatures
Look for Snow White's furry rabbit friends carved into the lower portion of the stone walls outside the attraction's *queue* area. You can find the rabbits in several locations along the wall.

Request a Flashlight
Sometimes small children can get scared while traveling through the dark corridors of this attraction, and a little bit of light goes a long way to ease their fears. You may request a flashlight for your little ones from cast members at the boarding area to lighten the encounter with the scary looking evil queen and the journey through the castle's shadowy passageways.

#41 Pinocchio's Daring Journey
Mild Ride
Follow the adventures of Pinocchio as he attempts to turn into a real boy in Pinocchio's Daring Journey. Watch as Pinocchio performs in Stromboli's Marionette show, visits the amusements at Pleasure Island, watches Lampwick turn into a donkey and runs into Monstro the Giant Whale among other adventures. You'll board a four-person woodcarvers cart and ride through scenes from Disney's animated Pinocchio film in this indoor Fantasyland ride. Stay on the lookout for Geppetto's wiley cat Figaro, Cleo the smiling goldfish, the helpful Jiminy Cricket and the magical Blue Fairy as you make your way through the story of Pinocchio.

Alpine Architecture
Take a close look at the charming architecture and details that went into the design of the building, which was inspired by Disney's Pinocchio film.

Painted Mural
Be sure to get a good look at the large mural painted on the wall in the vehicle

loading area before climbing into your woodcarvers cart. The mural depicts several scenes from Pinocchio's story.

Ticket Booth
The small kiosk used to control the ride in the boarding area is designed to look like a ticket booth for Stromboli's Marionette show. You pass this booth in your cart vehicle just as you leave the boarding area for the first room in the attraction.

Stromboli's Marionette Show
Be sure to take a look at the Marionette Show mounted over the attraction's entrance as you enter the ride *queue*.

#42 King Arthur Carrousel
Mild Ride
Climb aboard one of the 68 lavishly painted wooden horses as they spin around a central mirrored core on in this classic turn of the century carrousel. Ornate artwork, hand carved horses and an Arthurian theme make this a one of a kind carrousel experience. The King Arthur Carrousel was featured in Disneyland's opening day telecast in 1955, and has remained a classic ever since.

Knights of the Round Table Shields
If you look towards the top of the carrousel from the outside you can spot several different lavishly painted shields. These represent the shields carried by the Knights of the Round Table. See how many different shields you can spot on the carrousel.

Sleeping Beauty Panels
Around the central core of the carrousel is nine panels depicting scenes from Disney's animated tale about *Sleeping Beauty*. Look for them hanging up above the mirrors around the carrousel's center.

#43 Casey Jr. Circus Train
Mild Ride
Ride the rails above the *Storybook Land Canals* inside an ornate animal cage or sleigh-style train car in this classic Fantasyland attraction. The Casey Jr. Circus Train battles to make it up the hills and chugs around bends as you enjoy a birds-eye view of the canal boats and miniatures found in *Storybook Land*.

"I Think I Can!"
Listen for the train engine to say "I think I can" over and over as it climbs up a hill. Then, after it makes it to the top, you can hear the little engine proclaim: "I thought I could". Listen closely, sometimes it's hard to hear over the other noises surrounding the attraction.

Monkey Cage
Climb inside the monkey cage train car for a memorable ride through the rolling hills of storybook land. This car in particular has been a favorite of Casey Jr. fans since the attraction opened in 1955.

#44 Dumbo the Flying Elephant
Mild Ride

Soar through the sky with the flying elephant Dumbo as he circles around a central spire above Disneyland in this classic aerial carrousel-style ride. You will be handed a magic feather before entering the flight area to help your elephants achieve flight. Choose one of the 16 Dumbo elephants and climb aboard. Just before takeoff your feather is collected (because Dumbo doesn't actually need a feather to fly), and then your spinning elephant takes flight. You can use the lever found inside your elephant to maneuver it up and down while you fly. A pool of water below the elephants adds to the attractions beauty as you soar through the air.

Visit the Old Band Organ

Most people miss it, but walk around to the rear of the attraction to see a 1915 band organ housed in an enclosed kiosk behind the ride. Sometimes referred to as a "fairground organ," this mechanical music machine still bellows out music for the attraction.

Timothy Mouse

Look for Dumbo's friend balancing on top of a hot air balloon height above the flying elephants in the center of the attraction.

Dumbo the Flying Elephant

Look for a separate Dumbo ride vehicle under a small shaded kiosk outside the attraction. You're welcome to climb inside the elephant to have your picture taken.

#45 Peter Pan's Flight
Mild Ride

Board a flying pirate galleon for an aerial adventure over Victorian London, Neverland Island, Skull Rock and other majestic sights. Encounter characters such as Wendy, Michael, John, Captain Hook and Peter Pan along the way. Unlike other indoor Fantasyland rides, Peter Pan's Flight has a track hanging from the ceiling - you'll feel like you're flying through the air! This is the only indoor ride at Disneyland where you're expected to look down instead of up or straight ahead. Combine this feature with the fields of glowing stars and miniature islands viewed below the boat and Peter Pan's Flight becomes one of the most innovative and beautiful rides in the park.

London Clock Tower

View the iconic clock tower from Disney's Peter Pan looming over the outside of the attraction building before you enter the attraction *queue*.

Peter Pan Mural

View a colorful mural depicting the adventures of Peter Pan in the vehicle loading area as you wait to board the attraction.

New Visual Effects

An overhaul of the attraction in 2015 led to the addition of spectacular new visual effects. Most notable is the new effects surrounding Big Ben as you fly over London, which has been wowing fans of the attraction since the additions were unveiled earlier this year. Be sure to keep an eye out for them as you ride the attraction.

#46 Mr. Toad's Wild Ride
Thrill Ride

Join the absent-minded Mr. Toad as he takes a rambunctious journey in his motorcar "to nowhere in particular." Start by entering J. Thaddeus Toad's elegant home known as Toad Hall before boarding an open air motorcar and following one of Mr Toad's frantic adventures. Avoid brick walls, falling barrels and other obstacles as you drive through Toad Hall, Mr Winky's Pub, and the streets of London in this out of control motorcar ride.

"Nowhere in Particular" Mural

This mural features several scenes from Disney's animated film about Mr Toad. Separating the images in the center of the mural is a sign post with the words "Nowhere in Particular" on it, a reference to Toad's proclivity for adventure and constant wish to travel "Nowhere in Particular" in the film. Find this entertaining mural in the loading area where your board the ride's vehicles.

Mr. Toad Statue & Bust

Look upward before entering Toad Hall to see a stone statue of Mr. Toad holding out his glass monocle just above his family coat of arms. Then look higher on the building for a bust of Mr. Toad sitting just below one of the roof's peeks. Finally, look closely at the ornamented trim along the roof; the ornaments are actually little Mr. Toad heads.

Mr. Toad's Car

Look for Mr. Toad's convertible motorcar out in front of the Mr. Toad's Wild Ride attraction. Climb inside for a photo that commemorates your wild ride through the land of the Wind in the Willows.

#47 Mad Tea Party
Thrill Ride

Climb inside a giant teacup and spin in circles in this ride based on the *Alice in Wonderland* stories. Turntables in the base of the attraction's platform send all of the cups careening around the tea party area while a wheel in the center of each teacup allows guests to control the spin of their cup. With each of the 18 tea cups seating 3-4 people, the attraction can spin about 72 guests at a time.

Tea Cup

Look for the giant tea cup along the walkway near *Mr Toads Wild Ride* and climb inside for a memorable Mad Tea Party photo

#48 Alice in Wonderland
Mild Ride

Follow Alice as she adventures through the miraculous world of Wonderland in this indoor vehicle ride. Board cars in the shape of Absolem (Wonderland's hookah-smoking caterpillar) and ride through iconic scenes featuring the Cheshire Cat, the Queen of Hearts' croquet match, the March Hare, the Mad Hatter and his tea party and more. The ride even ventures outdoors for a while and gives guests an excellent second story view of Fantasyland. A 2015 update to the ride introduced new digital effects and other great additions.

Giant Mushroom

Look for the attraction's famous giant mushroom out in front of the ride *queue*. This used to serve as the attraction's ticket booth back when Disneyland rides required tickets.

A Somewhat Hidden Cheshire Cat

Look for this statue of Wonderland's mysterious Cheshire Cat recessed into the wall outside the attraction. Facing the attraction *queue* and entrance, walk to the left around the corner of the attraction building towards the Fantasyland public restrooms, and look upward. You should be able to see the Cheshire Cat staring down at you.

White Rabbit Statue

It's often overlooked, but a statue of the tea party's infamous white rabbit can be seen around the corner from the Alice in Wonderland building in front of the Fantasyland restrooms. Don't forget to have your photo taken next to the *White Rabbit Statue* before you leave.

#49 Storybook Land Canal Boats
Mild Ride

This seven minute ride through the Storybook Land Canals celebrates Walt Disney's love of miniatures. Guests board twelve person boats and tour tiny models of famous Disney buildings and landmarks along the banks of the Storybook Land Canal. Each miniature scene is build at 1/12 scale, using one inch of the models to represent each foot of the life-sized structures. During the ride your pilot will give a live narration about each of the intricately built models; each complete with tiny landscaping, charming music and special lighting effects.

Storybook Land Topiaries

Look for the words "Storybook Land" spelled out in bushes cut into letters along the front of the attraction. Other topiaries such as spiral trees can be seen around the attraction.

Striped Lighthouse

Sitting just outside the attraction *queue* is Storybook Land's iconic red and white striped lighthouse. This lighthouse is a reproduction of the ride's original ticket booth back when Disneyland attractions required tickets.

Monstro the Whale

Watch the infamous Monstro from Disney's animated feature *Pinocchio* (1940) closely as you pass through his mouth. Although he appears to be still, some say that if you watch him closely you can see his eyes blink and steam rise from his blow hole.

Sound Recordings

Listen carefully as you pass the miniatures for the sounds of characters singing or working. Sometimes they can be hard to hear over the narration and other sounds in the area.

New Frozen Additions Added for 2015

Look for new miniatures of the land of Arendelle from Disney's *Frozen* (2013). The additions were just recently unveiled to the delight of *Frozen* fans everywhere.

Casey Jr. Circus Train

View the famous train from Disney's *Dumbo* (1941) carrying it's passengers on tracks far above the Storybook Land Canal. Feel free to give these guests a wave if you feel so inclined.

#50 Brave Meet & Greet
Walk-Through Attraction

Meet the fearless heroine Merida at her special meet and greet location near *It's a Small World* at the north end of Fantasyland. See the *Disneyland Entertainment Times Guide* for operating times.

#51 It's a Small World
Mild Ride

Enjoy a leisurely boat ride past more than 350 audio-animatronic children from all over the world and 250 moving toys. The singing dolls gleefully harmonize the *It's a Small World* song in perfect unison throughout the indoor ride. Outside the attraction guests can enjoy a beautiful gold leaf building facade, trees trimmed into the shapes of animals and an animated clock tower. During the winter holiday season the attraction is transformed into *It's a Small World Holiday*, with winter holiday decorations and new songs added to ring in the holidays.

Topiaries

These trees and other foliage shaped like animals are found along the banks of the river and in areas surrounding the attraction. Look for a dolphin, moose, elephant, horse, lion and more.

The Disneyland Railroad

Disneyland's railroad can be viewed passing through the front of the 'It's a Small World' attraction from outside the building. Keep an eye out for it while waiting in the attraction *queue*.

#52 Matterhorn Bobsleds
Thrill Ride • Single Rider Line • Rider Swap • Height Requirement 35"

Climb aboard a three person bobsled for a high speed ride through Switzerland's Matterhorn Mountain. This roller coaster thrills guests with high-speed banked turns, dips and twists as they keep a look-out for the ferocious yeti lurking inside the mountain. The ride ends with a splashdown in a glacial lake at the base of the mountain that slows the speeding bobsleds and cools guests on hot days. Outside the mountain, climbers can periodically be seen descending from the Matterhorn's peak.

Mountain Climbers

When the Matterhorn Bobsleds premiered in 1959 one of the attraction's main features was actual human mountain climbers climbing up and down the mountain as the roller coaster sped by below. They were discontinued for a while, but recently they have been seen climbing the mountain again. So be on the lookout for actual mountain climbers using their ropes and carabiners to repel up and down Matterhorn Mountain. Ask a cast member if they are likely to appear on the day you visit.

The NEW Yeti

A ferocious mountain Yetti has been known to roam about these parts. Keep a sharp eye out for him, as he may surprise you. 2015 additions to the attraction have made the Yeti effects better than ever.

Expedition Equipment

Keep your eyes peeled for evidence of other previous explorers as you travel through the mountain.

#53 Snow White's Grotto
Walk-Through Attraction

At this enchanting garden getaway visitors can explore the wishing well, fountain, waterfall and statues of Snow White and the Seven Dwarfs tucked away among the lush foliage. There are benches to rest on, and the serene backdrops make for lovely photos. This spot is so beautiful it has become known as THE spot at Disneyland to make marriage proposals or other declarations of love.

The Fountain & Waterfall

Guests love to have their photo taken standing along the edge of the cobblestone walkway with their backs to the grotto's glimmering pond, showing the fountain, waterfall and statues behind them.

Wishing Well

Strike a pose at the wishing well for a memorable photo.

#54 Pixie Hollow: Tinker Bell & Her Fairy Friends
Walk-Through Attraction

Magically shrink down to fairy-size and enter Pixie Hollow to meet with Tinker Bell and her fairy friends in this character meet and greet attraction. Just outside the hollow you will find peaceful ponds and tiny waterfalls where you can try to spot fairies hidden among the banks and foliage. After you shrink you can find your favorite fairies among the oversized blades of grass and other fauna. Find Pixie Hollow between *Sleeping Beauty Castle* and the entrance to *Tomorrowland*.

See the World as a Fairy Would

Inside Pixie Hollow the giant objects such as plants, flowers, mushrooms, snowflakes and teapots make guests feel fairy-sized. Take a look around the area and see how many ordinary objects now appear to be enormous.

Fairies Hidden Around the Pond
The walkway up to Pixie Hollow passes by Pixie Pond, a small body of water with an enchanting fountain and little waterfalls. Be sure to inspect the pond and it's surrounding banks carefully: there are fairies hidden throughout the area.

Pixie Pond Water Show
At nighttime guests can watch as the ponds in front of Pixie Hollow come to life in a dazzling show of brightly colored dancing water.

Photos with the Pixies
Inside Pixie Hollow guests get the chance to have their photos taken with each of their Fairy friends. The attraction usually has at least three different fairies in attendance at any one time.

Toontown
#55 Downtown Toontown
Walk-Through Attraction
One of the greatest appeals of Toontown is the vast array of things to explore there. Full of secrets and surprises, the buildings and landmarks of Toontown can provide hours of entertainment. Be sure to visit them all. Pull every lever, push every button, and open every door. You never know what you will find.

Building Puns
The buildings in Toontown are full of puns and gags. Be sure to explore them all before leaving the area.

Signs & Plaques
A keen observer can spot a number of humorous signs & plaques throughout Toontown. Keep your eyes peeled for cartoon-themed signs, and see how many of them you can spot.

#56 Roger Rabbit's Cartoon Spin
Thrill Ride • FastPass
This zany automobile ride takes you through a maze of cartoon adventures while seated in a spinning cab. In the attraction's *queue* you'll walk through dark alleys in Toontown while encountering characters from the film until you eventually reach the boarding platform and climb inside *Lenny the Cab*. From here the ride vehicle continually moves forward as you control the spin of the cab by turning a central steering wheel.

Who is "Lenny the Cab?"
In Roger Rabbit's Cartoon Spin you ride inside a cartoon cab named Lenny, but who is he and where did he come from? Lenny is the identical cousin to "Benny the Cab," a well known cartoon cab character from the *Who Framed Roger Rabbit* (1988)

film. Early in the attraction we see Roger Rabbit driving Benny, so guests must board his cousin Lenny instead.

Attraction Queue Mayham

Pay attention to everything you pass in the line to the boarding platform. This queue is full of secrets for you to discover.

#57 Goofy's Playhouse
Walk-Through Attraction

The Goofy's Playhouse attraction is intended for little kids, and it's divided into two areas: an outside garden playground area and an inside living room area. The outside area features slides, tunnels, boxes and other things for your kids to climb on. Various wind chimes, mobiles and scarecrows decorate the garden. Inside Goofy's humble home kids can find plenty of oversized chairs to sit on, a cartoonish piano, a wardrobe and other things to explore. Don't forget to glance up toward the upstairs area while you're there.

Windmills & Scarecrows

Take a look at the variety of humorous scarecrows and wind-powered mobiles that inhabit Goofy's garden, as they are sure to entertain both kids and adults. Many of these mobiles can be found along the front of Goofy's garden fence, but the laundry wheel towards the back of his garden is particularly hilarious.

Goofy's Car

You can find Goofy's car out in front of his playhouse, just waiting for you to climb inside for the perfect photo.

#58 Donald's Boat
Walk-Through Attraction

Climb aboard Donald Duck's house boat and explore the home of Disney's number one duck. Down below in the hold, you can view Donald's living quarters, favorite photographs and artwork. A staircase leads up to the pilot house where you can find the boat's whistle, steering wheel, intercom and nautical controls. Be sure to look through the portholes and take in the view, and then head out on deck and explore the outside of the boat.

Animation Cells & Photos

Look for a variety of photos and animation cells decorating the walls throughout Donald's boat, you may recognize some of your favorite characters in them. You can even find a painting of Donald's ship being build if you look hard enough.

S.S. Miss Daisy

Take a close look at the name of Donald's boat, the "S.S. Miss Daisy." Donald named his houseboat after his favorite cartoon gal, Daisy Duck. The words painted underneath the boat's name indicate that the S.S. Miss Daisy sails out of Toon Lake.

#59 Minnie's House

Take a self-guided tour of Minnie's house. Once inside, you can explore Minnie's living room, bedroom and kitchen before moving on to her outdoor garden and gazebo area. Take advantage of Minnie's "paws-on policy" while you explore the house and test out all of her cabinets, drawers and appliances - you never know what surprises you might find.

Tea Time with Minnie

Have your photo taken with Minnie as she entertains at teatime in her backyard gazebo.

#60 Mickey's House
Walk-Through Attraction

Get a chance to meet Mickey Mouse and tour his home when you visit the main mouse's house in Toontown. A chalkboard out in front of the house displays a message from Mickey letting you know he's waiting for you out in his Movie Barn. You must walk through his house to get there, navigating through a maze of rooms filled with Mickey's photos, art, books, cartoon memorabilia and other personal effects. His house holds many secrets, so keep your eyes out for that special artifact that will bring back fond memories of your favorite mouse. After touring the house you'll be entertained with some of Mickey's favorite cartoons in his screening room while waiting in line to meet him.

Mickey's Car

Find Mickey's favorite wheels out in front of his house. Feel free to climb inside for a memorable photo. Be sure to note that his license plate reads "MICKEY1".

Piano Car

Climb aboard this silly car inside the Movie Barn for that perfect photo. Look for it just before you enter the screening room and get in line to meet Mickey.

Mickey Mouse

At the conclusion of this attraction you'll get the chance to meet and have photos taken with Mickey Mouse. After a walk through the house and garden join the line in the screening room to meet the top mouse. Mickey will greet you on one of four different movie sets, each with a unique theme based on a popular Mickey Mouse cartoon - *Steamboat Willie* (1928), *The Band Concert* (1935), *Thru the Mirror* (1936) and *Fantasia* (1940). Mickey dresses up in a different themed outfit for each of these rooms. Your meet and greet room is chosen at random, so there in no way to predict which movie set or Mickey costume you will get to see, but if you return to Mickey's house each time you visit Disneyland you may eventually get to see all four.

Skip the Meet & Greet If You Are Pressed for Time

If you just want to tour the house and don't wish to wait in a lengthy line to meet Mickey at the end, you can leave through a somewhat hidden exit located just behind the Piano Car in the room directly before the movie screening room. You won't get to meet Mickey, but his is a great option if you are pressed for time.

#61 Gadget's Go Coaster
Kids Thrill Ride • Rider Swap • Height Requirement 35"

Climb inside a green acorn pod for a roller coaster ride around Toon Lake. Hold on as the acorn train twists, turns and speeds it's way across roller coaster tracks past the soup cans, combs and spools of thread that Gadget scavenged for her creation. Towards the end of the ride a group of frogs attempt to squirt water on you as your roller coaster car rolls by.

Great for Kids

Although this is a roller coaster, it was designed with small children in mind and kids should have no trouble enjoying it.

A Tough Fit for Adults

The "acorn pod" cars are very small because they were designed for children. Usually either 2 children or one adult and a child can fit comfortably in each car. Trying to squeeze two adults into one car can be an uncomfortable experience.

#62 Chip 'n' Dale Treehouse
Walk-Through Attraction

Visit the home of Disney chipmunks Chip 'n' Dale inside an old redwood tree. The Treehouse was designed to be a small playland for young children. Kids start their treehouse adventure by crawling through the entryway, then climb a winding staircase into the heart of the tree. Then, at the top of the treehouse they can enjoy a fantastic view of Toontown before climbing back down to ground level. Adults are of course welcomed to climb inside the treehouse too, but some areas inside the tree can be a tight squeeze for adult sized bodies.

How to Tell Chip from Dale

There is a simple trick you can use to tell these two chipmunks apart. Chip has a small black nose like a "chocolate chip", where as Dale has a big red nose. Remember that Chip has a "chocolate chip," and you will never confuse these two characters again.

Tomorrowland
#63 Astro Orbitor
Mild Ride

The Astro Orbitor spins guests in small 1-2 person space crafts in circles around a central core. Guests use a lever inside the craft to raise and lower themselves as they spin. This classic ride was modeled after a drawing made by master artist and inventor Leonardo da Vinci five centuries ago. The distinguishing symbols along the tail fins of each rocket are astrological symbols, allowing each rocket to represent an astrological sign. If you're cleaver and fast enough, you can sit in the rocket that represent's your own astrological sign.

Ride Along

Parents can ride along with small children and help them to control the craft.

Two adults are allowed to ride together in a single spacecraft, but it's a tight fit and can be fairly uncomfortable.

#64 Buzz Lightyear Astro Blasters
Mild Ride

Join Buzz Lightyear as he attempts to defeat the evil Emperor Zurg and his plot to steal all the batteries used to power toys. This interactive ride-through adventure allows you to shoot at moving and stationary targets hanging on a variety of space dwelling creatures from within your moving spacecraft. Enter your Buzz Lightyear spacecraft, pick up your space blaster and start shooting at every target you see. A joystick in the center of the vehicle allows you to rotate your space craft left and right to get a better view of your targets. Points are scored for each target you hit and displayed on a score counter in front of you. At the end of the ride your total score is displayed and you receive a ranking from "Space Cadet" to "Galactic Hero". Up to two guests can ride in each vehicle. Each rider gets their own blaster and score counter.

Ride Photo

An automated camera snaps a photo of you towards the end of the attraction. The photos can then be viewed and sent to your email for FREE at photo kiosks found towards the attraction's exit. The photo also contains your score from the game.

#65 Star Tours – The Adventures Continue
Thrill Ride • FastPass • Rider Swap • Height Requirement 40"

Walk through a bustling spaceport terminal on your way to a Star Tours shuttle bound for another planet. Along your trip through the terminal meet R2D2 and C3PO, watch as droids inspect suspicious luggage and pass through galactic security check points. Then board a Star Tours shuttle for a motion filled 3-D adventure to strange places and distant worlds. A computer randomly chooses your shuttle's destinations, which characters you will encounter - everything about the scenario you'll experience. Every time you ride it's a different adventure. Disney partnered with George Lucas, the creative force behind the *Star Wars* films, to create this unique attraction.

Departure Monitor

While waiting inside the Star Tours terminal, watch the enormous departure monitor sitting high up on the wall. It displays several different video loops inbetween departure schedules to entertain you. Try to see how many different videos there are for you to watch.

C3PO & R2D2

Pay attention to the antics of C3PO and R2D2 as you wait in the *queue*, they put on an entertaining show while you wait.

Baggage Security

The droid operating the baggage security scanner may try to interact with you. Listen to what it has to say, it's quite a character. Pay special attention to the X-rays appearing in the baggage scanner, they are hilarious and they're always different.

Boarding Window

As you walk up the winding attraction *queue*, you can see a window displaying the shadows of several different Star Wars characters as they walk towards their shuttles. See how many different characters you can identify.

Security Check Droid

At the security check point in the *queue* the Security Droid may attempt to talk to you. It's droll spiel is worth a listen.

Thermal Imaging Scanner

Just before walking through the security scanner you can see a thermal image displayed on the scanner's glass panel. The image is generated from a camera on top of the scanner pointed down at the scanner's entrance. By waving your hands or making some other unique gesture you can see proof that the scanner glass is indeed displaying a thermal image of you. Have fun with it.

The other side of the scanner glass is interesting too, watch the glass as you walk through the scanner.

Pre-Show

Be sure to watch the pre-show video as you wait in the final *queue* to enter the Star Tours shuttle, it reveals a lot about the attraction's plot, and provides quite a few humorous moments as well. Pay particular attention to what's happening with C3PO and the Shuttle Pilot, and keep a sharp eye out for any.. ahem.. Imperial Probe Droids.

#66 Starcade
Walk-Through Attraction

In early 2013 this futuristic arcade went retro and introduced 26 classic arcade games from the 1980's. Look for this arcade next to the *Star Trader* shop, between the exit to *Space Mountain* and the exit to *Star Tours*. Unfortunately a 2012 expansion of the Star Trader took over a large section of the classic Starcade, but it's fantastic reproduction of an 1980's arcade and respite from the sun and crowds outside still make it a great place to take a break.

25¢ Tokens

All of the games except the free *Fix It Felix Jr.* require game tokens rather than quarters, which can be purchased from good old-fashioned token machines located near the entrances to the arcade. The bad news here is that you can't use your loose change to play the games, the machines require ones or fives to dispense tokens. The good news, however, is that almost every game in the arcade only costs a single 25¢ token to play, a low price we haven't seen since Kevin Flynn got sucked into his TRON video game back in 1982.

Play Fix It Felix Jr. FREE

A classic platform-style video game created to promote the Disney film *Wreck-It Ralph* (2012). At first I found it frustrating, but after spending a few minutes discovering the game's mechanics it actually turned out to be really fun to play. And you can't beat the price: FREE! There are currently 4 of the machines in Starcade, but some or all of them may be removed after enthusiasm for the film dies down. 1 or 2 player. Cost: FREE!!

#67 Tomorrowland Theater
Theater Attraction

This historic venue (formerly known as the *Magic Eye Theater*) features state of the art visual and motion effects that gives it's audience a very unique viewing experience. Though it usually hosts the *Captain EO Starring Michael Jackson* attraction, the show is occasionally replaced with other Disney films. The theater is currently closed down at the time this book went to press, but it's expected to reopen with a special preview of *Star Wars: Episode VII - The Force Awakens (2015)* very soon. Check to see if it has reopened yet when you visit the park.

Captain EO Starring Michael Jackson

This 3-D movie adventure with motion effects stars pop sensation Michael Jackson in an unusual outer space adventure. Michael and his inept star ship crew are tasked with bringing a special gift to "The Supreme Leader" (academy Award winning actress Anjelica Huston) of a world full of menacing cyborgs and rotting, twisted metal. The film was executive produced by George Lucas, the creative force behind the *Star Wars* films, and directed by Francis Ford Coppola (*The Godfather Trilogy, Apocalypse Now.*) Occasionally this attraction is temporarily displaced to make room for the motion picture previews listed below.

Motion Picture Previews

The *Magic Eye Theater* that serves as the home to Captain EO has recently been used to show other films as well, such as special 3D previews of upcoming Disney films with unique special effects that you will only be able to experience in this theater. If it looks like the Captain EO show is closed, stop by the theater anyway and you may get invited to one of these special once in a lifetime screenings.

#68 Space Mountain
Thrill Ride • FastPass • Rider Swap • Height Requirement 40"

(See Space Mountain Ghost Galaxy in the Top Halloween Attractions section at the front of this book.)

#69 Cosmic Waves
Walk-Through Attraction

At the Cosmic Waves fountain in front of *Space Mountain* guests can try their hand at turning the giant 1000 pound granite ball found floating on a thin sheet of water. This enormous, perfectly round boulder appears immovable, yet the constantly flowing water creates a low friction environment allowing even the youngest of guests to rotate it by simply pushing on the ball in any direction. Guests young and old can marvel at their ability to move this massive object with a simple flick of their wrists. Be sure to visit the Cosmic Waves fountain if you have a few extra minutes on your hands.

#70 Marvel Action Heros Meet & Greet
Charter Meeting

Now that the Innoventions building has permanently closed in March 2015, two of your favorite meet & greet opportunities from that attraction have found a new home across the road under the old people mover platform. Visit with *Thor* and *Captain America* in Tomorrowland daily. Look for the *Avengers* next to the *Tomorrow Landing* shop.

#71 Autopia
Guest Controlled • FastPass • Rider Swap • Height Requirement 32"

The Autopia lets drivers of all ages get behind the wheel and drive a small-scale convertible car around a series of roads throughout Tomorrowland. Travel over bridges, around bends - even off-road through the dirt. You control the gas and steering in these cars, giving you an authentic driving experience. Each car seats one to two guests.

Three Different Cars

Tomorrowland's Autopia actually has three distinctly different cars for you to drive, each with their own name and style. Each of the three cars come in several different colors, creating the diversity of cars you see on the Autopia track at any give time. The cars are *Suzy* the cute coupe, *Dusty* the off-road vehicle, and *Sparky* the stylish sports car.

Pick Up Your FREE Autopia Drivers License Card in the Attraction Queue

While you are waiting in line for the attraction you will get the chance to receive a FREE souvenir Autopia Drivers License in one of three designs. Look for them after exiting the interior portion of the attraction *queue* and passing through a turnstile. Sometimes cast members will stand there and hand out the licenses, and at other times you may simply pick one up from the table next to the turnstile as you pass though it.

Complete Your Driver's Licence

After completing your drive on the Autopia track you can personalize your license by taking it to one of the Driver's License Photo Booths located just outside the Autopia exit. Here your name and photo can be added to your licence for $5.

#72 Finding Nemo Submarine Voyage
Mild Ride

In this undersea adventure you board a submarine and travel under water into the world of Disney's feature film *Finding Nemo* (2003). See and hear Nemo, Squirt, Marlin and other characters from the film as you follow them on a marvellous adventure.

N.E.M.O.

Observant guests will note that their research submarine is from the "Nautical Exploration and Marine Observation Institute," also known as "N.E.M.O." This is of course a reference to the film the attraction is based on.

Animatronic Seagulls

Walking from Tomorrowland to Fantasyland, between the Finding Nemo lake and the Matterhorn Mountain, look across the lake and you will see three animatronic seagulls sitting on a buoy. Watch them for a minute and they will turn their heads, open their beaks and squawk like real seagulls. Listen carefully and you will discover that they are saying "Mine, Mine, Mine," just like the Seagulls in *Finding Nemo* (2003).

#73 Disneyland Monorail
Mild Ride

This futuristic single track train system transports guests back and fourth between Tomorrowland (inside the Disneyland Park) and the Disneyland Hotel side of Downtown Disney. The monorail is always free, but you must have a Disneyland Park ticket to ride it. The monorail usually opens at the same time the Disneyland park opens. This futuristic train is not only fun to ride, it's a great time saving way to enter the park, particularly in the morning when crowds form at the Disneyland entry gates. Find the monorail station near the west end of Downtown Disney. You can also use the monorail to leave the park and return to Downtown Disney for a quick lunch, a stop at your hotel, or to exit the park at the end of the day.

Closes Early

The monorail often stops running a half hour or more before the park closes. If you don't make it to the monorail station before it closes, you can always walk thought the Disneyland park and Downtown Disney shopping district to return to your hotel.

Ride Round Trip

You can also ride the monorail round-trip without getting off at the next station. This gives you a unique birds eye view of both Disneyland and Disney's California Adventure. Every once in a while the monorail operators will not allow round-trip travel - like during the fireworks show or any other time there may be safety concerns. But don't worry, you will be warned before boarding about any restrictions on riding round-trip.

California Adventure

Red Car Trolley
#01 Ride the Classic Red Car
Mild Ride

Enjoy a tour of the Buena Vista St. and Hollywood Blvd. of yesteryear inside this replica of the public transportation system of 1930's Los Angeles. Climb aboard and exit at your choice of four different stops, or ride the trolley round trip. Electric trolleys in Los Angeles date all the way back to 1887, but the Red Car Trolley attraction in California Adventure is based on the Pacific Electric Red Car Trolleys that ran from 1901 to 1961. You may board and exit the trolley at any of the four stations listed here: *Buena Vista Street*, *Carthay Circle* (Buena Vista Street), *Hollywood Boulevard* (Hollywood Land), and *Tower of Terror* (Hollywood Land).

Buena Vista Street
#02 Meet Oswald the Lucky Rabbit
Meet & Greet

Look for Oswald between his tire shop on Buena Vista Street and the *Chamber of Commerce* building. He will be happy to sign autographs and have his picture taken with you. Oswald only recently returned to the Disney family after a long-fought attempt by the company to purchase him back from Universal. Ever since his return home in 2006 Disney has been looking for a good use for the lucky rabbit, and now they have found it in his very own meet and greet location. Look for Oswald's debut in the animated short *Poor Papa* (1927) and many other shorts that followed.

#03 Buena Vista Bugle
Activity

This quarterly old-fashioned newspaper can be found at a little newsstand outside the *Chamber of Commerce* on Buena Vista Street (and on rainy days inside the *Chamber of Commerce*). It's always FREE to guests, so be sure to stop by and pick up a copy.

The Buena Vista Bugle debuted in the summer of 2012 following the opening of California Adventure's massive expansion project, and it's still going strong today. Look for helpful information about the park, advertisements for food and attractions, and articles that are just plain hilarious. In addition to outside the *Chamber of Commerce*, you can also find the Buena Vista Bugle at the *Carthay Circle Information Booth* and inside the *Fiddler, Fifer & Practical Café*.

#04 The Citizens of Buena Vista Street
Interactive Activity

Disney has hired a number of actors to dress in period costumes and entertain

115

guests as they walk thought Buena Vista Street. They are fun to interact with, and they may even give you something fun to bring home with you. Look for these characters as you stroll through the land and strike up a conversation. They tend to stick out among the modern dressed guests.

Officer Calvin Blue

This 1920's police officer strolls the streets in his classic blue uniform. He is friendly and attentive, and loves to chat. But watch out, if you get too chummy he might write you a citation for "Having the best smile" or "Being the friendliest person around."

Phiphi the Photographer

Phiphi is an experienced world traveler, taking photos throughout her voyages of interesting people and fun experiences she encounters. Ask her about her adventures, she will be happy to tell you about them.

Donna the Dog Lady

Donna loves dogs as much as she loves to socialize. She's a bit of a gossip, but her dog is cute and hilarious. Ask Donna if her dog knows any tricks.

Molly & Milly the Messengers

These uniformed messenger twins ride around Buena Vista Street delivering packages and parcels from their tricycles. If you see them, ask them how their deliveries are going.

News Boys

These 1920's newsboys wonder the streets delivering newspapers to everyone that needs them. Stop and chat with them about the news business if they have the time. They may even give you a copy of the local newspaper if they have any left. Their names are: *Patches*, *Speedy*, *Pushover*, and *Smalls*.

Hollywood Land
#05 Disney Animation
Walk-Through Attraction

The Disney Animation Building is full of animation-themed activates to fascinate young and old. Watch clips of classic Disney films, record yourself singing a song, and interact with a talking turtle in this fascinating building. You can even take a class on how to draw your favorite Disney character if you want. Take a look at the fun-filled activates listed below.

Animation Courtyard Gallery

The first room you enter in the Disney Animation Building is a vast courtyard full of giant animation screens and plenty of benches to rest on. This is a great place to relax and take a breather as you watch classic moments from Disney animated features projected larger than life on the many giant screens throughout the room.

Animation Academy

Take a class on drawing popular Disney characters. Classes are held about every half hour every day, and each class focuses on a different Disney cartoon character. See the list of class times and characters at the entrance to the animation building.

Sorcerer's Workshop

The mysterious Sorcerer's Workshop takes you through two separate attractions based on the principals behind animation:

Magic Mirror Realm - See examples of simple animation techniques deep in the cavernous dungeon of a spooky medieval castle. Then make your very own unique animation and bring it to life using the Magic Mirror Realm's unique animation tools. Take a good look around this room while you are here, there are many hidden treats to see here.

Beast's Library - Find out which Disney character you are most like in this interactive experience inside The Beasts library. Sit down in one of Beast's tall comfortable library chairs, open the book before you, and watch as it magically comes to life and guides you through the process of discovering the Disney character inside you. The room itself is full of fascinating memorabilia, so take a good look around before you leave.

Turtle Talk with Crush

Sit down and have a talk with the lovable turtle Crush in this unique interactive experience. He'll ask you all sorts of questions, respond to you, and even let you in on a few fascinating facts. Stop by and say hello, the performances are held every few minutes all day long.

#06 Frozen Fun
Stage Shows & Activities

For a limited time Disney has converted it's *Hollywood Studio* area in *Hollywood Land* into a *Frozen* (2013) themed wonderland, opening on January 7, 2015. Some of the *Frozen Fun* activities did already end in May 2015, but the following still remain open today.

Anna & Elsa's Royal Welcome - Stop by Anna & Elsa's new home in *Hollywood Land* to receive a royal reception. At *Anna and Elsa's Royal Welcome* you can meet the sisters, have your photo taken with them, get autographs, and even ask them a few questions about life in Arendelle. This meet and greet opportunity has temporarily moved from it's typical home in Disneyland for the *Frozen Fun* event. Look for it inside the *Disney Animation* building in *Hollywood Land*. Disney Fastpasses are required to meet the sisters, so stop by early in the day to get one.

Frozen at the Animation Academy - Learn how to draw some of *Frozen's* (2013) most lovable characters inside the *Disney Animation* building in *Hollywood Land*. Instructors will take you through the process step by step. The class really can be taken by anyone, so don't be shy about your drawing skills. I'm pretty much terrible at drawing anything, and when I took the class I did fine. Drawing supplies are provided for the class free of charge, and classes begin about every half hour.

For the First Time in Forever: A Frozen Sing-Along Celebration - This kids-oriented sing-along show features the characters from Disney's animated hit *Frozen* (2013) singing some of the film's greatest hit songs. Join Anna, Elsa, Kristoff, and the royal historians of Arendelle as they sing hits such as "Let it Go". Guests of all ages are encouraged to sing along. Look for this show at the *Crown Jewel Theatre*, a new space temporarily occupying the recently closed *Muppet Vision Theater* in the *Hollywood Studios* area of *Hollywood Land*.

Meet Olaf - Look for the lovable snowman from *Frozen* (2013) in the *Stage 17* area of Hollywood Land, near the *Crown Jewel Theatre*.

#07 Monsters, Inc. Mike & Sulley to the Rescue!
Mild Ride

Take a ride in a taxi through the monster-filled world of Monstropolis and follow along with the story from the hit animated film *Monsters, Inc.* (2001). Watch as Mike & Sulley attempt to hide a human child named Boo. While protecting Boo they try to outsmart the treacherous monster Randall Boggs while the entire town of Monstropolis suffers from widespread panic at the thought of a human child on the loose. This indoor ride is great for kids but fun for guests of all ages.

Jokes in the Attraction Queue

While in the queue, take a good look at the props found there. There is a lot to see, but examine as much as you can. Pay attention to posters on the walls, restaurant menus, instructions for monsters, telephone books and anything else monster-related that crosses your path. The items in the vending machines and the newspaper articles are hilarious.

Smells

Take a good sniff inside the sushi restaurant section of the ride, you can smell the ginger from the sushi served there. Keep your nose out for other scents during the ride as well.

Roz

Don't be afraid to strike up a conversation with Roz when you meet her at the end of your journey. She's interactive, and will respond to you in a number of hilarious ways. She may even comment on a hat or shirt you are wearing.

#08 Diamond Mad T Party
Walk-Through Attraction

This music-filled outdoor dance party held in the center of the *Hollywood Studios* area fills the air with flashing lights, smog machines, bright neon, live music and outrageous performances. The party has been revamped for *Disneyland's 60th Anniversary Diamond Celebration*. The creative costumes and fast paced music give the illusion that you are at some sort of rave party, but the whole event is closely monitored and kept safe for guests of all ages to enjoy.

Dance

The White Rabbit DJ will keep the beets going as you dance the nigh away. Guests of all ages hit the dance floor as the music, lights and effects fill the air around them.

Bands

Listen to cover songs ranging from oldies to current pop hits performed by the Mad T Party Band on the main stage. Occasionally local guest bands are invited to perform as well.

Performance Art

Watch as aerialists perform magical feats dangling from ropes high above the audience. Their act will astound you.

Mad T Party Characters

Meet the bazar characters of the Mad T Party as they walk through the crowd. A guest-favorite is the giant pink flamingo people. They operate the 12 foot high flamingos with such precision that they can even have the birds eating out of your hand.

T Party Lounge

Between the *House of Cards* beverage stand and the dance floor sits an outdoor lounge area filled with oversized *Alice in Wonderland* themed chairs. This is a great spot to rest, have a drink, take in the show, and even regroup with your party. A second lounge area has recently opened up between the *Disney Performing Arts Stage* and the *Drink Me* beverage stand.

Air Hockey

Test your skills against your friends in a friendly game of Air Hockey while you enjoy the ambiance of the Mad T Party. This group of 4 retro-arcade air hockey tables are located behind the *House of Cards* bar. With each game only costing a quarter this is one of the best deals in the park. These tables require at least two people to play; there is no single player version of air hockey.

Face Painting & HiDef Tattoos - Get your face painted or choose from a large selection of high quality temporary tattoos at this stand in the *Mad T Party* area. Prices very for face painting and tattoos based on the design you choose.

#09 The Twilight Zone Tower of Terror
Spooky Thrill Ride • FastPass • Rider Swap • Height Requirement 40"

(See <u>The Twilight Zone Tower of Terror</u> in the <u>Top Halloween Attractions</u> at the front of this book.)

A Bug's Land

#10 It's Tough to Be a Bug!
Theater Attraction

Head down into an underground bug lair for a little bug-style entertainment. This 3D film follows the characters from *A Bug's Life* (1998) on a new adventure as they attempt to put on a live stage show for their human friends. Join Flik, Chili, The Termite-ator, Claire De Room, and a cast of a million bugs in this 3D film experience. The theater also includes a number of other special effects to amaze and entertain you. As the poster outside the theater states, "The Crickets Agree... It's a Hit!"

#11 Heimlich's Chew Chew Train
Mild Ride

Climb aboard Heimlich the caterpillar and take a train ride through the lush green fields of A Bug's Land. Heimlich also narrates the trip as you ride in him. You will pass giant sized portions of foods such as carrots, Brussels sprouts, watermelon, candy corn and animal crackers.

#12 Princess Dot Puddle Park
Kids Walk-Through Attraction

This little park in the heart of A Bug's Land is a great place for little kids to cool down on hot summer days. Kids can play in the puddles as water sprays down from the giant garden faucet over head.

#13 Flik's Flyers
Mild Ride

Soar through the air in one of Flick's cleaver inventions, a hot air balloon made from takeout food containers and leaves inflated with air. Climb into one of several discarded food containers and then lift into the air amidst the whirling sounds of the leaves above you and the clanking sounds of the gears. You have several food containers to choose from, including a Chinese food container, an apple "Super Snack Pack" box, a box of raisins, and an animal cookies box.

#14 Francis' Ladybug Boogie
Kids Thrill Ride

Climb inside a ladybug and spin around in this Mad Teacup style ride designed with kids in mind. You don't need to do anything to make your bug spin, just sit back and take in the music as your bug spins in a figure eight motion under a colorful canopy.

#15 Tuck and Roll's Drive 'Em Buggies
Kids Thrill Ride • Rider Swap • Height Requirement 36"

Hop inside a pill bug and bump into other cars in this new take on the classic bumper cars attraction. Drive around in large circles under a big top circus tent and try to hit as many other cars as you can. This ride was designed with little kids in mind, so the cars move slow and steady across the driving area.

Cars Land
#16 Mater's Junkyard Jamboree
Thrill Ride

Take a seat in a trailer pulled by an adorable little tractor in this swinging and spinning thrill ride. The lovable tow truck Mater has gathered a lively group of little tractors for a good old-fashioned square dance, and you have been invited to join in on the fun. The tractors pull open-air trailers that hold one to three guests. They swing rapidly in one direction or another as the tractors spin in a big figure eight shape across the dance floor.

Junkyard Decorations

Old tires, hubcaps, oil drums, and license plates decorate Mater's junkyard square dance. Pay particular attention to the states listed on the license plates, they are hilarious puns.

Mater's Petting Zoo

A tractor from the ride is sitting just outside the attraction's entrance in a pen labeled "Mater's Petting Zoo." Stand next to the tractor and have your photo taken.

#17 Meet Cars Characters
Meet & Greet

Pull up to the *Cozy Cone Motel* and meet one of your favorite Cars characters. McQueen and Mater take turns meeting guests in front of the motel, so one or the other will be there when you stop by. Lately Red the fire engine has been spotted greeting guests here as well. This meet and greet opportunity is typically available all day long.

#18 Radiator Springs Racers
Thrill Ride • FastPass • Single Rider Line • Rider Swap • Height Requirement 40"

Climb inside one of the smiling cars of Radiator Springs and take off on an adventure through Ornament Valley. Each ride vehicle holds three guests in each of the two seat rows, allowing for a total of six guests to ride in each car. The enormous Radiator Springs Racers is currently know as the most expensive theme park ride ever built, costing more than two hundred million dollars to create. The attraction is like getting three different thrill-rides in one, with the leisurely ride through the outdoor Cadillac Mountains, followed by an indoor drive through a reproduction of Radiator Springs at night filled with *Cars* characters and an interesting storyline, and finally culminating with a head to head race with another car full of guests. With all this packed into a single attraction, it's easy to see why this has become the favorite ride of many guests.

The Cadillac Mountains

The Cadillac Mountain range in Radiator Springs Racers is made up of tall mountain peaks. But take a closer look at these mountains and you will notice that their peaks form the shapes of tail fins from Cadillac cars in the 1950s 1960s.

Ornament Valley Tourist Guide

Be sure to stop by the Ornament Valley tourist viewing area along the west edge of the attraction. There you can take in a breathtaking view of the Cadillac Mountains and learn about the area from the Ornament Valley guide posted there. You can read about the different mountain ranges, plant life, Stanley's Oasis, the Tail Light Caverns, and many other interesting articles about the area. Be sure to pay carful attention to the wording in the guide, it's full of puns.

Radiator Springs Racers Is on a Separate Fastpass Network

Normally you can only have one *Fastpass* at a time, but this ride is on a separate Fastpass network. This means that you can get a Fastpass for this ride first thing in the morning and then get a Fastpass for another attraction without having to use your Radiator Springs Racers Fastpass first. You can have a Fastpass for Radiator Springs Racers and any other attraction at the same time.

Every Ride Is Different

The path your car takes once inside the nighttime reproduction of radiator springs is randomly generated, sometimes taking your car through a set of activates inside *Luigi's Casa Della Tires* and other times taking you through different activities inside *Ramone's House of Body Art*. Later in the ride a head-to-head race is randomly generated, so you never know who will win.

In-Ride Photo

Smile for the in-ride camera located on the last hill you go up just before you pass the finish line at the end of the big head-to-head race. Your photo will be available for purchase near the exit of the attraction.

Golden Vine Winery
#19 Explore the Vineyards
Walk-Through Attraction

Give yourself a tour of the vineyard area. Here you can learn all about the winemaking process, which is an important part of California culture. Throughout the grounds you will find exhibits on growing, fermenting, and packaging wine grapes. If you are interested in wine, this is one exhibit you won't want to miss.

Live Grape Vines

See an exhibit featuring a variety of different types of live growing grape vines. Learn all about the different varieties of red and white wine grapes as well as about the different growing seasons. View this exhibit along the pathway that runs from the front entrance of The Golden Vine Winery to the *Wine Country Trattoria* restaurant.

Grape Press

Take a look at the old fashioned grape press on display between the *Grape Vines* exhibit and the *Mendocino Wine Bar* courtyard.

Taste & Terrior

View this exhibit about California's many wine regions near the entrance to the *Blue Sky Cellar* attraction.

Growing the Cork & Crafting the Barrel

View a live growing cork tree in this exhibit in the *Sonoma Terrace* courtyard. Learn about the art and science behind crafting wine barrels and how cork is harvested from trees to seal wine bottels.

Aging Well

Take a look at the aged grape vine and informational plaque in the "Aging Well" exhibit on display at the entrance to the *Al Fresco Lounge*. Here you can learn all about the vine pruning process.

#20 Blue Sky Cellar
Walk-Through Attraction

This preview center provides information on upcoming Disneyland and California Adventure attractions. The exhibit changes every couple of months as new attractions open and more information becomes available. You will often get to see rare blueprints, models, sketches and drawings of up incoming or recently opened attractions, making this a necessary stop for all die-hard fans of Disney theme parks. You can get the inside scoop on your favorite attractions and learn all sorts of new secrets. Stop by each time you visit the park and see what is on display.

Screening Room

Sit on a bench towards the back of the cellar and watch an informative video about Disney Imagineering.

Disney Quiz

Test your Disney I.Q. and see how much you know about Disney films and theme parks. A few of the wine barrels stacked along the wall have touch screen monitors in them, allowing you to test your Disney knowledge by taking a trivia quiz.

Pacific Wharf
#21 Boudin Bakery Tour
Walk-Through Attraction

Take a walking tour through a working sourdough bread bakery. Hosts Rosie O'Donnell and Colin Mochrie will talk you through the bread making process and the history of the famous Boudin sourdough bread bakery from San Francisco, California.

Free Bread Samples

Get a FREE sample of freshly baked sourdough bread while you tour the exhibit.

The Cannery Row Exhibit

View a photographic exhibit on the famous Cannery Row area of California in a display case outside the building. California's historic Cannery Row area is also explored in the famous novel *Cannery Row* by John Steinbeck.

Paradise Pier

#22 Caricature Drawings & Full Color Portraits
Art

Take a seat and pose for your own hand drawn caricature or color portrait at this stand along the boardwalk. It has recently moved to a new location at the entrance to the *Treasures in Paradise* shop. Hand-Painted Caricatures range between $17.95 - $32, Full Color Portraits between $17.95 - $35.95, and a wood frame is $13.95.

Top Halloween Items: Request a Halloween theme added to your Caricature Drawing, such as your head in a Halloween costume like Buzz Lightyear or a Storm Trooper.

#23 Meet Donald Duck
Meet & Greet

Step up to the gazebo next to *Cove Bar* and meet with your favorite troublemaking duck. As one of the characters actually created by Walt Disney, Donald holds a special place in many fans' hearts. See the California Adventure *Times Guide* for the times you can meet Donald.

> *"One of the greatest satisfactions in our work here at the studio is the warm relationship that exists within our cartoon family. Mickey, Pluto, Goofy, and the whole gang have always been a lot of fun to work with. But like many large families, we have a problem child. You're right, it's Donald Duck."*
> - Walt Disney

#24 California Screamin'
Thrill Ride • FastPass • Single Rider Line • Rider Swap • Height Requirement 48"

Strap yourself in for a screaming fast ride on a classic metal frame roller coaster. California Screamin' was designed to look like one of the old wooden-track roller coasters from the early 1900's, but it reaches the speeds of today's most advanced coasters. You will twist, dive, turn, and even go upside down during the ride's famous loop section.

Different Countdowns

Rather than having to listen to the same countdown spiel every time you ride California Screamin', you get to listen to one of four randomly chosen recordings of Neil Patrick Harris. Listen for the differences in the countdown recordings each time you ride the attraction.

In-Ride Photo

A camera snaps your photo just as you round the last bend in the track. Photos may be purchased at the nearby *California Scream Cam* shop.

#25 King Triton's Carousel
Mild Ride

Sit on top of ornately decorated sea creatures on this ocean themed carousel. Choose your seat on one of the dolphins, flying fish, garibaldi fish, sea horses, sea lions, sea otters, whales, or stationary water chariots. There are a total of 56 sea creatures and two chariots on the carousel to choose from.

Amusement Park Signs from the Past

Look for signs from past ocean-front amusement parks along the outer edge of the carousel's canopy. Signs from amusement parks such as Lick Pier (1923), Virginia Park (1939) and Nu-Pike (1930) can be found here. There are a total of 17 classic signs to view, see if you can find them all.

#26 Toy Story Midway Mania!
Interactive Mild Ride

This combination ride and interactive 3D game lets you compete for points against other players in five different mini-games inspired by the classic midway games of yesteryear. Board your game vehicle and allow it to take you to different game playing stations inside the attraction. The vehicle will zip along it's path, turning and spinning along the way. Then aim your cannon at the targets in the games and fire as fast as you can. Each game has a different theme, such as tossing hoops or throwing darts.

Your score is shown on the panel in front of you as you play the game. At the end of the ride you are awarded a virtual prize (a graphic displayed on the score board) according to your score, and your individual score is compared to the scores of the other players in your ride vehicle. Each vehicle holds up to eight players.

Mr. Potato Head

While waiting in the ride queue be sure to have a chat with Mr. Potato Head. He is interactive and will respond to you in a funny way.

Posters

Take a look at the funny midway game posters found throughout the queue and the game. They are not only entertaining, but many of them give you a preview of what you can expect on the ride.

#27 Meet the Characters from Toy Story
Meet & Greet

Meet the characters from the Toy Story series of films and videos at this brand new meet and greet. Look for this chance to meet your favorite characters between *Mickey's Fun Wheel* and *Paradise Gardens*. See the California Adventure *Times Guide* or ask a cast member for meet and greet times. Different characters show up throughout the day, so you may want to check back a few times to see if your favorite character has arrived.

A Great Photo Opportunity

A colorful Toy Story themed diorama is left at the meet and greet location even when the characters aren't there. This gives you the opportunity to get a memorable photo even when it's not an official visiting time.

#28 Games of the Boardwalk
Interactive Games

Try your luck at these classic boardwalk games of skill and chance. It costs money to play each game, but you can earn real prizes if you win. Credit-card style "Play Cards" which hold your game credits (called "points") can be purchased from vending machines near the games. This is so you don't have to keep handing over cash each time you want to play. You have four different games to choose from:

Goofy About Fishin' (250 points)

Sink your fishing poll into the stream below you and bring up a fish. The prize you win is determined by what's inside the fish you reel in, but every player wins a prize.

Casey at the Bat (8 balls for 500 points)

Try to pitch your ball through the hole in the catcher's mitt in this classic boardwalk skill game. Pitch three balls into the mitt to win a prize.

Dumbo Bucket Brigade (250 points)

Race against other players as you squirt water into a target to move your clown up the ladder. The first player to get their clown to the top wins a prize.

Bullseye Stallion Stampede (250 points)

Race against other players to roll your ball up a ramp and into holes worth different amounts of points in this skee ball type game. The more points you score, the faster your horse moves towards the finish line in the race above you. The first player to get their horse across the finish line wins the plush animal at the top of their skee ball ramp.

#29 Face Painting & Henna Tattoos
Art

This cart located just outside the *Point Mugu Tattoo* shop offers you a variety of face painting options costing $12, $14 or $17. Children can have their faces painted in a variety of colors, designs and styles at the face-painting booths located inside California Adventure. Choose your favorite style from the sample photos provided on the booth, and then sit down to have your face turned into a walking work of art. Face painting is also available at a stand in the Mad T Party while the nighttime show is on.

You may also have a henna tattoo artist paint a temporary tattoo on you at this same stand. Henna Tattoos use natural dyes that fade over time, usual lasting for several weeks. The Tattoos cost from $7 - $30 depending on the design, with a rather large selection available from the stand's catalog.

Top Halloween Items: Ask for Halloween Themed Temporary Tatoos and Face Painting Designs.

#30 Mickey's Fun Wheel
Gentle/Thrill Ride

Ride inside this classic Ferris wheel with a twist. Some of the gondolas on the wheel stay fairly stationary as the wheel rotates. The others swing fiercely on an internal track, sliding you from side to side and tipping you dramatically. This additional movement adds some thrill to the ride, but guests sensitive to motion may prefer the calmer stationary gondolas. Once you reach the top of the wheel take in a breathtaking look at the park from above. This is also a great opportunity to take some aerial photos even though the ride cadge may get in the way. (Although Perhaps they should be called "Earial" photos.)

#31 Silly Symphony Swings
Thrill Ride • Rider Swap • Height Requirement 40"

Strap yourself into this classic fairgrounds style swing ride. As *The William Tell Overture* plays in the background and a tornado begins to flurry your swing will take flight. Around and around you will go high above the waters of Paradise bay.

Canopy Illustrations

Look for classic illustrations from the animated short *The Band Concert* (1935) on the ride canopy as you spin through the air. As the canopy extends upward it reveals more of the illustrations.

#32 Goofy's Sky School
Thrill Ride • FastPass • Single Rider Line • Rider Swap • Height Requirement 40"

This classic fairgrounds style compact roller coaster serves up its thrills from its frequent sharp turns and fast dips. Climb aboard a flight training vehicle from Goofy's less than perfect flight school and take off into the sky. As you zig and zag around the track keep your eye out for Goofy's helpful flying lesions on topics like "How to Fly" and "How to Turn", they are hilarious.

This ride was redesigned from the former Mulholland Madness ride that occupied the same spot from 2001 to 2010. While the basic track layout was kept the same, the new theming of the attraction better fit with the new California Adventure esthetic that was emerging.

Flight School Information

The attraction queue is full of fun things to look at, like the "Flying the Goofy Way" illustration above the drinking fountains and the bulletin board full of hilarious notices. Also take a close look at Goofy's "official" flight school permit as you pass it.

#33 Jumpin' Jellyfish
Kids Thrill Ride • Height Requirement 40"

This parachute drop style ride for young kids lifts you up into the sky and then back down to earth over and over again. With it's sea life themed decorations it's as fun to look at as it is to ride. At the top of the 40 foot tall tower you can get a great view of California Adventure from above.

#34 Golden Zephyr
Mild Ride

Take a ride in a shiny metallic Zephyr inspired by the space ships in old serial movies like *Flash Gordon* (1936) and *Buck Rodgers* (1939-1940). The ride spins six twelve-seat Zephyrs up into the air and over the waters of Paradise Bay. The ride is fairly relaxing and the view from the Zephyr is beautiful.

#35 The Little Mermaid: Ariel's Undersea Adventure
Mild Ride

Venture "under the sea" and relive the story of the Little Mermaid in this enchanting ride. Board a clamshell that seats one to three guests and be miraculously transported under water where you will meet many of the characters from Disney's *The Little Mermaid*. The amazing special effects that transport you under water, lively animatronic characters and catchy music make this an attraction you won't want to miss.

#36 Fun Wheel Challenge
Interactive Games

New to California Adventure is a fun interactive game that lets you pit your skills against the players around you in Paradise Pier. Since November 16, 2013, guests have been able to connect their smart phones to a special wifi network just before the World of Color show begins and compete against other guests for control of the lights on Mickey's Fun Wheel. If you win you get to control the attraction's massive multi-color lights until another guest wins. The original idea behind the game was to give guests who are waiting for the World of Color to start an opportunity to talk and interact with the other guests around them, but anyone in the area can play the game once they connect to the special wifi network.

Stand somewhere in the Paradise Pear land of California Adventure and connect to the game's free wifi network labeled "PierGames" with your web browser enabled smart phone. The signal is strongest near the World of Color viewing areas, so if you are having trouble finding or connecting to the network then try to move towards one of those areas. The special wifi network and interactive game are available from 45 minutes before the World of Color show starts until the lights are shut down on the Ferris Wheel when the show begins. The amazing thing about the game network is that you don't even need to download a special app or enter a website address to play. As soon as you connect to the special wifi network it opens a website window on you phone and you can begin playing. This means that just about any type of web enabled smart phone can connect and play.

All of the *Glow with the Show* mouse ears in the area also light up in unison with the lights on Mickey's Fun Wheel as you play, so if you win, you are not only controlling the colors on the Fun Wheel, but also the colors on all of the *Glow with the Show* mouse ears in Paradise Pier!

To play the game, simply watch Mickey's Fun Wheel and try to match the attraction's light patterns on the game board presented on your smart phone. If you win, you gain control of the lights on the wheel! Get more information at the game's official website:

http://funwheelchallenge.com

Grizzly Peak
#37 Grizzly River Run
Thrill Ride • FastPass • Single Rider Line • Rider Swap • Height Requirement 42"

This thrill ride promises to get you soaking wet as you ride down the treacherous Grizzly River on an eight-person raft. You will spin around corners, crash over rapids and drop down tall waterfalls, all while surrounded by the beauty of the California wilderness. The attraction is named after Grizzly Peak, the bear shaped rocky mountain that looms high above the river. You will get wet on this ride. Very wet.

Legend of Grizzly Peak

Look for a large rock near the entrance to the attraction with the Legend of Grizzly Peak carved into it. This will give you the story behind the ride.

Frog Jump Falls

If you would like to cool down on a hot day, noting beats standing at the edge of the railing at Frog Jump Falls and allowing the waves of water to wash over you as rafts crash down at the base of the river's tallest plunge. Look for Frog Jump Falls towards the attraction entrance end of Mountain Road, a walking path that cuts through the attraction.

River Guide Artifacts

While moving through the queue, take a look at the artifacts left by various river guides. You can find tools, posters, books, radios, even a canoe made into a bookcase. Be sure take a look at the chalkboard with notes about the various rivers on it. It has some funny things to say about them.

#38 Route 49 Binoculars
Walk-Through Attraction

In the grand tradition of tourist areas throughout California's great state and national parks, coin-operated binoculars have been left for you at key viewing spots along Route 49. There are two Binocular areas, one on the west side of *Grizzly River Run* towards the entrance to the Grand California Hotel, and another set of Binoculars on the south side of Grizzly River Run towards the path to Paradise Bay. The binoculars were placed in their particular locations for a reason, so look through them and see if you can spot something special. The best thing about *these* binoculars is that the coin slots have been removed and *they are FREE!*

Mill Artifacts & Equipment

View a large variety of artifacts and equipment as you walk along Scenic Route 49 around the perimeter of the Grizzly River Run attraction. Some of the artifacts have plaques posted near them that tell you about the significance of the piece. Look for plaques about the The Pelton Wheel, The Steam Donkey, and other artifacts.

#39 Redwood Creek Challenge Trail
Walk-Through Attraction

This attraction is spread-out over a large plot of land and was made to resemble California's many national and state parks. Trails through the woods, a campfire circle, climbing, crawling, sliding, jumping, hanging, and more await you in this fun filled outdoor recreation area. There are a large number of activities to do here for kids of all ages, so expect to spend an hour or two here.

Get a Map

Be sure to ask the ranger at the entrance to the attraction for a map to Redwood Creek. These maps are very helpful and point out many of the activities, sights and trails found inside the attraction.

Earn Your Wilderness Explorer Badges

The maps obtained from the Redwood Creek rangers also tell you how to earn your Wilderness Explorer Badges and become a Senior Explorer. Fulfill the requirements for each badge listed on the map. The 6 badges are: Tracking, Bravery, Rock Climbing, Wolf Howl, Animal Spirit and *Puzzle Solving*. Then meet at the Ahwahnee Camp Circle for your *Senior Wilderness Explorer Ceremony*.

Meet Russell & Dug

Occasionally you will get the chance to meet with Russell & Dug in Redwood Creek. Say hello, have your picture taken, and ask for an autograph if you have an autograph book handy. They often appear near the *Camp Circle* just after the *Senior Wilderness Explorer Ceremony*, but sometimes you can also catch them walking down the trails inside Redwood Creek. If you spot Russell & Dug inside Redwood Creek, be sure to have your picture taken with them. Cast members should be standing by to assist you.

Explore the Trails

Redwood Creek has a lot of trails and paths to explore, but the three main trails are marked by signs. Use your Redwood Creek map to help you find and navigate these trails.

Mt. Lassen Lookout

Look through the room at the base of the tower, and then climb up top to enjoy the view. You can find the Mt. Lassen Lookout at the tail end of the *Quail Trail* (pun intended.) There is a lot to look at inside the first story of the lookout post. A labeled mineral collection, tagged animal skulls, plant specimens, a two way radio, an old camp stove, informative posters, photos, plaques, and much more. Take a good look around and see what you can discover. Communicate through code with the radio at the *Mt. Whitney Lookout*. Instructions at the radio tell you how to operate it. Take a look through the Binoculars mounted on the top floor of the tower. They are FREE to operate. Play the ring toss game found out on the observation deck level of the tower. Pick a rope bridge and head to your next destination. They are fun to walk through as the sway around. Take a look at the wealth of information this lookout has to offer on plants, minerals, and animals through posters, maps, collections, and specimens.

Eagle's Ascent

Climb up the expansive series of rope bridges and ramps in this fun activity for anyone young at heart.

Squirrel Scramble

This small set of rope bridges and ramps is more geared towards younger kids.

The Spirit Cave

Walk inside the cave and place your hand on the paw print in the cave wall to discover your spirit animal. Look for ancient hieroglyphic drawings on the exterior of the cave. They feature bears, moose, and other animals. Learn about the unique characteristics of each spirit animal from a sign across the path from the cave entrance. You may even encounter a reference to Kevin, the bird from film *Up* (2009).

Boulder Bears

Climb around these boulders in the shapes of bears from the films *Brother Bear* (2003) and *Brother Bear 2* (2006).

Rock Slide

Climb up a short set of rock stairs and then slide down the short slides toward the ground below. This slide is intended for small children, but anyone young at heart can enjoy it.

Mt. Shasta Lookout

Enjoy the forestry maps and posters before walking out to the edge of the lookout and taking in the beauty of the park. Take a look through the Binoculars mounted on the top floor of the tower. They are FREE to operate. Take a look at the sighting tool used to find fires, it's mounted in the center of the tower. Instructions on how to operate the fire Finder are found attached to its base.

Hoot-N-Holler Logs

Slide through hollowed out logs from the top of the Mt. Lassen Lookout to the ground below. The activity is named after the logs themselves, one is called "Hoot" and the other is called "Holler." Don't forget to practice your Wolf Howl as you slide through the logs.

Shake-A-Log

Climb through this three-segment log that shakes and sways as you move through it. The name for the Shake-A-Log is a pun on the saying "Shake a leg", which means to do something quickly.

Mt. Whitney Lookout

Climb up to the observation tower and take in the view of Redwood Creek. Use the other end of the two-way radio to communicate through code to guests over at the *Mt. Lassen Lookout*. Instructions at the radio tell you how to operate it.

Sequoia Smokejumpers

Climb the training tower and then slide downward along a long rope from a tire swing. When you are finished you will have earned your bravery badge. This activity is only for children. You must be age 12 or younger and between 42" to 63" tall to jump. Smokejumpers are firefighters who parachute into a remote area to combat wildfires. The first use of smokejumpers in California was in the Sequoia National Forest in 1944, hence the name of this activity.

Cliff Hanger Rock Climb
Climb across a rock face in this fun activity for all ages.

Millennium Tree
View the history of California through the rings in this impressive tree segment from the birth of the tree in 818 A.D. till it fell in 1932. Signs will explain how to use the tree's rings to date it, and plaques on the tree segment itself will highlight the tree rings that correspond to important historical events. Learn about the history of this tree as well as the history of California from the many signs and plaques found here.

Big Sur
Walk through the split tree trunk of a giant redwood, named and themed after the famous split trunks of giant living redwood trees that tourists can walk through in the central costal area of Big Sur in California. Listen carefully as you walk through and you may hear some interesting sounds.

Grizzly Peak Airfield (formerly Condor Flats)
#40 Soarin' Over California
Thrill Ride • FastPass • Single Rider Line • Rider Swap • Height Requirement 40"
In this simulated flight experience, you will be strapped into a multi-seat hang glider and taken on a vast adventure over key parts of California. From wave-filled beaches to snow covered mountains, you will get to see some of the best sights California has to offer while your hang glider simulates the motion you would experience if you were really in the air. The effects and images in this attraction are fantastic, which is why it remains one of the most popular rides in the park.

Wings of Fame
Take a look at the portraits of famous California planes and aviators adorning the walls of queue inside the hanger. Near each photo is a plaque describing the significance of the person or plane in the photo. The interesting thing about this exhibit is that each side of the hanger has different photos, so you will get to see one version of the exhibit if you wait in the *Fastpass queue* and an entirely different version of the exhibit if you wait in the Standby queue.

Scents
During the attraction several scents fill the room at the appropriate times in the film. Look for these scents: *Citrus*, *Pine*, *Sagebrush*, and *Ocean*.

Dining

The Disneyland Resort is full of unique culinary experiences, covering a wide variety of food genres. With so many great choices at hand, guests can afford to be choosey. There's no reason to just settle for any old restaurant that crosses your path. People have been known to travel to the resort just for the dining opportunities alone. Many others look forward to their meals as much as the attractions. You should treat your Disneyland dining experience as a chance to have a truly special meal. Use the guide below to help you find that special restaurant. Halloween themed meals and snacks have also been listed in the *Top Halloween Dining* section for your spooky pleasure.

Disneyland

Main Street, U.S.A.
01. Carnation Café
Full Service

As the only remaining full service sit-down restaurant on Main Street, the Carnation Café combines an 1890's small town charm with delicious American fare like soups, sandwiches and meatloaf. This café has been famous for years for it's elaborate desserts. The restaurant's quaint outdoor seating area is a favorite people watching spot on Main Street, where guests can be seen strolling down Disney's largest shopping district at any time of the day or night. *Guest Favorites:* Baked Potato Soup, Fried Pickles with Dipping Sauce, Sourdough Bacon Cheese Melt, and Chicken-Fried Chicken.

02. Coca-Cola Refreshment Corner
Quick Service

At the tail end of *Main Street*, just before the *Central Hub*, sits a small street-corner eatery called the Coca-Cola Refreshment Corner. Here guests can find hot dogs, chili bowls, hot pretzels, beverages and a few other snacks. The Refreshment Corner is sponsored by soft drink giant Coca-Cola, and has been serving guests since the park's opening day in 1955. Seating is available at the adjacent outdoor tables, where guests can listen to live piano performances throughout the day as they enjoy their meal. *Guest Favorites:* Mac & Cheese Hot Dog, Hearty Chili in a Sourdough Bread Bowl, and Cherry, Raspberry, & Vanilla Coke.

03. Little Red Wagon
Quick Service

This little food stand contained within an old-time red delivery truck has become a Disneyland favorite. It really only serves one entrée, but it serves it well: Disneyland's gigantic delicious corn dogs. *Guest Favorites:* Hand-Dipped Corn Dog.

04. Plaza Inn
Quick Service

The Plaza Inn serves classic American meals with all the sides for breakfast, lunch and dinner. As one of Walt Disney's favorite dining spots, the inn is decorated with authentic 19th-century furnishings, Victorian stained glass and ornate woodwork salvaged from a historic Los Angeles home. Although it originally went by the name Red Wagon Inn, the restaurant has been serving guests delicious food such as it's world famous fried chicken since the park opened in 1955. *Guest Favorites:* Plaza Inn Specialty Chicken, Pot Roast, and Cobb Salad.

Breakfast with the Stars

The *Disney Character Breakfast* at the Plaza Inn includes the chance to meet with favorite Disney stars while you dine on delicious breakfast fare. This fixed-price buffet offers fresh-baked pastries, waffles, made-to-order omelets and more as guests spend their morning collecting autographs and taking great souvenir photos with their favorite Disney characters.

Birthday Parties at the Plaza Inn

Celebrate your child's birthday at the Plaza Inn with host Pat E. Cake. You'll get music, cake decorating and special appearances by Mickey and Minnie Mouse. Reservations are required. Call Disney Dining (714) 781-DINE to make a reservation or get more information about this special birthday event.

05. Jolly Holiday Bakery Café
Quick Service

Replacing the under-utilized Plaza Pavilion building and the overly crowded Blue Ribbon Bakery, this newly opened café features a large variety of delicious baked goods, specialty coffee drinks, quality sandwiches, creative salads and soups that change daily. The building has a *Mary Poppins* theme, with artifacts on display to inspire fond memories of the classic 1964 Disney film. Seating is available in front of the building in the ample outdoor dining area. *Guest Favorites:* Jolly Holiday Combo (Toasted cheese sandwich with tomato basil soup), Roast Beef & Blue Cheese on Traditional Baguette, Jolly Holiday Salad, Assorted Pastries, Muffins, Cookies, and Specialty Coffees.

06. Main Street Fruit Cart
Carts

This old fashioned street cart sits in front of the *Market House* on *Main Street*. Fresh whole fruit, hummus and veggie cups offer a healthy alternative to sugar and fat-filled snacks. *Guest Favorites:* Mango Slices, Berry Bowl, Hummus, and Veggie Cup with Ranch Dip.

07. Market House
Coffee & Dessert

This historic café has been serving piping hot coffee since Disneyland opened in 1955. It's a great place to get a simple cup of coffee, an expertly crafted cappuccino, tea, hot cocoa and a variety of baked goods. A renovation and reopening at the end of 2013 brought a whole new look to the Market House and introduced Starbucks to the Disneyland park. *Guest Favorites:* Specialty Coffees and Assorted Baked Goods.

08. Gibson Girl Ice Cream Parlor
Coffee & Dessert

This turn of the 20th century inspired ice cream parlor offers up a generous helping of charm and style. Recently renovated and reopened in 2012, the parlor serves a delicious variety of ice cream by the scoop and great ice cream sundaes. This is THE location in Disneyland to get your ice cream. Many seasoned guests never leave the park with out stopping by here at least once. *Guest Favorites:* Chocolate Chip Cookie Hot Fudge Sundae, Firehouse Dalmatian Mint Sundae, and Ice Cream by the Scoop.

09. Candy Palace & Penny Arcade
Coffee & Dessert

Disneyland's iconic Candy Palace spills over into the Penny Arcade with a variety of freshly made candy, including ornately decorated candy apples and the shop's famous buttered peanut brittle. You can watch candy being made through the stores large glass windows as you shop for hand-dipped chocolates and delicious baked goods. During holiday seasons a variety of special holiday-themed candy apples and hand-made candy canes bring in the patrons in record numbers. Prepackaged candy and cookies are also available, and guests love to mix and match from the store's huge wall of assorted jelly beans and Goofy Mostly Sour Power Candy display. *Guest Favorites:* Pecan Brittle, Disney Theme Candy Apples, and Assorted Fudge.

10. Central Plaza Cappuccino Cart
Coffee & Dessert

Located at the west side of the Central Hub between the pathway to *Frontierland* and *Fantasyland's* new *Fantasy Fair* area, this cart serves gourmet specialty coffees, fresh whole fruit and a few assorted pastries. *Guest Favorites:* Espresso, Cappuccino (Hot or Iced), Café Mocha (Hot or Iced), Café Latte, Coffee, Hot Tea, Hot Cocoa, Whole Fruit, and Assorted baked Goods.

Adventureland
11. Bengal Barbecue
Quick Service

This outdoor food stand features deliciously seasoned beef, chicken and vegetable skewers. The skewers are made to order, each is sold separately for a very affordable price. Many die-hard fans will also swear that their famous Tiger Tail Breadsticks are the best snack food in Disneyland. A few other assorted snacks are also available.

Guest Favorites: Banyan Beef Skewer (Hot & Spicy), Chieftain Chicken Skewer in a Polynesian Sauce, and Safari Skewer (Bacon Wrapped Asparagus).

12. Tropical Imports
Cart

Enjoy a selection of fresh tropical fruits, ice cold drinks, plus a few other healthy snacks at this small outdoor marketplace located between the entrance and exit to the *Jungle Cruise* attraction. A few adventurous souvenirs can also be found here. *Guest Favorites:* Mango slices, Whole fruit, and Iced Tea.

13. Tiki Juice Bar
Coffee & Dessert

The history of the Tiki Juice Bar goes all the way back to 1976 when the Dole Pineapple Company started sponsoring the *Enchanted Tiki Room* Attraction. Sitting right at the entrance to Adventureland's famous *Enchanted Tiki Room*, the Tiki Juice Bar's tropical thatched-roof hut serves the "Dole Whip Float," a unique take on the traditional ice cream float. This unique dessert features Dole pineapple juice poured over a large serving of pineapple soft serve ice cream, topped off with a cherry and a decorative paper umbrella. With both the front and back sides of the hut capable of serving thirsty guests, the floats may be purchased both outside and inside the *Enchanted Tiki Room*'s waiting area. *Guest Favorites:* Dole Whip Float, Pineapple Dole Whip Soft-serve, Fresh Pineapple Spear, and Dole Pineapple Juice.

New Orleans Square

14. Blue Bayou
Full Service

This amazing sit-down service restaurant has been a guest favorite since it opened in 1967 inside the Pirates of the Caribbean attraction. Diners get the unique experience of enjoying the restaurant's delicious selection of gourmet New Orleans specialities as Pirates of the Caribbean's guests sail past their table in small boats. Sitting under the restaurant's perpetual nighttime sky and false outdoor veranda create the fantasy that patrons are dining out along the Louisiana bayou, adding an unparalleled charm to this unique dining experience. This is easily the fanciest sit down restaurant available to guests in Disneyland, with dinner prices ranging from about $35 to $60 per person. *Guest Favorites:* Royal Street Seafood Jambalaya, Broiled Filet Mignon, Cajun-Spiced Salmon, Mint Julep, and Louisiana Lemonade.

15. Café Orléans
Full Service

This quaint sit-down restaurant at the heart of New Orleans Square features a number of creole masterpieces for lunch and dinner. Guests can dine either inside the New Orleans themed dining room or outside in the covered patio looking out over New Orleans Square's walking promenade. *Guest Favorites:* New Orleans Gumbo, Pommes Frites, Monte Cristo Sandwich, and Chicken Gumbo Crepe.

16. Royal Street Veranda
Quick Service

This quick-service restaurant features a few creole specialties such as Steak Gumbo, Vegetarian Gumbo and New Orleans Fritters. Located just to the right of the Pirates of the Caribbean attraction, the restaurant's rather small outdoor seating area offers a delightful view of New Orleans Square's promenade, across from which you can see the *Rivers of America* and *The Pirate's Liar on Tom Sawyer's Island*. *Guest Favorites:* Steak Gumbo, Vegetarian Gumbo, and the Trio of New Orleans Fritters.

17. French Market Restaurant
Quick Service

This cafeteria-style sit down restaurant features expertly prepared meals at a reasonable price. Guests may enjoy the restaurant's chicken, roast beef, salmon, pasta and other specialty dishes with all the trimmings for about $12 - $15 per plate. Seating is available outside in the restaurant's covered patio. A stage towards the far end of the patio features New Orleans' inspired musical performances at various times throughout the day. *Guest Favorites:* Red Beans and Rice with Andouille Sausage, Jambalaya, and Creole Seafood Pasta.

Halloween Themes: Take in the *The Nightmare Before Christmas* (1993) and other Halloween themed decorations along the restaurant's outer fence and seating area.

18. Mint Julep Bar
Coffee & Dessert

This bar doesn't serve alcohol but the small outdoor counter service stand built into the rear of the *French Market Restaurant* serves refreshing nonalcoholic mint Juleps, a variety of special coffee drinks, their famous Mickey-shaped Beignets (a New Orleans style donut-like pastry), soft drinks and other assorted beverages. Diners may enjoy their snacks and beverages in the *French Market Restaurant's* nearby seating area. *Guest Favorites:* New Orleans Mint Julep , Mickey-shaped Beignets, Espresso, Cappuccino, Café Latte, and Café Mocha.

19. New Orleans Square Coffee Cart
Coffee & Dessert

Find this specialty cart near the entrance to the building it was styled after, the *Haunted Mansion*. It features piping hot coffee and a few snack items. *Guest Favorites:* Regular & Decaf Coffee, Hot Cocoa and the Giant Cinnamon Roll.

Critter Country
20. Harbour Galley
Quick Service

This riverfront shack serves delicious soups and salads along the famous *Rivers of America* at the entrance to Critter Country. Designed to look like a weathered harbor from a time gone by, the restaurant's unique seating on top of a rustic wooden pier gives diners an amazing view of old sailing ships, paddle wheel steamboats and canoes as they sail past on the adjacent river. Nearby trees and umbrellas provide some shade in the hot summer months, and diners can get a close-up view of the

Mark Twain Riverboat and the *Sailing Ship Columbia* docked in the harbor when not in use on the river. *Guest Favorites:* Lobster Roll, Barbecue Chicken & Slaw Baked Potato, and Broccoli Cheddar Soup.

21. Hungry Bear Restaurant
Quick Service

This woodland-inspired two story restaurant serves as the main eatery in Critter Country. With seating available on both levels of it's outdoor wooden decks, diners get a magnificent view of the *Rivers of America* as they enjoy the restaurant's unique specialties including a fried green tomato sandwich, sweet potato fries and tiny hand-made pies. The surrounding trees add to the forest feel of the area, and large seating areas provide plenty room for large numbers of guests. *Guest Favorites:* Fried Green Tomato Sandwich, Pioneer Chili Cheeseburger, Trixie's Pies (Available seasonally), and Sweet Potato Fries.

22. Pooh Corner
Coffee & Dessert

This rather large *Winnie the Pooh*-themed souvenir shop at the tail end of Critter Country carries freshly made candy, baked goods and snacks in the bakery area towards the front of the shop. Its isolation from the hustle and bustle of Disneyland's more popular areas can provide a nice quiet place to relax with a snack without having to battle with the crowds found in the more centrally located areas of the park. *Guest Favorites:* Gourmet Candy Apples, Chocolate Caramel Cashew Pretzel Rod, and a variety of other baked goods.

Frontierland
23. Big Thunder Ranch Barbecue
Full Service

This all-you-can-eat family-style table service experience features a delicious selection of country favorites including ribs, chicken and smoked sausage. Although a savory vegetarian tofu version of the meal is available, it lacks the variety found in the regular meal. Guests enjoy being served plate after plate of their favorite barbecued meats and sides at outdoor tables in front of the *Big Thunder Stage*. The Thunder Ranch Barbecue only operates during very limited hours, so be sure to check it's operating hours before attempting a visit. Typically the restaurant is open for Lunch (Adults $23.99 / Kids $11.99) 11pm-3:45pm, and Dinner (Adults $29.99 / Kids $12.99) 4pm-7pm. Lunch includes *BBQ Chicken, Ribs, Cookie's Cole Slaw, Ranch Beans*, and *Corn Bread*. Dinner includes lunch menu plus *Smoked Sausage* and *Corn Cob Wheels*. Desserts are extra. *Dessert favorites:* Ranch Hand Sundaes, S'mores Bake, and Chef Cookie's Deep Dish.

24. Rancho del Zocalo Restaurante
Quick Service

Nestled in a quite corner of Frontierland is the Rancho del Zocalo Restaurante, a nice counter service restaurant offering Mexican cuisine. Here guests can relax in the atmosphere of Old Mexico as they enjoy burritos, tacos, enchiladas, soups and a variety of desserts. Entrées cost about $10 to $14. *Guest Favorites:* Burrito Guadalajara, Red Chile Enchilada Platter, and Tostada Salad.

Seasonal Themes: Look for Día de los Muertos decorations throughout the restaurant, food service, and dining room areas. Pay particular attention to the displays around the fireplace just before the checkout counters.

25. The Golden Horseshoe
Quick Service

Nothing beats the old West atmosphere at the Golden Horseshoe. Sit in a lavishly decorated replica of a pioneer-style theater as you enjoy a quick meal and some of the best desserts in Disneyland. You may want to have a seat in second story balcony, the view is great and it's an excellent place to enjoy your meal while watching the show below. Although a few fast-food style entrées are served here such as Chicken Nuggets and Fish & Chips, this restaurant is best at delivering quick snacks and delicious desserts. *Guest Favorites:* Chili Cheese Fries, Hot Fudge Sundae, and the Golden Horseshoe Ice Cream Float.

26. Stage Door Café
Quick Service

Designed to conjure up images of a small food service stand in an old west theater, this little counter-service restaurant provides hurried guests with a quick meal. To relax and eat, try the nearby outdoor seating area located along the main walkway through Frontierland. *Guest Favorites:* Hand-Dipped Corn Dog, Fish & Chips, and House-Made Funnel Cakes.

27. River Belle Terrace
Quick Service

Sitting on the further-most corner between Adventureland and Frontierland, this quaint little counter-service restaurant features gourmet carver style sandwiches and salads in an atmosphere inspired by riverfront eateries in the day's of *Mark Twain*. In the morning you can find the park's most popular breakfast item, Mickey Mouse shaped pancakes. Because of it's location at the tail end of both lands, entrances to the restaurant can be found on both sides of the building in Adventureland and Frontierland. Dining is available in both indoor and outdoor seating areas; and the food service is usually lighting fast. The indoor dining room provides a classic Southern decor with shade and air conditioning on hot days, while the outdoor terrace gives guests the opportunity to view the *Mark Twain Riverboat* travel down the *Rivers of America*. *Guest Favorites:* The Messy Mississippi BBQ Pork, River Belle's Sirloin & Cheddar, and Becky Thatcher's Vegetarian Chopped Salad.

28. Shipping Office
Quick Service

Across from the entrance to the Big Thunder Mountain Railroad and just to the right of the Mark Twain Riverboat dock is a delightful quiet riverfront deck hanging over the waters of the rivers of America. Attached to it is a little outdoor stand offering Disneyland's famous Giant Turkey Leg, Chimichanga, Corn on the Cob, and Coffee.

Fantasyland

29. Village Haus Restaurant
Quick Service

This recently renovated eatery serves gourmet burgers, flat bread pizzas and salads inside a thatched-roof building from Pinocchio's home village. Pinocchio-themed artwork and lavish decorations adorn the walls of this restaurant's charming indoor dining room, making this one of my favorite places to eat inside Disneyland. *Guest Favorites:* Angus 1/3 lb Pastrami Cheeseburger, BLT Flat Bread Pizza, and Apple & Cheddar Salad.

30. Edelweiss Snacks
Quick Service

This small counter-service stand was designed to match the Swiss theme of the nearby *Matterhorn Bobsleds* serving quick entrées like Disney's famous Jumbo Turkey Leg. Head behind the restaurant to find dining tables on a landing that floats over the old Motor Boat Lagoon. *Guest Favorites:* Jumbo Turkey Leg, Glazed Pork Shank, Chimichanga, and Buttered or Chili-Lime Corn on the Cob.

31. Troubadour Tavern
Quick Service

At the rear end of Fantasyland sits a large food stand designed to look like something you would find alongside a knight's jousting tournament. This purveyor of medieval food is a bit out of the way, but it's a convenient place to buy a quick snack from both inside and outside the new *Fantasyland Theatre*. *Guest Favorites:* Bratwurst, Tavern Nachos, Pretzel Bites with Cheese Sauce, and Cinnamon-Apple Baton.

32. Maurice's Treats
Cart

This small food stand serves unique snacks to hungry guests outside the *Royal Hall* in the new *Fantasy Fair* area. The stand opened in March 2013. *Guest Favorites:* Strawberry Twist, Chocolate Twist, Cheddar Garlic Bagel Twist, and Boysen Apple Freeze.

33. Fantasia Freeze
Coffee & Dessert

This *It's a Small World* themed stand sits near the *Storybook Land Canal Boats*, across the main Fantasyland walkway from *Edelweiss Snacks*. The stand's specialty is frozen lemonade with a cherry or raspberry "flavor shot". The stand also serves coffee and hot cocoa in an optional souvenir travel mug.

Mickey's Toontown

34. Daisy's Diner
Quick Service

Donald Duck's girlfriend Daisy has an entire food stand dedicated to her. This is pretty remarkable considering she is rarely, if ever, mentioned in the rest of the park. Daisy first appeared in the Disney cartoon *Mr. Duck Steps Out* (1940), where her date with Donald Duck is interrupted by Donald's attention-seeking nephews Huey, Dewey and Louie. Daisy's Diner serves a fast-food style mini-pizza and a very limited selection of desserts. *Guest Favorites:* Pepperoni Pizza, Cheese Pizza, and Assorted Desserts.

35. Pluto's Dog House
Quick Service

Pluto first appeared as Minnie Mouse's dog "Rover" in *The Picnic* (1930), but he's known as Mickey Mouse's non-speaking pet dog in later Disney cartoons. This food stand named after Pluto and his iconic dog house serves exactly what you might expect: hot dogs. A very limited selection of desserts are also available. *Guest Favorites:* Premium Hot Dog with sliced apples or chips and assorted desserts.

36. Clarabelle's
Quick Service

Named after Disney's Clarabelle Cow character, this quick service food stand offers a very limited selection of pre-made sandwiches and salads. Ample seating is available for diners in the outdoor tables surrounding Toontown's Town Square and in front of the many building facades in the area. These seating areas are also shared with the nearby *Daisy's Diner* and *Pluto's Dog House* food stands. *Guest Favorites:* Slow-roasted Turkey Sandwich with Chips, Chef Salad, and Mickey Ice Cream Sandwich.

37. Toon Up Treats at Goofy's Gas Station
Cart

This elaborate set of carts is located in the middle of Toontown next to the gas pumps at Goofy's Gas Station. Fresh fruits and cold beverages await guests in the ice-filled carts, providing a quick healthy snack for guests on the run. Pineapple Spear, Mango Slices, and Hummus.

38. Goofy's Freez Time
Dessert

This vacation trailer is located just outside Goofy's Playhouse. The name "Freez Time" is a play on words that mixes the idea of vacation "free time" with the "frozen" drinks found there. The trailer serves up frozen slushy style drinks in 3 flavors: *Frozen Apple*, *Blue Raspberry*, and *Wild Cherry*. *Chips* are also available.

Tomorrowland

39. Tomorrowland Terrace
Quick Service

This open air counter service restaurant sits in the center of Tomorrowland serving burgers, sandwiches and fries to guests as they enjoy shows on the Tomorrowland Terrace stage. The restaurant supplies guests with a generous amount of outdoor seating and the multiple service windows serve diners their meals quickly. *Guest Favorites:* Roasted Portobello & Vegetable Sandwich, Grilled Chicken Chop Salad, and Angus 1/3 lb. BBQ Bacon Cheeseburger.

40. Redd Rockett's Pizza Port
Quick Service

This restaurant supplies pizza by the slice, whole pizza pies, pasta and specialty salads to Tomorrowland guests. Pizza slices provide an instant meal for guests on the go, while ordering a whole pizza may take a little more time. A variety of sides, snacks and drinks are also available. The restaurant's plentiful seating offers you the choice of indoor or outdoor dining, with two separate outdoor dining patios located on either side of the building. *Guest Favorites:* Supernova Pizza Special Mega Slice, Asian Chicken Salad, and Count Down Chicken Fusilli.

41. The Spirit of Refreshment at the Moonliner Rocket
Cart

As it states below the Moonliner rocket, this Coca-Cola sponsored refreshment stand is tasked with "Delivering Refreshment to a Thirsty Galaxy." This small stand serves ice cold beverages to thirsty guests in front of Redd Rockett's Pizza Port. Even if you are not in the market for a cold soft drink, stop by to get a look at this magnificent part of Disneyland history.

Fantasmic! Dining

Dinner Packages

Guests may purchase special *Fantasmic!* dining packages at the restaurants listed below. These special packages include either a "Grab & Go" meal or a 3-course prix fixe dinner, as well as special *Fantasmic!* reserved seating. Visit the *Fantasmic!* dining page to make a reservation or get more information.

disneyland.disney.go.com/dining/disneyland/fantasmic-dinner-packages/

Reservations are highly recommended: (714) 781-DINE (3463).

Aladdin's Oasis [Grab & Go meal]
$22.99 (adults) / $13.99 (children 3 to 9).

River Belle Terrace [3-course prix fixe dinner]
Starting at 3pm: $41.99 (adults) / $21.99 (children 3 to 9).

Blue Bayou Restaurant [3-course prix fixe dinner]
Starting at 4pm: $61.00 (adults) / $23.00 (children 3 to 9).

California Adventure

Buena Vista Street

01. Carthay Circle Restaurant
Full Service

Easily the most elegant, popular, and expensive restaurant in the entire Disneyland Resort, the Carthay Circle Restaurant serves up exquisite gourmet dishes, meticulously selected wine tasting flights, and a charming dining atmosphere. The ornate building which houses the restaurant is a reproduction of Los Angeles' historic Carthay Circle Theatre, the movie theater that premiered Walt Disney's first feature length film *Snow White and the Seven Dwarfs* (1937). From the dark wood paneling to the classically inspired wait staff uniforms; every aspect of this restaurant was designed to transport you back in time to the day Walt's masterpiece premiered. The restaurant's menu changes seasonally, so use the highlights below to get an example of the types of food you can expect. *Starter Favorites:* Carthay Signature Fried Biscuits, Fire Cracker Duck Wings, and Blue Cobia Ceviche. *Entrée Favorites:* Tempura-fried Shrimp, Thick-Cut Pork Chop, and Grilled Angus New York.

02. Carthay Circle Lounge
Full Service

Stop by this period-accurate lounge for unique drinks and appetizers, and get fully immersed in the world of 1937 Los Angeles. This bar area located adjacent to the *Carthay Circle Restaurant's* lobby is also a great place to relax with a drink while you wait for your dinner table to be ready. Here you will find unique cocktail recipes, local beer on tap, and a variety of beer, wine, and spirits tasting flights to complement the lounge's delightful appetizer menu. *Appetizer Favorites:* Lobster Pad Thai Imperial Roll, Carthay Flat Bread, Vietnamese Twice Cooked Beef Taco, and Duck Confit Sliders. *Cocktail Favorites*: Tasting Flights of a Variety of Spirits, Locally Brewed Beer on Tap, Unique Cocktails.

03. Fiddler, Fifer & Practical Café
Quick Service

This café serves a variety of gourmet Starbucks coffee drinks, hot and cold sandwiches, soups, pastries and desserts in a classic coffee shop atmosphere. With ample seating and a centralized location, this café is an ideal stopover for weary travelers. *Guest Favorites:* Roasted Beef and Cheddar Sandwich, Turkey Apple Cheddar Salad, Soup of the Day, and Specialty Coffee Drinks.

04. Mortimer's Market
Quick Service

This open air-fruit stand at the beginning of Buena Vista Street offers fresh fruit and quick healthy snacks. The stand is named after Mortimer Mouse, the name Walt Disney almost gave to his Mickey Mouse character, until his wife Lillian talked him out of it. *Guest Favorites:* Whole or Sliced Fruit, Healthy Snacks, and Ice Cold Drinks.

05. Clarabelle's Hand-Scooped Ice Cream
Quick Service

Ice cream sundaes, scoops, and cones are served in this delightful old-fashioned ice cream parlor at the south end of Buena Vista Street. The shop also specializes in custom, made to order hand dipped ice cream bars. *Guest Favorites:* Chocolate Chip Cookie Hot Fudge Sundae, Hand Dipped Ice Cream Bars, and Ice Cream Cones.

06. Trolley Treats
Quick Service

Enjoy freshly made candies and baked goods in this large 1920's themed candy shop on Buena Vista St. *Guest Favorites:* Fancy Character Themed Candy Apples, English Toffee, Pecan Brittle, Spicy Peanut Brittle, and Assorted Gourmet Fudges.

Hollywood Land
07. Award Wieners
Quick Service

This large hot dog stand on Hollywood Blvd offers a nice selection of specialty dogs and toppings. *Guest Favorites:* Chili Cheese Dog, Barbecue Hot Link, and Vegetarian Portobello-Mushroom Philly.

08. Fairfax Market
Quick Service

This outdoor fruit stand offers a large variety of fresh fruits and healthy snacks. *Guest Favorites:* Whole or Sliced Fruit, Apples with caramel dipping sauce, Pickle, Veggie Cup with Ranch, Hummus, and other healthy snacks.

09. Schmoozies
Quick Service

This fruit smoothie stand offers a nice variety of blended fruit drinks as well as gourmet coffees and hot cocoa. *Guest Favorites:* Specialty Fruit Smoothies, Fresh Fruit Juices, Make Mine Mocha (Frozen chocolate espresso), Gourmet Coffee, and Ultimate Hot Cocoa.

10. House of Cards
Quick Service • Limited Hours

This large Alice in Wonderland themed stand in the far corner of Hollywood Land offers you a small selection of beer and unique cocktails while you enjoy the *Mad T Party*. *Guest Favorites:* Wonderful Underland Cotton Candy Lemonade, Fuze Juice Drinks, Specialty Alcoholic Mixed Drinks, and Royal Milliner's Brews (Blue Moon or Fat Tire Amber Ale on Tap).

11. Drink Me
Quick Service • Limited Hours

Themed after the famous "Drink Me" potion in the Alice in Wonderland stories, this stand offers alcohol and non-alcohol cocktails while the *Mad T Party* is happening. *Guest Favorites:* Wonderful Underland Cotton Candy Lemonade, Fuze Juice Drinks, Specialty Alcoholic Mixed Drinks, and Royal Milliner's Brews (Blue Moon or Dos Equis Beer on Tap).

12. Fuze Catering Truck
Quick Service • Limited Hours

The Fuze-beverage-sponsored catering truck found at the south-east end of the Mad T Party is hard to miss with its bright neon purple and green color scheme. The truck's 2012 Mad T Party makeover left it with a distinct Mad T Party playing cards theme. It's Non-alcoholic specialty drinks feature unique flavors that can only be found at the Mad T Party. The Non-Alcoholic *Twisted Cheshire Concoctions* include: "Tweedle Blue" (Cotton Candy), "Hatter's Mandarian Fury" (Mandarian Orange), "Jabberwocky Juice" (Granny Smith Apple), or "Cheshire Chiller" (Desert Pear).

Cars Land

13. Flo's V8 Café
Quick Service

This 50's style car themed diner offers good old American fare such as NY strip stakes, milk shakes and freshly baked pies. *Guest Favorites:* BBQ Pork Ribs, Turkey Dip, Veggie Tater Bake, Flo's Pie-O-Ramas Mini Pies, and Flo's Classic Shake.

14. Cozy Cone Motel
Quick Service

This unique restaurant features five different traffic cone themed food stations, each with a unique menu. It's as if Radiator Springs has it's own food court. *Guest Favorites:* Chili Cone Queso, Chicken Verde Cone, Pretzel Bites with Cheesy Sauce, Churro Bites with Cinnamon Spiced Chocolate Sauce, Soft Serve Ice Cream, "Route" Beer Float, Cinnamon Spiced Hot Cocoa, and a variety of Flavored Popcorns.

15. Fillmore's Taste-In
Quick Service

This groovy tidied geodesic dome tent is owned by none other than Fillmore the VW van from the *Cars* films. Here you can find a variety of fruits and other healthy snacks. *Guest Favorites:* Whole Fruits, Sliced Fruits, and Fruit Bowls, Dill pickles, and assorted chips.

Golden Vine Winery

16. Wine Country Trattoria
Full Service

This delightful eatery in the center of California Adventure offers fine Italian dining surrounded by the beauty of the California Wine Country. Located at the heart of the Golden Vine Winery, a relaxing atmosphere and charming scenery complement the delicious meals served here. *Guest Favorites:* Pasta Your Way Shrimp Scampi, Osso Buco, Wine Tasting Flight, Trattoria Blend Press Pot Coffee and other Specialty Coffees.

17. Alfresco Tasting Terrace
Full Service

This open-air bar located a floor above the *Wine Country Trattoria* offers majestic cocktails and fantastic views. Enjoy the relaxing atmosphere as you sip on fine wines and dine on gourmet appetizers. *Guest Favorites:* Wine Country Shrimp, Trio of Beef Tenderloin Sliders, Flatbread Two Ways, Wine Tasting Flights, and White Sangria.

18. Mendocino Terrace
Quick Service

This small outdoor wine bar offers the park's largest selection of wine tasting flights with plenty of seating around the bar. *Guest Favorites:* Variety of Wine Tasting Flights, Mendocino Bar Special (Mimosa), and Mendocino Cheese Box.

19. Sonoma Terrace
Quick Service

Sit under the shade of the old cork tree as you sip on signature wines or more than 15 selections of local craft beers. Formerly the counter service for the *World of Color* picnic dinners, the Sonoma Terrace was transformed in summer 2013 into the ultimate beer-lovers paradise, combining unique bottled beers with a picturesque environment in which to relax and take in the scenery. *Guest Favorites:* Local California Craft Beer in Bottles, Wine by the Glass, Cold Cut Plates, and Warm Bavarian Pretzel.

Pacific Wharf
20. Lucky Fortune Cookery
Quick Service

This small eatery serves up delicious wok style Asian foods at lightning fast speeds. *Guest Favorites:* Asian Rice Bowls, Edamame, Fresh Mango Slices, and Bottled Sapporo Beer.

21. Pacific Wharf Café
Quick Service

This San Francisco themed eatery offers signature soups, unique salads, and delightful sandwiches along the waters surrounding Pacific Wharf. Margaritas can be obtained from the nearby *Rita's Baja Blenders* or draft beer from the *Pacific Wharf Distribution Co.* to complement your meal. *Guest Favorites:* Chinese Chicken Salad, Turkey Pesto Club, and Clam Chowder.

Boudin Bakery Cart

Find a modest selection of freshly baked sourdough breads from the on-site bakery of San Francisco's world famous Boudin bakery company at this small cart outside the *Pacific Wharf Café*. The freshly baked loafs are not only nice to take home, but you will often see guests walking around snacking on them all day. *Guest Favorites:* Classic Freshly Baked Sourdough Breads and Character Shaped Breads.

22. Cocina Cucamonga Mexican Grill
Quick Service

This counter service restaurant serves classic Mexican-American dishes with a modern flair. Expect to find tacos, burritos and tamales here filled with a variety of different meets or vegetables. While you are here try a delightful draft Mexican beer (Dos Equis Amber or Tecate) with your meal. *Guest Favorites:* Fire-Grilled Citrus Chicken, Carne Asada and Chicken Tamale, Soft Tacos Monterrey, and Burrito Sonora.

23. Ghirardelli Soda Fountain
Coffee & Dessert

Enjoy amazing deserts featuring ice cream and Ghirardelli chocolate inside this reproduction of San Francisco's iconic chocolate factory. This combination soda fountain and chocolate shop offers a wide range of ice cream desserts, chocolate candy and unique drinks. *Guest Favorites:* The Earthquake, The World Famous - Hot Fudge Sundae, Nob Hill Chill Shake, and Ice Cream by the Scoop.

24. Rita's Baja Blenders
Outdoor Bar

Rita, no doubt named after the signature margaritas served here, offers up refreshing blended fruit drinks in both alcoholic and non-alcoholic varieties in her small tropically-themed stand. *Guest Favorites:* Margaritas and Non-Alcoholic Blends.

25. Pacific Wharf Distribution Co.
at the Karl Strauss Biergarten
Outdoor Bar

This Karl Strauss delivery truck-turned beer service stand offers a variety of draft Karl Strauss beers. You may pick up a beer here to complement your meal from any of the nearby restaurants. *Guest Favorites:* Karl Strauss Handcrafted Beers and Warm Pretzels.

Paradise Pier
26. Ariel's Grotto
Character Dining Breakfast or World of Color Lunch & Dinner

Dine "under the sea" in this unique character dining experience along the relaxing waters of *Paradise Bay*. Breakfast features a prefix menu while you meet Ariel from *The Little Mermaid* (1989). Later in the day you can enjoy a prix fixe lunch or dinner menu before departing for your specially reserved *World of Color* seats. The restaurant also makes full use of *Cove Bar* upstairs - offering you a wide range of wines, beers and cocktails. Serves a pre-fix *Ariel's Disney Princess Celebration Breakfast,* and a *World of Color* Lunch or Dinner.

27. Cove Bar
Bar & Full Service Dining

Even though it is technically a bar, I'm listing *Cove Bar* here as a full service restaurant because the venue's spectacular food is rivaled only by its amazing bay-front views and relaxing kick up your heals atmosphere. The establishment's full bar, local brews on tap, and small but amazing food menu make this often overlooked culinary treat one of California Adventure's best kept secrets, and one of my favorite dining haunts. Try the lobster nacho's, you won't be disappointed. Yes, you, ..outside the book, I'm talking to you. TRY THE LOBSTER NACHOS! *Guest Favorites:* Lobster Nachos, Trio of Tri-Tip Sliders, Specialty Flatbread Pizza, Locally Brewed Beer, Fine Wines, and Full Bar.

28. Boardwalk Pizza & Pasta
Quick Service

This Italian eatery at the heart of *Paradise Gardens* offers pizza, pasta, salads and draft beer surrounded by a Victorian-era themed outdoor dining courtyard. *Guest Favorites:* Featured Pizza Slice, Chicken Sun-Dried Tomato Pesto, Italian Chef Salad, *60th Anniversary Cake, and Draft Karl Strauss Featured Beer.

29. Paradise Garden Grill
Quick Service

This outdoor stand offers fast access to Mediterranean themed foods inside the *Paradise Gardens* area. Choose your meat and your sauce to create a unique Mediterranean meal. *Guest Favorites:* Mediterranean Skewers, Greek Salad, Baklava.

30. Corn Dog Castle
Quick Service

This medieval castle-themed stand offers freshly-made batter-fried hotdogs, hot link sausages and cheese on a stick. The stand's yellow and red striped awning was designed to evoke the memories of your favorite corn dog toppings, mustard and ketchup. Following a 2011 redesign the stand's banner that flies overhead now features the "Corn Dog King" flying a plane, a tie-in to the *Goofy's Sky School* attraction next door. *Guest Favorites:* Original Corn Dog, Hot-Link Corn Dog, and Cheddar Cheese Stick.

31. Don Toma's
Quick Service

This little old Italian-themed stand in Paradise Pier's Midway area offers you Disney's famous smoked Jumbo Turkey Legs and affordable Chimichangas. *Guest Favorites:* Chimichanga, Jumbo Turkey Leg, and Corn on the Cob (Buttered or Chili-Lime).

32. Hot Dog Hut
Quick Service

This stand conveniently located in the center of the *Midway* offers hot dogs and corn on the cob. *Guest Favorites:* Hot Dog and Corn on the Cob.

33. Paradise Pier Ice Cream Co.
Quick Service
    This little outdoor stand brings back memories of the beach front ice cream stands of yesteryear, allowing you to cool down with soft serve cones and root beer floats on warm days. *Guest Favorites:* Soft Serve Ice Cream and Beachfront Float.

34. Gourmet Coffee
Quick Service
    This outdoor stand in the plaza on the northeast edge of Paradise Park offers a variety of specially coffees and pastries. *Guest Favorites:* Specialty Coffee Drinks and Various Baked Goods.

35. Bayside Brews
Outdoor Bar
    This small-boardwalk themed stand by the *Silly Symphony Swings* offers *Paradise Gardens* patrons easy access to draft beer and wine by the glass. *Guest Favorites:* Beer on Tap, Wine by the Glass, and Warm Jalapeño Cheese-filled Pretzel.

Grizzly Peak Airfield *(formerly Condor Flats)*
36. Smokejumpers Grill
Quick Service
    This aerial firefighters themed restaurant next to the *Soarin' Over California* attraction was created inside an authentic-looking aircraft hanger. The specialties here include gourmet burgers and sides like onion rings and chili fries. *Guest Favorites:* Bacon Cheddar Burger, Chili Cheeseburger, Chili Cheese Fries, Smokin' Onion Rings, Ice Cream Shakes, Red Sangria, and Ice Cold Draft Beer.

37. Refreshment Point
Quick Service
    This California parks themed refreshment stand mixes the roadside vacation stops of yesteryear with fun new technologies. Let the state of the art Coka-Cola machines pour the perfect soda after choosing from a large variety of flavors and mixtures from the device's digital touchscreen interface. It's as much fun to operate these machines as it is to drink the concoctions they create. *Guest Favorites:* Create your own masterpiece by mixing several different soda flavors together.

38. Popcorn
Cart
    This California parks themed cart next to the *Soarin' Over California* hanger offers piping hot popcorn to nearby guests. *Guest Favorites:* Regular or Caramel Popcorn.

World of Color Dining
Dinner Packages

Guests may purchase special World of Color dining packages at the restaurants listed below. These special packages include a 3-course prix fixe dinner and special *World of Color* reserved seating. Visit the World of Color dining page to make a reservation or get more information.

https://disneyland.disney.go.com/dining/world-of-color-dining/

I highly recommend that you reserve your World of Color dinner packages as soon as possible, as they have been known to sell out long before the show starts. Call (714) 781-DINE (3463) or visit the web page above to make your reservation.

Ariel's Grotto
$48.58 (adults) / $26.98 (children 3 to 9).

Wine Country Trattoria
Lunch: $34.55 (adults) / $22.66 (children 3 to 9)
Dinner $ $48.58 (adults) / $26.98 (children 3 to 9).

Carthay Circle Restaurant
Lunch: $44.29 (adults) / $23.76 (children 3 to 9)
Dinner $66.96 (adults) / $27.01 (children 3 to 9).

Downtown Disney & Resort Hotels

Downtown Disney

01. Catal Restaurant
Full Service

Gourmet Mediterranean cuisine served inside a Mediterranean themed Dining room, or on a balcony with an amazing view of Downtown Disney. Great selection of signature cocktails, wine, draft beer, and non-alcoholic cocktails. *Guest Favorites:* Seafood Paella Mixto, Slow Roasted Prime Rib, Filet Migno, Seared Jumbo Diver Scallops, Catalan Seafood Stew. The restaurant accepts reservations at: (866) 9-PATINA.

www.patinagroup.com/catal | (714) 774-4442
1580 Disneyland Dr, Anaheim, CA 92802

02. Downtown Disney Starbucks
Coffee & Dessert

This coffee franchise in a modern designed building was the most recent Starbucks to open in the resort, offering guests the coffee shop's standard fair.

www.starbucks.com | (714) 817-7387
Suite 105, 1570 S. Disneyland Drive, Anaheim, CA 92802

03. Earl of Sandwich
Quick Service

Enjoy amazing hot sandwiches, salads, soups, and bottomless soft drinks . This is my favorite spot for lunch in Downtown Disney, and their refillable cup of coffee (while you dine) is a great morning treat. *Sandwich Favorites:* The Full Montagu, Hawaiian BBQ, Chipotle Chicken Avocado, and Holiday Turkey.

www.espnzone.com | (714) 300-3776
1545 Disneyland Dr., Anaheim, CA 92802

04. ESPN Zone
Full Service

High-end burgers, wings, and other sports-fan's favorites are served in rooms filled with sports memorabilia and art. *Guest Favorites:* Cheese Fries, Highlight Reel Sampler, Barbecue Brisket Sandwich, Barbecue Ribs and Chicken, Smoked Cajun Pasta, Grilled Angus Top Sirloin Steak Salad, and Middle Street Burger.

www.espnzone.com | (714) 300-3776
1545 Disneyland Dr., Anaheim, CA 92802

05. Crossroads @ House of Blues
Full Service

This combination restaurant, bar, and entertainment venue pleases the taste buds with their own twist on classic American dishes. *Guest Favorites:* Voodoo Shrimp, Char Grilled Citrus Marinated Steak Street Tacos, Jambalya with Shrimp, Shrimp and Grits, Lobster Mac & Cheese, Buttermilk Fried Chicken, and Build Your Own Signature Burger.

www.houseofblues.com/anaheim | (714) 778- BLUE (2583)
1530 S. Disneyland Dr., Anaheim, CA 92802

The Voodoo Lounge

The outdoor Voodoo Lounge area offers guests a relaxed atmosphere in which to enjoy cocktails and light meals. It features about the same menu as *Crossroads* above.

06. La Brea Bakery Café
Full Service or Quick Service

Soups, specialty salads, sandwiches, burgers, artisan pizzas, pastas, and amazing baked goods are available in both formal sit-down or quick service Dining rooms. *Guest Favorites:* Eggs in a Nest Artisan Pizza (brunch), La Brea Bakery Cheeseburger, and Turkey Avocado on a Pretzel Roll.

www.labreabakery.com/disneyland-bakery | (714) 490-0233
1556 Disneyland Drive, Anaheim, CA 92802

La Brea Bakery Express

This quick service counter attached to *La Brea Bakery Café* offers a faster way to enjoy freshly baked goods. *Guest Favorites:* Bacon & Egg Panini (breakfast), Quiche Lorraine (breakfast), Grilled Ham & Cheese Panini, Artichoke & Gruyere Pizza Ciccione, and assorted specialty soups.

07. Marceline's Confectionery
Dessert

This candy shop features hand made candies and baked goods. It was named after the small town Walt Disney grew up in; *Marceline, Missouri. Guest Favorites:* assorted jelly beans, Disney Theme Candy Apples, and Assorted Fudge.

Halloween Themes: Look for *The Nightmare Before Christmas (1993)* and other Halloween decorations hanging throughout the shop.

1580 Disneyland Dr #104, Anaheim, CA 92802 | (714) 300-7922

08. Naples Ristorante e Pizzeria
Full Service

A classic Italian restaurant featuring salads, pastas, seafood dishes, and of course authentic Neapolitan pizza. *Guest Favorites:* Garganelli Pasta, Gnocchi, Conchiglie, Pesce del Giorno (fish of the day), and Build Your Own Pizzas.

www.patinagroup.com/naples/ | (714) 776-6200

1550 Disneyland Dr, Anaheim, CA 92802

Napolini

This small quick service counter attached to *Naples Ristorante* offers a faster way to get your classic Italian pizza. *Guest Favorites:* Classic Cobb Cold Sandwich, Quattro Fromaggi Pizza By-The-Slice, and Vesuviano Calzoni.

09. Rainforest Cafe
Full Service

The unique rainforest setting INSIDE this restaurant is as entertaining as it is informative. Animatronic animals add movement to this unique forest setting as you enjoy burgers, seafood, sandwiches, and more. *Guest Favorites:* Volcanic Cobb Salad, Guacamole Burger, and Ribs, Steak & Shrimp Trio.

www.rainforestcafe.com | (714) 772-0413
1515 S. Disneyland Drive, Anaheim, CA 92807

10. Ralph Brennan's Jazz Kitchen
Full Service

This unique creole eatery features all of the dishes that made New Orleans famous. Live Jazz performances fill the air on select nights. *Guest Favorites:* Bourbon Street Sampler for Two, Gumbo Ya-Ya, Chicken Etouffée, BBQ Shrimp & Grits, Fried Chicken Po-Boy, and the Three Course Prix-fixe Dinner.

www.rbjazzkitchen.com | (714) 776-5200
1590 South Disneyland Drive, Anaheim, California 92802

Jazz Kitchen Express

This quick service version of the Jazz Kitchen features speedy service and delicious creole classics. And it's a lot cheaper than the regular restaurant too. For an authentic taste of New Orleans you MUST try the Beignets. *Guest Favorites:* New Orleans Platter, Gumbo Ya Ya, Jazz Kitchen Jambalaya, Classic Red Beans and Rice, Fried Popcorn Shrimp Po-Boy, and Original New Orleans Beignets

11. Tortilla Jo's
Full Service

Gourmet style Mexican cuisine favorites. Don't leave without sampling one of Jo's many specialty Margaritas or unique cocktails. This is also a great place to spend Happy Hour. And a number of great non-alcoholic alternatives (such as traditional Horchata, Agua de Tamarindo, and Agua de Jamaica) let everyone in your party enjoy Jo's. Reservations are accepted online or by phone. *Guest Favorites:* Tableside Guacamole, Ceviche Huachinango, Fajita de Tres, Steak Ranchera, Jo's Carnitas, and Enchiladas Suizas.

www.patinagroup.com/tortillaJos | www.facebook.com/tortillajos
1510 Disneyland Dr., Anaheim CA 92802 | (714) 535-5000

Taqueria at Tortilla Jo's

This quick service counter serves affordable taco, burrito, and other Mexican cuisine plates quickly to customers on the go. Don't leave without trying the Chips & Guacamole and the Mexican Brownie with Chocolate Sauce. *Guest Favorites:* Chilaquiles (breakfast), Carnitas Nachos, Tacos, and Burritos (with a choice of Meat).

12. Uva Bar & Café
Full Service

The Mediterranean-themed cuisine at Uva Bar & Café continues in their unique October-Fest menu throughout October. It may seem like an odd combination of ingredients, but try the Uva Street Fries w/ fried organic egg - You won't regret it. *Guest Favorites:* Chilaquiles (breakfast), Trio of Mediterranean Dips, Lamb Burger, and Albondigas and Brava Potatoes.

www.patinagroup.com/uva/ | (714) 774-4442
1580 Disneyland Drive, Anaheim CA 92802

Grand California Hotel
13. Napa Rose
Full Service

This upscale restaurant features California cuisine at it's finest. Gourmet seafood, stake, and poultry dishes await you here, as well as rare regional wines. Reservations available at (714) 781-DINE. *Starter Favorites:* Wood-fired Pizzetta of the Season, Seven Sparkling Sins, and The Sizzling Beach Rock. *Entrée Favorites:* "Smiling Tiger Salad", Herb-roasted Colorado Lamb Chop and Braised Lamb Brisket, Pan-roasted Angus Beef Filet Mignon, and Berkshire Pork Loin and Laughing Bird Shrimp.

Napa Rose Lounge

This beautiful lounge inside the Napa Rose restaurant features seats alongside an exquisite fireplace and other relaxing seating. If you are looking for a romantic spot to bring that special someone, this is the place. The bar features some very rare and unique beers on tap, as well as a nice variety of wines and spirits. *Guest Favorites:* Pappardelle Pasta, Pan-roasted Diver Scallops, and Wood-fired Pizzetta of the Season.

14. Storytellers Cafe
Full Service

This California folklore themed restaurant serves an amazing breakfast buffet with Disney characters present to brighten up your day. Call (714) 781-DINE for reservations. *Guest Favorites:* Breakfast or Dinner Buffet, Sautéed Clams and Mussels with Spanish Chorizo, Grilled 10 oz. New York Strip, Bone-In Pork Chop, and Grilled Lobster Tail Salad.

15. White Water Snacks
Quick Service

This restaurant features some unique takes on classic American fair, offering hamburgers topped with Carnitas, chicken nachos, and sandwiches with delicious ingredients. It's actually one of my favorite stops, and it's also one of the few park restaurants that still serves French fries alongside its burgers. The restaurant is so close to Disney California Adventure that you can see Grizzly Peak's *Scenic Route 49* walking trail just a few feet away from the restaurant's outdoor dining tables. *Guest Favorites:* Carnitas Angus Cheeseburger, Shredded Beef or Chicken Nachos, and Char-Broiled Chicken Sandwich.

16. Hearthstone Lounge
Bar

This popular bar inside the Grand California Hotel features the usual selection of mixed drinks, spirits, and fine wines. A limited selection of draft beer is also available here. Inside, the atmosphere is relaxed and the seating is plentiful. Outside, seating around the enormous Hearthstone fireplace should not be missed. *Guest Favorites:* Robusto Flatbread, Seafood Cocktail, Margherita Flatbread, and Sticky Spare Ribs.

Disneyland Hotel
17. Steakhouse 55
Full Service

Named after the year Disneyland opened, this fine Dining restaurant offers amazing cuts of steak, chops, and seafood. Try the "Chef's Tasting Menu", you will not be disappointed. And the "60 Carat Chocolate Diamond" desert is a nice complement to Disneyland's 60th Anniversary Celebration. Reservations accepted at (714) 781-DINE. *Guest Favorites:* Sautéed Sea Scallops (appetizer), Maine Lobster Bisque, Porterhouse Steak, Dry Rub Bone-In Rib-Eye, Filet Mignon, Slow-roasted Prime Rib, and Cold Water Lobster Tail.

The Lounge at Steakhouse 55

The casual lounge attached to the front of the hotel's famous steak restaurant offers a wide selection of wine, cocktails, and beer on tap. A full dining menu is also available here. *Guest Favorites:* Chimichurri Flat Iron Steak Salad, Meat Lover's Flatbread, Smothered Potato Chips, French Dip, and Maine Lobster Roll Sliders. New *60th Anniversary Celebration Cocktails* include the Magical Diamond Cocktail and Diamond Glow-tini.

18. Goofy's Kitchen
Full Service

Breakfast and dinner buffets offer "all-you-care-to-enjoy" American fair and a chance to meet Chef Goofy in person. Reservations are recommended by calling (714) 781-DINE. *Guest Favorites:*

19. Tangaroa Terrace
Quick Service

Experience casual island dining in this Polynesian themed restaurant that sits above the pools of the Disneyland hotel. Tropical music, tiki torches, and quick service foods such as Hawaiian cheeseburgers and slow roasted pork sandwiches await you here. Both indoor and outdoor seating on a tiki-themed deck are available here.

Guest Favorites: Loco Moco (breakfast), Ahi Poke, Angus Hawaiian Cheeseburger, Slow-roasted Kālua-style Pork Sandwich, Kālua-style Pork Flatbread, and Big Island Flatbread.

20. The Coffee House
Coffee & Dessert

Open only in the morning, this small shop offers piping hot coffee and a variety of baked goods to kick start your day. *Guest Favorites:*

21. Trader Sam's Enchanted Tiki Bar
Bar & Full Service

This amazing bar should not be missed. Full of secrets and surprises, Trader Sam's offers draft beer, wine, and a large variety of very unique and creative cocktails in an amazingly decorated tiki themed space. I'll even let you in on one of the secrets: You may think you're watching the tiki masks on the wall, but with closer inspection you will soon get the overwhelming feeling that it is THEY who are watching YOU. *Guest Favorites:* Pu Pu Platter, Kālua-style Pork Flatbread, Big Island Flatbread, Angus Hawaiian Cheeseburger, and Slow-roasted Kālua-style Pork Sandwich.

Paradise Pier Hotel
22. Disney's PCH Grill
Full Service

The Surf's Up! Breakfast Buffet with Disney characters and Beach Side Bonfire Dinner Buffet round out your only major restaurant choice inside the Paradise Pier hotel. Try the "Dry-rubbed Smoked Tri-Tip Beef" and "Littleneck Clams, Chorizo & Potatoes." Reservations are recommended: (714) 781-DINE.

23. Surfside Lounge
Bar

Cocktails, beer, wine, and some quick snack-type meals are offered at the laid-back lounge in the hotels main lobby area. *Guest Favorites:* Wood-fired Breakfast Flat Bread, Beer-battered Onion Rings, Crispy-breaded Cauliflower (better than it sounds), Baja California Caesar, Albondigas Soup, La Mesa Southwest Burger, and and Grilled Chicken Sandwich.

24. The Sand Bar
Bar

Enjoy cocktails, beer, wine, and a few snack foods at this pool-side bar. Open seasonally.

Shopping

The Disneyland Resort has a large variety of shops to choose from, carrying an eclectic range of merchandise. But selling souvenirs is not the only function of these stores, and if you take a little bit of time to really explore them you can find a myriad of secrets and historical information hidden inside them. From detailed reproductions of life in the 1890's to hidden views of galactic heros, the shops at the resort contain unparalleled details to delight adventurers young and old. Use this guide not only to locate the Disneyland merchandise you are looking for, but also to extend your Disneyland adventure by seeking out many of the little details that make this theme park the fully immersive experience it has become. *Top Halloween Items* have also been listed under each store listing for your shopping pleasure. Happy shopping!

Disneyland

Main Street USA

01. Newsstands

These small old-fashioned newsstands let guests purchase last minute souvenirs, candy, snacks, personalized mouse ears, hats, pins and postcards just inside and outside the Disneyland entry gates. Although the shops do not have a large selection, this is a great place to get that last minute item as you leave the park. Four different Newsstands exist in Main Street USA; with stands just outside the *entry gates* west of the turnstiles, just inside the gates to the west of the turnstiles, on the west side of *Town Square* after passing though the tunnel under the *Disneyland Railroad* tracks and on the east side of *Town Square*. *Guest Favorites:* Disney Pins, Postcards, Candy, and Snacks.

Top Halloween Items: A few last minute Halloween gifts such as Pins and Light Up Jack-O-Lantern Wands.

02. Disneyana & The Disney Gallery

This combination souvenir shop and art gallery sits on the edge of *Town Square*. One of a kind Disney artwork can be seen on display and for sale in this unique shop, with different Disney artists featured in seasonally changing art shows in the rear of the building. The shop's authentic 1916 bank vault is often used to highlight special art collections and the former bank teller windows are now used as the store's checkout counter. Guests may also browse and select artwork prints from automated Art on Demand kiosks found near the check out counters at the front of the shop. *Guest Favorites:* Original Disney-Inspired Paintings, Models of Disneyland Buildings, and Art on Demand.

Halloween Themes: The gallery typically features a spooky Halloween themed show. 2014 featured the *Ghostly Materials* art show, with original Haunted Mansion themed art works for viewing and sale. Be sure to stop by and take a look at the ghoulish collection of original paintings, prints, dioramas, and hand crafted figurines found here.

Top Halloween Items: Halloween Themed Pokit Pals (decorative cast resin boxes), and Haunted Mansion Figurines, Signs, Original Artworks, Keys, and Mugs.

03. The Mad Hatter

This shop features a huge selection of specialty Disney hats and mouse ears. Choose from wizard, princess, Goofy and many other Disney hat choices. Walking around Disneyland wearing mouse ears with your name stitched on them is a tradition leading all the way back to the park's opening. At the Mad Hatter shop this tradition is continued with personalized embroidery available for hats and ears purchased inside the store. *Guest Favorites:* Custom Embroidered Mouse Ears and Disney Clothing.

Top Halloween Items: Halloween Ears Hats, Ear Headbands, and *The Nightmare Before Christmas* (1993) Hats.

04. Disneyland Emporium
101 Main Street

As the largest store on Main Street, the *Emporium* contains just about every souvenir available to buy at Disneyland. You can find books, clothing, toys, key chains, Vinylmation, photo frames, candy, snacks, mugs, tea, coffee, and pins in this enormous shopping space. The shop also merges seamlessly with the *Crystal Arcade* at its north end. *Guest Favorites:* Disney Mugs, Trading Pins, and Autograph Books.

Top Halloween Items: This shop has just about everything Halloween-related that you can find at other shops throughout the park.

05. Crystal Arcade

The Crystal Arcade is a collection of several different stores joined together in one large space, including a rather significant entry area filled with Disney products to purchase. It also provides alternate access to the *Emporium, The Storybook Store* toy shop, the *Jewelry Shop* and the *Fortuosity Shop. Guest Favorites:* Plush Animals, Autograph Books, and Large Selection of Disney Pins.

06. Jewelry Shop

A wide assortment of jewelry and watches are available in this little old-time Jewelry Shop. Prices range from very cheap to very expensive, with rings available for as little as $4 inside the shop. If you are in the market to buy jewelry at Disneyland, this should be your first stop. *Guest Favorites:* Custom Beaded Jewelry, Disney Watches, Rings, Bracelets, Ear Rings, and Necklaces.

07. Fortuosity Shop

Rare gifts, jewelry, curios and watches adorn this fancy little wood-paneled shop. You can also find tee-shirts, unique purses and scarves here. Inside you can watch featured artists creating unique drawings of Disney characters and scenes, which are then shrunk down and placed inside "Artisan Watches" to be sold as one of a kind hand illustrated watch faces. The shop also has a large selection of cast resin *Pokitpals*, which depict popular Disney characters, places and scenes on small magnetically closed boxes that can be used to store small items in your pocket. *Guest Favorites:* High End Disney Watches, Artisan Watches, Pokitpals, and Men's Dress Hats.

Halloween Themes: This store goes all out with it's Halloween decorations, and it's famous for its hundreds of black ravens looking down from perches high within the shop.

Top Halloween Items: Disney villain themed bags, purses, and clothing.

08. The Storybook Store

Located inside the Crystal Arcade building, this toy shop features Disney versions of popular board games, figures, dolls and playsets of iconic Disneyland vehicles such as the monorail, parking tram and Disneyland railroad. The 1890's toy shop motif gives it the look and feel of a toy store from another time. *Guest Favorites:* Disney Editions of Popular Board Games, Toy Guns & Swords, and Disneyland Playsets.

Costume Items: Toy Swords, Guns, and Bows to complement your Halloween costumes.

09. Disney Showcase

Children's costumes inspired by many favorite Disney characters are the highlight of this clothing shop on Main Street. Here kids can dress up like pirates, Toy Story characters, Carsland mechanics, Minnie Mouse, princesses and more. Figurines, plush animals and a limited selection of toys are also available at the shop. Disney Character Costumes and Disney Figurines.

10. Main Street Magic Shop

This magic shop features a vary large selection of magic tricks, gags, magic books, puppets, masks and, of course, the requisite rubber chicken. Browse the enormous collection of tricks on display along the shops southern wall and feel free ask the store's expert staff any questions about magic you may have. The shop is staffed with actual magicians who can demonstrate a trick for you after you purchase it. *Guest Favorites:* Magic Tricks, Gags, Magic Books, and Puppets.

Costume Items: High-end Latex Monster Masks, Creepy Puppets, Elvis Sideburn Glasses, and a full body Pink Gorilla Costume.

11. 20th Century Music Company

This small-town music shop offers Disney pins, music CDs, movies on DVD & Blu-Ray discs and other select merchandise such as Disney-themed iPhone covers. *Guest Favorites:* Disney Animated Features on Blu-Ray and Disney Music CDs.

12. Disney Clothiers, Ltd

This replica of an 1890's clothing store mixes the display of antique clothing and accessories with the sale of modern Disneyland inspired apparel. *Guest Favorites:* Tee-Shirts & Sweatshirts, Disneyland Messenger Bags, and Inexpensive Jewelry.

Top Halloween Items: *The Nightmare Before Christmas* (1993) Tee Shirts, Hats, and Scarves, Minie Mouse Dresses, and Día de los Muertos themed clothing.

13. Castle Bros.

This collegiate-themed shop offers sweatshirts, tee-shirts, jerseys, hats and other clothing items presented inside a collage-of-yesteryear theme. Guests get the chance to view old-time collage memorabilia as they peruse the modern clothing for sale in the shop. *Guest Favorites:* Disneyland Track Suits, Tee Shirts, and Sweatshirts.

14. Chester Drawer's

This children's clothing store is found behind the *Castle Bros.* shop. As the stores "Togs for Toddlers" slogan infers, this shop offers a large variety of Disney and non-Disney theme clothing for toddlers and young children. The shop's stock will often change seasonally, with Halloween costumes and Christmas fare offered around the holidays. *Guest Favorites:* Princess Dresses, Kid's Tee-Shirts & Hats, and Children's Purses.

Top Halloween Items: Halloween themed shirts and dresses for kids.

15. Crystal Arts

Elaborate crystal castles, detailed figurines, hand-made statues and beautiful jewelry can be found inside this unique Disneyland shop. Guests may purchase fine crystal cups, mugs, plates and collectibles here. Custom engraving is always free on crystal items. While you are there be sure not to miss the giant crystal gem and vases on display in the shops front window. *Guest Favorites:* Crystal Jewelry, Color Figurines, and Jeweled Tiaras.

Top Halloween Items: Crystal Figurines of Dragons and other scary creatures, and Crystal Embedded iPhone Cases Featuring Pirates of the Caribbean or Other Scary Characters.

16. Silhouette Studio

Creating hand-cut silhouettes is a Disneyland tradition. At Main Street's Silhouette Studio individual or group portrait Silhouettes are created for you in a minute or less while you wait. The silhouettes are $9 per person for TWO copies of your silhouette, and it's an additional $9 to add a character silhouette such as Mickey or Minnie Mouse to your image. The classic black and gold frames are an additional $9.95. Smaller framed silhouettes of Disney characters are available pre-made for $6.45. The silhouette shop is able to create all of these unique keepsakes very quickly. They'll even hold on to them for you until you leave the park.

17. China Closet

Fine seasonal gifts such as Christmas ornaments, porcelain & china collectibles, tea pot sets, mugs, speciality teas and ground or whole coffee are available inside this quaint shop. The shop has two different entrances, one on *Main Street* and one around the corner in the alley that crosses *Main Street*. *Guest Favorites:* Fancy Snow Globes, Disney Figurines, and Disney Inspired Fine China.

Top Halloween Items: Limited Edition Collectible Halloween Figurines, *The Nightmare Before Christmas* (1993) Christmas stocking and ornaments, and Haunted Mansion Bottle Stopper, Coaster Set, jewelry Box, Hour Glass, and Candle Holder.

18. Main Street Photo Supply Co.

As it states above the shop's main entrance, "A Picture Is Worth a Thousand Words." This old-time camera shop was created to take care of your every photographic need and send you home with a lifetime of memories. Use this little shop to get your Disneyland photopass photos developed. While you're there you can purchase a number of photo-related supplies such as batteries, memory cards, picture frames and photo albums. *Guest Favorites:* Photopass Photo Development, Camera Memory Cards, Batteries, Photo Frames, and Albums.

Adventureland

19. Tropical Imports

This tropical-style street bazaar sits between the entrance and exit to Adventureland's famous Jungle Cruise attraction. In addition to the cold beverages, fresh fruits and other healthy snacks it offers weary travelers there's also a small selection of adventurous souvenirs such as rubber snakes and plush animals. *Guest Favorites:* Rubber Creatures, Plush Animals, and Fresh Fruit.

Top Halloween Items: Scary Rubber Creatures.

20. Adventureland Bazaar

The Adventureland Bazaar's enchanting old-world theme has drawn in guests since Disneyland's opening day in 1955. The shop sits directly across from the *Enchanted Tiki Room's* exit, offering unique collectibles from adventurous locations around the globe. Designed to resemble a street bizarre from an exotic local, guests can find hand-made African musical instruments, African masks & art, jungle-themed mouse ears, hats, tee-shirts, plush animals, toys and Vinylmation throughout the shops rugged sandstone interior. *Guest Favorites:* African Drums & Other Musical Instruments, African Masks, and Wind Chimes.

Top Halloween Items: Pirate swords, guns, flags, and accessory kits, perfect to add to your Halloween costume. They also have a small selection of Día de los Muertos shirts.

21. South Seas Traders

Connected to both the *Adventureland Bazaar* and the *Indiana Jones Adventure Outpost*, the South Seas Traders shop offers a variety of beach-themed clothing and merchandise for adventurers visiting from around the world. *Guest Favorites:* Adventure Clothing, Hats, and Vinylmation.

Top Halloween Items: Spooky pins and adventure clothing.

22. Indiana Jones Adventure Outpost

This Indiana Jones inspired shop features everything the young adventurer needs, from toy guns to fedora hats. The shop offers toys, clothing, souvenirs and a very limited Disney pin collection. You can also find official Indiana Jones merchandise, bags of gem stones from the Chamber of Earthly Treasures and adventure maps. *Guest Favorites:* Toy Guns, Swords, Whips, Indiana Jones Clothing, and Rubber Creatures.

Costume Items: Indiana Jones themed hats, whips, guns, spiders, snakes, maps, and costume sets, perfect for dressing up like an adventurer for Halloween.

New Orleans Square

23. Port Royal

This Caribbean seaport themed "Curios & Curiosities" shop features pirate and *Haunted Mansion* inspired merchandise including t-shirts, sweatshirts, hats, backpacks, mugs and a limited selection of pins. The shop's stock changes seasonally but they usually have a large supply of *Nightmare Before Christmas* merchandise on hand, particularly around the Halloween and Christmas seasons. *Guest Favorites:* Hunted Mansion Playing Cards and Board Games, The King's Ransom (fill-yourself jewel bags), and Fancy Dress Hats for Men and Women.

Halloween Themes: Look above merchandise shelves and up along the ceiling for a myriad of spooky skulls, jack-o-lanterns, cob webs, and other Halloween decorations.

Top Halloween Items: A very large selection of *The Nightmare Before Christmas* (1993) and *Haunted Mansion* merchandise.

24. Pieces of Eight

This *Pirates of the Caribbean* themed shop next to the exit of the *Pirates of the Caribbean* attraction offers a large selection of pirate gear, hats, clothing, toys, & pins. *Guest Favorites:* Iron Keys from Pirates of the Caribbean, Pirate Swords, Guns, Hats, Boots, Eye Patches, and Outfits.

Top Halloween Items: Pirate or Pirate Princess Costumes, Hats, Swords, Guns, Eye Patches, and other gear. They also carry an interesting selection of Día de los Muertos Shirts, Bags, and Purses.

25. Cristal d'Orleans

Famous for it's engraving on crystal products purchased in the shop, this store offers a wide variety of fine crystal and glassware products similar to those found at the *Crystal Arts* shop on *Main Street*. *Guest Favorites:* Personalized Crystal Engravings, Crystal Figurines, Crystal Jewelry.

Top Halloween Items: Crystal Figurines of Dragons and other scary creatures, and Crystal Embedded iPhone Cases Featuring Pirates of the Caribbean or Other Scary Characters.

26. Le Bat en Rouge

This is primarily a woman's clothing store with a few gothic and *Nightmare Before Christmas* items thrown in. The unique atmosphere created by the shop's intriguing dark red exterior and various eerie looking artifacts make this a destination that should not be missed. *Guest Favorites:* Nightmare Before Christmas collectibles, Women's Hats, Purses, and Clothing.

Halloween Themes: This shop maintains a spooky Halloween feel year round, be sure not to miss it.

27. La Mascarade d'Orleans

This shop recently traded it's Disney Pins and Vinylmation in for a specialty jewelry collection hosted by Pandora jewelers (pandora.net).

Top Halloween Items: This shop has it's usual fair, but the decorative Chat Noir (Black Cat) Tin of specialty soap would make an excellent Halloween gift for that special someone.

28. Mlle. Antoinette's Parfumerie
20 & 24 Orleans St

This little shop specializes in a large selection of high-end designer perfumes. Disneyland created a partnership with LVMH (Moët Hennessy Louis Vuitton), an outside perfume company based in France, to provide this one of a kind perfume shopping experience inside the park. A large variety of perfumes are available to browse, sample and buy in this unique store. In addition to classic fragrances from Givenchy, Guerlain, Christian Dior, Acqua di Parma, and Emilio Pucci the shop offers two scents that are exclusive to Disney theme parks. *Guest Favorites:* Fine Imported Perfumes, Holiday Perfume Sets, Scents Exclusive to Disney Theme Parks.

29. Personalized Parasols

The Personalized Parasols stand is located towards the end of Orleans St, near the French Market Restaurant. It offers personalized, embroidered parasols. The parasols are $17.95 for a large parasol with one name and hearts (or flower) accents, or $11.95 for a mini parasol with one name and hearts (or flower) accents. An additional $5 is charged for optional artwork such as a rainbow or carrousel horse.

Top Halloween Items: Look for hand drawn Halloween designs on display at the parasol cart throughout the season. A large selection is available to choose from including: bats, cobwebs, spiders, grave stones, vampires, werewolves, and more. More and more designs will become available as it gets closer to Halloween. Ask an artist at the cart about what is currently available. Some artists will also even draw unique art on the spot for you.

30. Jack Skeleton Carriage Cart

This specialty stand shows up during the Halloween and Christmas seasons over by the *Haunted Holidays* edition of the *Haunted Mansion*. It features Jack Skeleton themed souvenirs including hats, sweatshirts, mugs, bobble heads and other *The Nightmare Before Christmas* (1993) items.

Top Halloween Items: A variety of *The Nightmare Before Christmas* (1993) themed items.

Critter Country

31. Briar Patch

This *Splash Mountain* inspired shop near the entrance to *Critter Country* offers a very large selection of themed hats and mouse ears, as well as a limited selection of barrettes, combs and crowns. Custom embroidery of hats and ears is available with a choice between *Basic Embroidery* ($3) or *Premium Embroidery* ($7). *Guest Favorites:* Custom Embroidered Mouse Ears, Disney Theme Hats, and Princess Crowns.

Top Halloween Items: Halloween Ear Hats, Ear Headbands, and *The Nightmare Before Christmas* (1993) Hats.

32. Prof. Barnaby Owl's Photographic Art Studio

This little stand just outside *Splash Mountain*'s exit primarily sells prints of the photos taken on the attraction. Guests can also find frames, cameras, photo albums, autograph books and other photo related accessories here. *Guest Favorites:* Splash Mountain Photos, Photos Frames, and Autograph Books.

33. Pooh Corner

This combination candy store, bakery and souvenir shop sells *Winnie the Pooh* themed plush animals as well as other souvenirs, clothing, & pins. *Guest Favorites:* *Winnie the Pooh* Plush Animals, T-Shirts & Sweat Shirts, and Custom Bead Jewelry Station.

Top Halloween Items: Halloween Mugs, Pins, Statues, and an Infant Tigger Onsie Costume.

Frontierland

34. Westward Ho Trading Company

This Frontierland store boasts the largest selection of pins in the park. Wall after wall of pins are available for purchase here and cast members are always ready to trade. Guests can also find a variety of sheriff badges with unique messages on them and a few other Wild West themed souvenir. *Guest Favorites:* Disney Pins & Pin Starter Kits, Pin Lanyards, Folders, & Bags , and Sheriff Badges.

Top Halloween Items: Halloween Pins, Pin Sets, and Lanyards.

Costume Items: Speciality Sheriff badges.

35. The Leather Shop

These two famous Frontierland stands located in front of the *Pioneer Mercantile* offer guests a large variety of leather products that can be personalized with names or messages. Cast members inside the two stands are ready to help guests select the perfect leather product and then personalize them while you wait. Both stands, located on either side of the *Pioneer Mercantile* entrance, tend to carry the same products. Guest can find hats, belts, buckles, bracelets, key chains and even sheriff badges here. *Guest Favorites:* Personalized Leather Goods and a Sheriff Badge with your name on it.

36. Pioneer Mercantile

Originally named Davy Crockett's Pioneer Mercantile after the famous home-spun hero of the American frontier, the Pioneer Mercantile supplies young frontiersmen and frontierswomen with Davy's signature coonskin cap among other adventure supplies. The coonskin cap fad dates back to the 1950's when Disney promoted their Davy Crockett television series heavily throughout Frontierland and American children went crazy over the unconventional headwear. Although the fad is long gone, the caps are sill for sale today. Don't be surprised to see adults wearing the caps to celebrate the heroes of their youth and kids wearing them to become new members of a time-honored Disneyland tradition. The shop also sells a large variety of toys, collectibles, clothing, hats and mugs. Personalized mouse ears can also be purchased and embroidered here. *Guest Favorites:* Coonskin Caps, Personalized Mouse Ears, Pocahontas Merchandise.

Top Halloween Items: Halloween Figurine Statues, Hats, Scarves, and Plush Animals.

37. Bonanza Outfitters

This storefront facade shares a common shop space with the *Silver Spur Supplies* and the *Crockett & Russel Hat Co.*, creating the illusion of three separate buildings while camouflaging the single large clothing store that runs behind all of them. The store stocks a large variety of clothing including hats, shirts, purses and more. *Guest Favorites:* Sweatshirts, Tee Shirts, Hats, and Waterproof Sandals.

Fantasyland

38. Fairy Tale Treasures

Found between the *Royal Theatre* and the exit to the *Royal Hall* in the new *Fantasy Fair* area, this medieval princess-themed souvenir shop offers guests the opportunity to buy royal gowns and knightly swords in a fairy tale atmosphere. *Guest Favorites:* Princess Dresses & Accessories, Knight Swords, and Princess Autograph Books.

39. Enchanted Chamber

This small toy shop is located inside *Sleeping Beauty Castle* and offers a variety of dolls and toys primarily for girls. The shop's castle ambience and princess theme delights girls of all ages. *Guest Favorites:* Princess Themed Play Sets, Princess Coloring and Sticker Books, and Miniature Disney Hats.

40. Bibbidi Bobbidi Boutique

This one of a kind Disneyland shop offers kids costumes and costume accessories to transform young ones into their favorite Disney characters. Here you can purchase a variety of dresses, crowns, hats, play jewelry, swords, shields, make up kits and other costume accessories for girls and boys. *Makeover Services* are also available to transform your child into a knight or princess. *Guest Favorites:* Magic Wands, Swords and Shields, and Costumes and Dresses.

Top Halloween Items: Halloween Themed Mouse Ear Headbands, Halloween Mini Mouse Dresses, and Matching Orange Witch Hats. This shop also carries its usual stock of costuming apparel and accessory to turn children into knights and princesses, the perfect place to get a Halloween costume.

41. Castle Heraldry Shoppe

This specialized gift shop allows guests to look up, view and purchase their family's coats of arms and family history in a building just inside the gates to *Sleeping Beauty Castle*. Family crests can be placed on tee-shirts, hats, golf towels, metal shields, framed parchment and embroidered wall hangings. A variety of decorative metal swords, daggers, axes and shields can also be purchased at the shop and then mailed to your home. These weapons are not toys however, and they are not meant for children. While you are inside the shop take a look at the antique suits of armor and other reproductions of medieval antiquity on display outside and inside the store. *Guest Favorites:* Family Coat of Arms, Family History, Fancy Metal Swords, Daggers, Axes, and Shields.

42. Carrousel Candies

This medieval carriage themed souvenir stand is found in the courtyard of *Sleeping Beauty Castle*. It used to supply a large variety of candy, but now it offers a combination of souvenirs, toys and a small selection of candy and prepackaged baked goods. *Guest Favorites:* Glow in The Dark Souvenirs, Minnie's Bake Shop Character Cookies, and Disney Themed Candy.

Top Halloween Items: Halloween Pins and Pin Sets.

43. Stromboli's Wagon

This "Pinocchio's Village" inspired covered wagon offers hats, toys and other souvenirs along the tail end of Fantasyland just before reaching the *Big Thunder Trail* that leads into *Frontierland*. Stromboli also sells autograph books, bubble makers, sunblock and a fairly good selection of candy at his wagon. *Guest Favorites:* Plush Animals, Disney Hats, and Autograph Books.

Top Halloween Items: Halloween Mouse Ear Head Bands, Orange Mouse Ear Witch Hats, and Light Up Skull Lanyards.

44. Mad Hatter

This famous Fantasyland hat shop offers a huge selection of unique hats & mouse ears. Custom embroidery of your name is available for all ears purchased in the shop. *Guest Favorites:* Mouse Ears with Custom Embroidery and Disney Hats.

Top Halloween Items: Halloween Ear Hats, Themed Hats, and Ear Headbands.

45. Le Petit Chalet

This small stand on the Eastern edge of Fantasyland offers Disney hats, mouse ears and toys. Like other Disneyland hat shops, custom embroidery services are available on mouse ears purchased at the shop. The shop was designed to match the Swiss theme of the nearby *Matterhorn Bobsleds*. *Guest Favorites:* Mouse Ears with Custom Embroidery, Disney Hats, and Autograph Books.

Top Halloween Items: Halloween Ear Hats, Themed Hats, and Ear Headbands.

46. Fantasy Faire Gifts

This open air souvenir stand along the path to *It's a Small World* features a limited selection of toys and other souvenirs, film, postcards and candy. The stand itself has a medieval Fantasyland tent theme. Plush Disney Characters, Light Up Swords, Candy, and Snacks.

47. "it's a small world" Toy Shop

This toy shop at the exit to the 'It's a Small World' attraction is primarily geared towards girls, although it does have some toys for boys as well. The shop features collectible dolls, figures, hot wheels, plush animals, Disney versions of popular board games, a limited selection of Disney pins and other Disney theme toys in an *It's a Small World* themed building. Disney Princess Doll Sets, Plush Animals, and Princess Crowns.

48. Fairytale Faces

This station is located next to the *Fairytale Scripts* stand and across the walkway from the *Matterhorn Bobsleds* attraction. Children can have their faces painted in a variety of colors, designs, and styles. Choose your favorite style from the sample photos provided at the booth, and then sit down to have your face turned into a walking work of art. The face painting costs $12-$17 depending upon the design you choose.

Top Halloween Items: Ask about a spooky Halloween face paint designs at the booth.

49. Fairytale Scripts

Guests can have their name made into a unique work of art at the *Fairytale Scripts* stand in Fantasyland, with each letter of their name crafted into a unique illustration. You may choose between having only the first letter of your name illustrated or every letter in your name made into a unique character. Plenty of samples are on hand to give guests a preview of what their name art may look like. Names with a single letter made into a unique drawing cost $18, where as names with 2-4 letters made into unique drawings cost $35, and longer names can cost $40 and up. You can also have your name artwork framed for you at the booth (Mats $10, Frames $35 and up). Look for the Fairytale Arts specialty stand next to Edelweiss Snacks at the north end of Fantasyland. The stand was also designed to match the Swiss theme of the nearby Matterhorn Bobsleds attraction.

Top Halloween Items: Name art that uses Fall themed colors and Halloween elements are now available.

Mickey's Toontown
50. Gag Factory / Toontown Five & Dime
This large souvenir shop has two different entrances with two different names for the single store that occupies this building. The shop features *Disney pins*, *vinylmation*, magic tricks, plush animals, Toon apparel, very few gag gifts and a variety of other toys and souvenirs. There is also a "make your own necklace or bracelet" station where guests can mix and match beads and charms to create their own unique souvenir and the shop's "Stich-O-Matic" can add your name to Disney hats and mouse ears purchased in the shop. *Guest Favorites:* Custom Embroidered Mouse Ears, Plush Animals, Collectible Packs, and Disney Toys.

Top Halloween Items: Halloween Pins and Vinylmation.

Tomorrowland
51. Little Green Men Store Command
The *Buzz Lightyear Astro Blasters* attraction exits into this Buzz Lightyear themed shop. The store offers a very large selection of Disney pins to choose from, as well as Buzz Lightyear and other Toy Story themed figures, toys and clothing. The shop is decorated with Buzz Lightyear murals and a matching bright green and purple color scheme. Disney pin trading between guests is available at tables provided just outside the shop. *Guest Favorites:* Disney Pins, Buzz Lightyear Toys, and Plush Animals.

Top Halloween Items: Halloween Pins, Pin Sets, and Lanyards.

52. The Star Trader
This rather large *Star Wars* themed merchandise shop is a favorite among fans of the franchise. *Star Wars* figures, toys, clothing, collectibles and vinylmation can be found here in abundant supplies. You can also find other toys, Disney souvenirs and a limited selection of pins. Mouse ears and name embroidery services are also available in the south end of the shop. Kids can enjoy choosing from a wide variety of parts and build their own lightsaber at the store's lightsaber station. If you see someone carrying an Ewok on their back and you'd like one of your very own, check out the backpacks here. Made to look like Yoda, Chewbacca and other Star Wars characters these backpacks are a park favorite. Knit hats resembling the heads of Ewoks and Storm Troopers are also becoming quite popular here. *Guest Favorites:* Build Your Own Lightsaber, Star Wars Droid Factory, and Star Wars Figures.

Top Halloween Items: Mickey and Minnie in Halloween Costumes Plush Animals,

Three Hitchhiking Ghosts Plush Animals, and Large Maleficent Dragon Toy, Haunted Mansion Products (Hour Glass and Candle Stick Holders), and a Large Selection of Halloween Clothing.

Costume Items: Star Wars Lightsabers, guns, and other Dress-Up accessories.

53. Spaceport Document Control
The small stand at the exit to *Space Mountain* sells prints of the photos taken towards the end of the roller coaster ride as well as a few unique *Space Mountain* and *Captain EO* themed souvenirs. The stand also offers cold soft drinks and snacks to weary space travelers. Photos can be previewed on screens located above *Space Mountain's* exit walkway, or on monitors at the stand itself. *Guest Favorites:* Space Mountain Photo Prints, Space Mountain T-Shirts, Picture Frames, Captain EO T-Shirts, and Captain EO Plush Animals.

54. Tomorrow Landing
This little hat shop offers a large selection of Disney theme hats and mouse ears tucked away under the former People Mover platform. Guests may have their name embroidered on their mouse ears here to give them that personal touch. *Guest Favorites:* Mouse Ears, Name Embroidery Services, and Disney Hats.

Top Halloween Items: Spooky Ear Hats, Halloween Ear Headbands, and Wearable Character Tails.

55. Autopia Winner's Circle
This small outdoor stand near the entrance to the *Autopia* attraction features miniature *Autopia* cars, apparel and a variety of collectible toys to choose from. Here transportation enthusiasts can find several Disneyland semi truck, monorail, railroad and thrill ride vehicle play sets as well as Cars Land cars and other miniature vehicles for sale. *Guest Favorites:* Disney Hats, Toy Cars, Disney Monorail Play Sets, and Disneyland Railroad Sets.

California Adventure

Buena Vista Street
01. Oswald's Tires
Oswald's was designed to look like an old-fashioned service station you might find in 1930's California. Located just past the California Adventure entry gates, this store is the first to greet you as you enter the park. The shop's unique exterior and interior design feature old-fashioned gas pumps, classic photos on the walls and old gas station memorabilia throughout the store. Although the shop offers a limited selection of merchandise, it's worth a look for the history lesson it offers alone.

Guest Favorites: Large Selection of Hats, Oswald the Lucky Rabbit Merchandise, and "Oswald's Tires" Gas Station Jackets & T-Shirts.

02. Los Feliz Five & Dime

This large shop was created to look like an old fashioned dime store you would find in 1930's America. Inside the shop you will find t-shirts, toys, collectibles, and a very large selection of hats. *Guest Favorites:* Large Selection of Mouse Ear Hats, Fancy or Casual Hats, and Disney Mugs.

Top Halloween Items: Spooky Hats, Mouse Ear Hats, Halloween Pins, Light Up Trick or Treat Bags, and a variety of Halloween Inspired Clothing.

03. Big Top Toys

Be transported inside the big top in this small circus-themed toyshop sandwiched between the large Los Feliz Five & Dime and the even larger Elias & Co. Department Store. This store offers you a wide selection of children's books, plush animals, and Disney themed play sets. *Guest Favorites:* Toy Play Sets, Plush Animals, Disney Themed Board Games, and Disney Children's Books.

Costume Items: Knight swords and shields, Bow & Arrows, Star Wars Lightsabers, Star Wars Guns, and other dress up accessories.

04. Youth Dept. at Elias & Co.

This is THE shop for children's clothing in California Adventure. Mini-Mouse themed dresses, shirts, and accessories fill the walls as well as the many other Disney-themed shirts for boys and girls that can be found here. *Guest Favorites:* Kids T-Shirts, Kids Casual Wear, Minnie Mouse Dresses, Purses, Shirts, Jackets, and Shoes.

Top Halloween Items: Youth Minnie Mouse Dresses and accessories.

05. Woman's Dept. at Elias & Co.

This classic women's clothing department features a large selection of California themed shirts, hats, belts and bags. *Guest Favorites:* Woman's Fashion (T-Shirts & Sweatshirts, belts, hats, bags, purses, Shoes, and Jewelry.)

06. Men's Dept. at Elias & Co.

This classic shop offers men's hats, shirts, jackets and accessories. *Guest Favorites:* The Hat Walt Disney Wore, Men's Jackets, Hoodies, Tee Shirts, Oswald merchandise, and Plush Animals.

07. Jewelry Dept. at Elias & Co.

The opulently decorated Jewelry Shop in Elias & Co. welcomes guests with ornate artwork and an extravagant chandelier dangling from the ceiling. Here you can find jewelry, watches and high-end clothing accessories. *Guest Favorites:* High-End Disney Watches and Pocket Watches, Jewelry, and Disney "Beautifully" Brand Makeup.

Top Halloween Items: Adult Minnie Mouse Dresses and Accessories, and Snow White inspired shirts.

08. Kingswell Camera Shop *(In the Elysian Arcade)*

This shop provides all of California Adventure's photography services, including the ordering of prints from all the *Photopass* photos taken by Disney parks photographers. The shop also offers a limited selection of photography supplies, frames, and albums. *Guest Favorites:* Photo Printing, Decorative Frames, Photo Albums, Memory Cards, Film, Batteries, Straps, Cases, and Other photo Accessories.

09. Julius Katz & Sons *(In the Elysian Arcade)*

This old-fashioned shoe and watch repair shop offers you a wide selection of Disney trading pins, Vinylmation, and other collectibles. *Guest Favorites:* Disney Bar-Ware, Red Car Trolley Magnets, Shirts, Posters, and Special Seasonal Items.

Top Halloween Items: Halloween Pins and Vinylmation, Haunted Mansion Bottle Stopper, Coaster Set, Jewelry Box, Hour Glass, and Candle Holder.

10. Atwater Ink & Paint *(In the Elysian Arcade)*

This fictitious art supply store is decorated with paints, brushes, paper, and other art supplies that would serve early animation artists. In reality the shop offers guests cooking supplies, cookbooks, gourmet teas & coffees, and a very large selection of Disney mugs. *Guest Favorites:* Disney Themed Kitchen Equipment, Disney Cookbooks, and Disney Mugs.

Hollywood Land

11. Gone Hollywood

From its' flashing neon sign to its' art deco interior, this reproduction of the typical Hollywood Boulevard shop offers many of the wares also found in that iconic Los Angeles neighborhood. Hollywood style scarves, sunglasses, hats and bags will make you think you are shopping on *The Boulevard* itself. *Guest Favorites:* Wide Selection of Sunglasses, Hats, Purses, Scarves, Mad Tea Party Gear, and Vintage Style Mouse Ear Headbands.

Top Halloween Items: Halloween Mouse Ear Headbands, Spooky Pins, and Lanyards.

Disney Junior Souvenir Stand

Look for this stand offering *Jake and The Never Land Pirates* (2011 - present), *Sofia the First* (2013 - present), *Doc McStuffins* (2012 - present), and *Miles from Tomorrowland* (2015 - present) merchandise across the sidewalk from the *Disney Junior Live On Stage* attraction. *Guest Favorites:* figures, toys, dresses, tee-shirts, and DVDs.

Costume Items: *Sofia the First* (2013 - present) dresses and accessories, *Doc McStuffins* (2012 - present) stethoscope, doctors smock, and doctors kit, and *Miles from Tomorrowland* (2015 - present) masks and dress up accessories.

12. Off the Page

This animation themed shop offers high end Disney collectibles including original sketches, paintings, illustrations, prints and animation cells. It has also recently become the only location inside California Adventure where guests can trade Vinylmation. *Guest Favorites:* Hand Drawn Character Sketches Created While You Watch, Original Paintings, Unique Dolls, Figurines, and Disney themed books. *New in 2015*: Painted Disney Vinal Records and Disney Themed Comic Books (featuring Disneyland attractions and characters, Star Wars, Marvel, and other Disney properties.)

Top Halloween Items: Unique Limited Edition Halloween Figurines, Halloween Themed Pokit Pals (decorative cast resin boxes), Halloween Pins, and Unique Disney Villain Artwork. You can also ask for a Halloween Theme to be added to your Hand Drawn Character Sketch.

13. Wandering Oaken's Trading Post

Purchase Frozen-themed apparel, collectibles, and toys at this newly-remodeled trading post based on the Oaken character from *Frozen* (2013). This stand replaces the previous Muppet-themed *Studio Store* found just outside the former *Muppet Vision Theater*.

Top Halloween Items: Light Up Skeleton and Mouse Eared Jack-O-Lantern wands, Mickey and Minnie in Halloween Costumed Plush Animals, and Halloween themed Pins.

Costume Items: *Frozen* (2013) dresses, crowns, and other dress up accessories.

Personalized Leather Accessories

Look for this stand offering free engraving on leather goods in front of *Wandering Oaken's Trading Post*. Bracelets, luggage tags, key chains, and a number of other leather products can be found here. Decorative rivets in a number of styles can also be added to your leather product for an additional charge.

14. Mad T Party Face Painting

Turn your face into a work of art at the Mad T Party's face painting stand, located at a booth at the east end of the Hollywood Studios area near the Mad Arcade. The stand is usually only open in the evening while the Mad "T" Party is happening. A variety of face painting colors, designs and styles are available.

15. Disney Diamond Anniversary Gifts

This small stand located between the *Mad T Party* and the *Hyperon Theater* offers a large selection of *60th Anniversary* gifts. *Guest Favorites:* Anniversary Mouse Ears, Diamond Mouse Ear Headbands, and a variety of light up wands.

16. Tower Hotel Gifts *(at the Hollywood Tower of Terror)*

This fancy hotel gift shop stuck in 1939 (the year lightening struck the tower and people disappeared) offers guests a unique collection of hotel souvenirs, Tower of Terror T-shirts and other apparel, Twilight Zone memorabilia, Disney pins and Vinylmation. And there are plenty of old photos and artifacts to look at while you shop. *Guest Favorites:* Hotel Items (Bathrobes, Towels, Mugs, and Do Not Disturb Signs), Bellhop Mouse Ears, Fancy 1930's Mouse Ear Headbands, Classic *Twilight Zone* TV Show Episodes on DVD, and Disney's *Tower of Terror* (1997) film on DVD.

Halloween Themes: Be sure to take a look at the display windows full of spooky Halloween artifacts set up in front of the store.

Top Halloween Items: Large Selection of *The Nightmare Before Christmas* (1993) merchandise, Twilight Zone Books and DVDs, the *Tower of Terror* (1997) film on DVD, Halloween Pins, Halloween Vinylmation, and Tower of Terror clothing.

Cars Land
17. Sarge's Surplus Hut
This military surplus store is located inside an old military hanger and offers you a large selection of Cars Land themed clothing, toys and books. *Guest Favorites:* Cars Pit Crew Jumpers and Tees, Cars Land Toy Playsets, Cars Land Children's Books, and Unique Cars Land Hats (Flying Tire or Traffic Cone.)

18. Radiator Springs Curios
This curios shop based on the *Cars* (2006, 2011) movies offers you Cars Land themed stickers, postcards and snow globes; exactly what you would expect from a rural stop along the desolate Route 66. The shop also sports a very large collection of trading pins for sale and recently started offering guests customized leather wristbands with your name or a short message engraved on them. *Guest Favorites:* Car Themed Designer Purses, Snow Globes, Cars Land Post Cards, and Bumper Stickers.

19. Ramone's House of Body Art
This classic 1950's style auto body shop from the *Cars* (2006, 2011) films boasts a bright field of neon outside its' classic small-town architecture. Inside the shop offers you a slew of automobile themed merchandise including purses, shirts, blouses, jackets, hats, and unique artworks. *Guest Favorites:* Limited Edition Air Brushed Art Work, Hand Drawn Cars Sketches, Cars Land T-Shirts, Hats, Posters, Automobile Decals, and Bumper Stickers.

Pacific Wharf
20. Ghirardelli Soda Fountain & Chocolate Shop
This iconic San Francisco chocolate maker opened up a shop right inside California Adventure to the thrill of fans everywhere. Look for boxes, bags, and gift sets of chocolate bars, hot cocoa, and other chocolate delicacies. Don't forget to pick up your **free chocolate sample** on the way in, and stay for a delicious gourmet sundae if you have the time. *Guest Favorites:* Cable Car Chocolate Bar Gift Sets, Individual Large Chocolate Bars, Large Bags of Assorted Chocolates, Jars of Fudge or Caramel, Hot Cocoa Mix.

Top Halloween Items: Seasonal Pumpkin Spice Caramel Chocolate Squares,

Halloween themed Premium Chocolate Assortment Tin, and other assorted Halloween themed chocolate collections.

Paradise Pier

21. Laod Bhang's Pin Traders

This souvenir cart offers a large selection of Disney Pins for sale and trade. It was designed to look like a Chinese fireworks cart from San Francisco's Chinatown area. The name of the cart, "Laod Bhang", is a pun referring to the "loud bang" that firecrackers make. *Guest Favorites:* Disney Pins, Pin Sets, Lanyards, and Other Pin Accessories.

Top Halloween Items: Spooky Pin Starter Sets, Pin Sets, and Pins Featuring the Haunted Mansion, Disney Villains, Pirates of the Caribbean, Monsters University, and Other Halloween Themes.

22. Treasures in Paradise

Boardwalk

From the dolphins and sea horses on it's ornate shop sign to the unique amusement park artifacts inside, this boardwalk themed shop portrays an oceanfront California of yesteryear. Inside find a variety of beach themed souvenirs, kids clothing and toys. *Guest Favorites:* Duffy the Teddy Bear with Various Duffy Outfits , Princess Dresses with Accessories, and Jewelry.

Costume Items: Wearable Disney Character Tails, Jedi, Pirate, Pirate Princess, and Disney Princess costumes and dress up accessories.

23. California Scream Cam *(At California Screamin')*

This boardwalk themed stand offers prints of your California Screamin' photos as well as a limited selection of California Screamin' themed souvenirs. *Guest Favorites:* Photo Prints, Frames, Disposable Cameras, and California Screamin' Merchandise (Pins, T-Shirts, Hats, Totes, and Cups.)

24. Midway Mercantile

This Toy Story themed shop at the exit to the *Toy Story Midway Mania!* attraction offers a variety of Toy Story merchandise. *Guest Favorites:* Woody & Jessie Cowboy/Cowgirl hats, Toy Story Tee Shirts, and Toy Story Toys (Plush Animals, Dolls, Figures, Play Sets, and Other Toys.)

Costume Items: Buzz Lightyear costumes, Toy Story Hats, Guns, and other Dress-Up Accessories.

25. Point Mugu Tattoo

Designed to replicate the classic California beachfront shop, this small boutique takes on a heavily tattoo-inspired theme. And like the sign says, all tattoos are "Guaranteed NOT to last for ever." This shop used to feature a nice selection of rub-on temporary tattoos, but about two years ago the shop stopped carrying them all together and opted for standard Disney souvenir fare instead. *Guest Favorites:* California Themed Clothing, Design-It-Yourself Bead Jewry, and Vinylmation.

Top Halloween Items: Halloween Themed Vinylmation, Pins, pin Sets and Lanyards.

26. Boardwalk Bazaar
This hat themed shop offers a very large selection of Disney themed hats and mouse ears. *Guest Favorites:* Wide Selection of Hats, Custom Embroidered Mousse Ears, Plush Animals, and Plush Animal Pillows.

Top Halloween Items: Halloween Themed Ear Heaadbands, Maleficent and Pirate Hats, Candy Corn, and Halloween Plush Animals.

27. Sideshow Shirts
This Big Top themed shop offers a wide selection of shirts inside the interior of a circus tent. *Guest Favorites:* Wide Variety of Tee Shirts Hats, Sweatshirts, Jackets, and Other Apparel.

Top Halloween Items: Halloween Shirts, Light Up Trick or Treat Baskets, and a very large selection of *The Nightmare Before Christmas* (1993) Merchandise.

28. Embarcadero Gifts
This ocean themed shop across from the *Ariel's Undersea Adventure* attraction entrance offers *Little Mermaid* merchandise, *World of Color* gear, and one of the park's largest selections of pins for sale. *Guest Favorites:* Little Mermaid Items (Shirts, Hoodies, Bags, Accessories, and Dolls), World of Color T-Shirts, Bubble Guns, Glow with The Show Ears, and a Large Selection of Disney Pins.

Top Halloween Items: *The Little Mermaid* (1989) costumes and Halloween Pins.

29. Seaside Souvenirs
This large souvenir stand located across the walkaway from the *Golden Zephyr* offers boardwalk gifts and supplies under an oceanfront themed canopy. *Guest Favorites:* Custom Embroidered Mouse Ear Hats, Grumpy Beard Hats (and Other Theme Hats), Sunblock, and Snacks.

Top Halloween Items: Halloween themed mouse ears, pins, hats, shirts, and antenna toppers.

30. Paradise Pier Sunglass Hut
This specialty stand located near the *Corn Dog Castle* offers a large selection of high-end sunglasses. Browse among the Ray-Ban, Michael Kors, Coach, Ralph Lauren, Versace, Prada, and other famous brands offered here. (Less expensive sunglasses can be found at the *Seaside Souvenirs* shop next door.)

Grizzly Peak

31. Rushin' River Outfitters

This outdoor supply shop located inside the wood cabin-style "Eureka Gold & Timber Co." building sits right on the edge of *Grizzly River*. Here outdoor enthusiasts can enjoy shopping for hats, clothing, and plush woodland animals among the displays of outdoor sporting equipment. This is also the place to purchase a poncho if you don't want to get soaking wet on the *Grizzly River Run* next door. The shop also offers a few prepackaged snacks and refrigerators full of ice-cold beverages. *Guest Favorites:* Furry California Bear Hats, Outdoor Adventure Gear (Hats and Clothing), Woodland Themed Plush Animals, and the Fill-a-Bag with Polished Rocks & Gems station.

Top Halloween Items: Halloween Pins, Pin Sets, and Lanyards.

Grizzly Peak Airfield *(formerly Condor Flats)*

32. Humphrey's Service & Supplies

This shop's combination of 1950's aviation and car racing themes provides a unique shopping environment full of memorabilia and unique souvenirs. It's pilot gear and large selection of model planes will satisfy any aviation enthusiast. It also contains one of the largest selections of pins for sale, and pin trading is commonplace here. Vinylmation is also big at this shop. A nice shaded seating area just outside the shop's side door provides a quiet place to rest for a few minutes at the benches, tables, and chairs provided. *Guest Favorites:* Special Edition Disney Pins, Model Airplanes, Flight Jackets, Hats, and Goggles.

Top Halloween Items: Halloween Pins, Pin Sets, and Lanyards.

Costume Items: Pilot hats, goggles, and flight jackets. Conservationist gear such as bird whistles.

Downtown Disney & Resort Hotels

Downtown Disney

01. Apricot Lane Boutique

A stylish clothing boutique that caters to young women.

02. Build-a-Bear Workshop

Design your own teddy bear from the paw up at this unique specialty shop. Choose from a variety off animal types, sizes, and outfits.

Top Halloween Items: Special Halloween themed bears and bear costumes are released throughout the Halloween season, with the first batch arriving in late September. Look for a werewolf in a skeleton suit, a cat in a witch outfit, and many more special Halloween designs.

03. D-Street

This cozy shop in the center of the Downtown Disney district specializes in Vinylmation, limited edition art, and unique tee shirts.

Top Halloween Items: Halloween themed vinylmation.

04. Disney Studio 365

This large shop give you access to a large selection of clothing and Disney costuming for kids outside the walls of the Disney theme parks.

Top Halloween Items: A small collection of Fall colored or Halloween themed skirts and shirts.

05. Disney Vault 28

This Disney specially merchandise shop offers woman's clothing, hats, jewelry, and bags.

Top Halloween Items: Maleficent and Evil Queen themed bags and purses, Día de los Muertos Tee Shirts, and Unique *The Nightmare Before Christmas* (1993) Bracelets. It also offers Haunted Mansion Picture Frames, Jewlery Boxes, Coaster Sets, and Wine Stoppers.

06. Disney's Pin Traders

This small shop next to the Monorail station offers a huge selection of Disney pins and pin accessories.

Top Halloween Items: One of the largest selections of Halloween Disney Pins, Specialty Pins, and Halloween Themed pin Accessories Such as Lanyards and Starter Sets.

07. ESPN Zone Studio Store

ESPN and other sports related clothing, art, and collectibles.

08. Fossil

The famous watch brand shows off it's creative watch styles here.

09. House of Blues Company Store

House of Blues and music themed clothing and souvenirs.

10. The Lego Store

This store specializes in a huge selection of Legos, with just about every set available from the famous toy manufacturer available here. Lego contests, activities, and more also await the Lego fanatic in your family.

11. LittleMissMatched

Cute socks, unique belts, and many other clothing accessory choices.

12. Pearl Factory

Real oysters guaranteed to have a pearl inside can be purchased at this unique stand. Pearl-based jewelry and other accessories can also be found here.

13. Quiksilver

Clothing and accessories based on the popular Quiksilver line of beach apparel.

14. Rainforest Café Retail Shopping Village

Rainforest and animal themed clothing, accessories, toys, and collectibles. And if you love plush animals, this is the shop to visit!

15. Ridemakerz

This unique shop lets you custom build your own remote controlled cars. Disney character themed cars are also available here among the shop's usual collection of racing cars and trucks.

16. Sanuk

Contemporary casual men's and women's footwear. This is a great place to get comfortable sandals to help you beat the Southern California heat, or replace your travel shoes after three days of hiking through the theme parks has eaten them.

17. Sephora

A very large specialty make up store.

18. Something Silver

A jewelry store that focuses on one particular precious metal. Yes, you guessed it: Silver.

19. Studio Disney 365

Princess and knight make-overs mixed with a variety of kids apparel.

20. Sunglass Icon

Your typical high-end sunglass shop.

21. WonderGround Gallery

A unique gallery featuring Disney inspired paintings, prints, and other art. They regularly have guest artists appear and create new works of art before your very eyes.

22. World of Disney

As the largest Disney shop in the resort, the World of Disney has just about everything you can find at other stores throughout the theme parks and hotels. This is an all in one stop for all of your Disney merchandise needs.

Halloween Themes: Look for special Halloween decorations and displays throughout the massive store.

Top Halloween Items: The official Halloween section is located just inside the shop entry at the east end of the shop (the side closest to the theme parks). There you can find the usual Halloween items found at shops throughout the resort. further inside you can find unique Halloween themed figurines, pins, vinylmation, costume pieces, accessories, and toys.

Grand California Hotel
23. Acorns Gifts & Goods
This small hotel gift shop offers a wide selection of Disney merchandise including clothing, watches, Disney pins, and much more. It also offers a few prepackaged snack food items.

Top Halloween Items: Halloween Pins, Light Up Jack O Lantern Trick or Treat Buckets (perfect for Mickey's Halloween Party), and Halloween light-up lanterns.

Disneyland Hotel
24. Fantasia Shop
This large hotel gift shop offers many Disney items found in the theme parks including clothing, Disney pins, and much more.

Top Halloween Items: Halloween Pins, Light Up Trick or Treat Bags (perfect for Mickey's Halloween Party), Jack O Lantern candle holders, and Halloween Plush Animals.

Paradise Pier Hotel
25. Mickey in Paradise
This rather large shop inside the main lobby to the Paradise Pier Hotel offers many of the standard Disney souvenirs found throughout the park as well as vacation supplies.

Top Halloween Items: Halloween Pins, Light Up Trick or Treat Bags (perfect for Mickey's Halloween Party), Jack O Lantern candle holders, and Halloween Plush Animals.

Made in the USA
Las Vegas, NV
07 December 2020